AN EXPENDABLE MAN

MARGARET EDDS

AN EXPENDABLE MAN

The Near-Execution of Earl Washington Jr.

New York University Press • *New York and London*

NEW YORK UNIVERSITY PRESS
New York and London

Library of Congress Cataloging-in-Publication Data
Edds, Margaret, 1947-
An expendable man : the near-execution of Earl Washington Jr. /
Margaret Edds.
p. cm.
Includes bibliographical references and index.
ISBN 0-8147-2222-9 (cloth : alk. paper)
1. Washington, Earl.   2. African american prisoners—Biography.
3. Death row inmates—United States—Biography.
4. People with mental disabilities and crime—United States—Biography.
5. Discrimination in criminal justice administration—United States.
6. Capital punishment—Moral and ethical aspects—United States.
7. DNA fingerprinting—United States.   8. Washington, Earl.   I. Title.
HV9468. W35E33 2003
364.66'092—dc21   2002155791

New York University Press books are printed on acid-free paper,
and their binding materials are chosen for strength and durability.

Manufactured in the United States of America

10 9 8 7 6 5 4 3 2 1

In memory of Virginia Barnes

Contents

All illustrations appear as a group following p. 82.

Acknowledgments

I AM GRATEFUL to many people who assisted in the writing of this book and particularly to those who put the public interest in dissecting a miscarriage of justice ahead of possible private interest in leaving the story untold.

Members of Earl Washington's defense team opened their offices and files to scrutiny and spent countless hours reconstructing pivotal moments and events. Attorney John Scott shared generously of his time, even though the spotlight's glare did not reflect kindly on his defense of Washington during the capital trial. Former Virginia attorneys general Stephen Rosenthal and William Broaddus, former deputy Gail Marshall and others provided insight into the state's handling of death cases, while former U.S. District Court Judge Robert R. Merhige and Chief Judge J. Harvie Wilkinson III of the U.S. 4th Circuit Court of Appeals helped explain the actions and mind-set of those who sit on the federal courts serving Virginia. Fauquier County Commonwealth's attorney Jonathan Lynn, who as a defense attorney in the 1980s represented Washington on several charges, was a keen observer of his former client's personality and response to authorities following his arrest; through letters, former death row inmate Joe Giarratano supplied similar analysis of Washington's temperament and behavior during his first years behind bars. Former gubernatorial counsels Walter McFarlane and Walter Felton described the inner workings of the gubernatorial clemency system, and Kay Mirick, Ruth Luckasson, and Richard Bonnie provided deeper awareness of mental retardation and its intersection with the criminal justice system.

Two members of Earl Washington's family, his sister Alfreda Pendleton and his half sister Shirley Cuesenberry, were especially helpful in exploring family dynamics, even as they worried about un-flattering portrayals of the Washingtons in various newspaper and magazine accounts.

Several members of Rebecca Williams's family were initially help-ful and then declined communication. Their ambivalence reflected con-tinuing confusion and pain about the case and Earl Washington's role in it. Among those who took a different view of events, I am particularly grateful to former Fauquier County investigator Terry Schrum and Culpeper Commonwealth's attorney Gary Close for their spirited de-fense of an opposing perspective. While I ultimately believed them to be in error, their arguments helped me understand pivotal points at which misunderstanding and miscommunication occurred. I regret that John Bennett, who prosecuted the case against Washington, chose not to share his views. Bennett declined both written and oral requests for interviews. Two other principals in the investigation of Earl Wash-ington—Deputy Denny Zeets and Special Agent Reese Wilmore of the Virginia State Police—are deceased. The Virginia Foundation for the Humanities provided workspace and helpful commentary on a work in progress. Thanks to Roberta Culbertson, director of the fellowship pro-gram, President Robert Vaughan, and other VFH staff members and fel-lows. Thanks also to my coworkers at the *Virginian-Pilot*—Patrick Lackey, Roger Chesley, Beth Williams, and Alan Sorensen—who as-sumed a heavier workload during my five-month leave of absence, and to more recent colleagues Dennis Hartig and Bronwyn Lance Chester for their enthusiasm. A number of other colleagues and friends pro-vided support and encouragement: Warren Fiske, Guy Friddell, Frank Green, Laura LaFay, Christina Nuckols, Larry Sabato, Joshua Scott, and Bill and Carol Wood. The staffs of the Library of Virginia and the Culpeper Circuit Clerk's office were unfailingly courteous in assisting with research. Several individuals read portions or all of the manuscript as it progressed. Keo Cavalcanti, Stephen Fleming, Glenn Frankel, Karen Owen, and Barry Weinstein offered invaluable observations and recommendations, and my appreciation to them is profound. Any re-maining errors in fact or judgment are my own. Thanks also to my agent, Noah Lukeman, for his belief in the project. The mainstays dur-ing the writing of this book were my family—Kate and Adam Lipper; Sharon, Brett, Taylor, and Lauren Halsey; Rachel Edds; Elliot Lieber-man; Charles and Eleanor Murray; Margaret and Jerwaine Simpson, and as always, Bob Lipper.

Timeline

June 4, 1982: Rebecca Lynn Williams, a nineteen-year-old mother of three, is raped and murdered during a midday assault at her apartment in Culpeper, Virginia. She is stabbed thirty-eight times but lives long enough to say that her attacker was a sole black man whom she did not know.

May 21, 1983: Earl Washington Jr. breaks into the home of an elderly neighbor in Fauquier County to steal a gun. When confronted by the woman, he assaults her with a chair. He is arrested early that morning in a nearby field. During police questioning, he confesses to a series of crimes, including the rape-murder of Rebecca Williams.

November 2, 1983: Based on the evaluation of a clinical psychologist at Central State Hospital (who determines that Washington has an IQ of 69, placing him in a category of mild mental retardation), a Culpeper County Circuit Court judge rules that Washington is competent to stand trial and that his confession was properly taken.

January 18–20, 1984: Washington is tried and convicted of capital murder. The jury recommends the death penalty.

May 13, 1985: The U.S. Supreme Court, following similar action by the Virginia Supreme Court, upholds Washington's conviction. Virginia officials set a September 5 execution date, even though Washington has no lawyer.

August 1985: After death row inmate Joe Giarratano initiates a class-action lawsuit on Washington's behalf (because of the lack of legal representation), the New York law firm of Paul, Weiss, Rifkind, Wharton & Garrison agrees to file a state habeas petition on Washington's behalf. The petition is filed and a stay granted on August 27, nine days before the scheduled execution.

December 19, 1991: A three-judge panel of the 4th Circuit Court of Appeals sends the case back to the federal district court for a rehearing after learning that Washington's blood type does not match the blood type of semen found on a blanket at the crime scene. (That fact was not introduced into evidence at Washington's trial, and earlier was rejected by state courts and a federal district court as evidence that Washington's trial counsel provided an inadequate defense.)

September 17, 1993: After the federal district court decides that the blood type evidence is inconclusive and that Washington would have been convicted with or without it, the 4th Circuit panel upholds the death sentence 2 to 1.

October 23, 1993: A DNA test done by the Virginia state laboratory finds genetic material on Williams's body that could not have come from Washington. Virginia's Twenty-One-Day Rule prevents Washington from going back to court.

January 14, 1994: On his last day in office, Governor L. Douglas Wilder reduces Washington's sentence from death to life in prison.

June 1999–January 2000: While preparing a documentary on prisoners who appear to be innocent, based on DNA testing, but remain in prison, a reporter for PBS's *Frontline* is shown the results of DNA tests that were conducted in 1993 but never shared with Washington's attorneys. Renewed in their belief of Washington's innocence, the attorneys begin petitioning Governor Jim Gilmore for a new round of more sophisticated DNA tests.

June 1, 2000: Gilmore orders new DNA tests.

October 2, 2000: After the tests reveal two sets of DNA, neither belonging to Washington, the prisoner is granted an absolute pardon from the governor. Gilmore does not issue an apology and says only that he believes a jury currently hearing evidence in the case would not convict Washington. The inmate remains in prison until he reaches a mandatory release date in the assault of the former neighbor, Hazel Weeks. Experts in Virginia's sentencing and parole procedures say that the prisoner would have been released years earlier in the assault of Weeks, save for the capital conviction.

February 12, 2001: Earl Washington Jr. is released from prison. He is expected to remain under parole supervision until 2004.

AN EXPENDABLE MAN

I

Countdown

SHARDS OF CRYSTALLINE LIGHT exploded inside Marie Deans's skull. A rainbow of refracted colors filled her mind's eye. Another August morning was dawning moist and heavy in Richmond, Virginia, a city struggling to break free of its Old South past. Another migraine was forming in the recesses of her brain.

Eleven-year-old Robert and his best friend Hashim still slept, nestled in a jumble of comic books, their latest passion. Lists of attorneys, addresses, and telephone numbers crowded Marie's own space in the low-rent, West End apartment that she shared with her youngest son. As the head of the Virginia Coalition on Jails and Prisons, she had spent these last months soliciting some five dozen Virginia lawyers, another dozen or so attorneys out-of-state, the pro bono committee of the District of Columbia Bar Association, six large firms in D.C., the Southern Prisoners Defense Committee, the NAACP Legal Defense and Education Fund, on and on, all to no avail.[1]

Where was some help, dammit? Somebody had to step forward. Nobody got themselves executed in America without a lawyer. Six prisoners sentenced to death by the state of Virginia had been turned over to Marie's care in this summer of 1985 alone, all of them spiraling toward the electric chair without a motion or a plea blocking the way. Earl Washington Jr. was sitting even now in a death cell at the Spring Street penitentiary, his habeas appeals not filed, the clock ticking day and night toward a September 5 execution date, less than three weeks to go.

The light show was passing. Soon the migraine would speed through her veins, and then there would be no stopping the pain and nausea. Then, the only choice would be to ride that demon, handed down from grandmother to mother to daughter, through a day of hell. Telephone calls and letters, the dread mandatory visit to Spring Street, cigarettes and coffee and supper with Robert, all would be backdrops to a throbbing, aching pain. Marie slipped a tiny tablet under her tongue, closed her eyes, and prayed for relief. She slid her five-foot, ten-inch frame into a skirt and blouse, headed for the kitchen to start coffee, lit a Marlboro, and forced herself to focus on the tasks at hand. Priority #1: get Earl Washington a lawyer.

She'd met Earl about a year earlier, not long after he arrived on death row at the Mecklenburg Correctional Center, deep in rural, south-side Virginia. Marie had driven the two-plus hours south from Richmond to get a personal sense of Washington and his case. She took it upon herself to keep track of the men on the row. Prior to her assignment by the Southern Coalition on Jails and Prisons to Virginia in 1983, no one—not even the state Supreme Court—kept an accurate count, much less a record of who had an attorney and when various filings were due. Now, when she could, Marie did an entrance interview to find out a few details of the case and, if possible, where the prisoner stood in the appeals process. Many of the men had no idea. Virginia did not automatically provide lawyers for state and federal habeas appeals, the critical part of the appeals process in which the possibility of improper imprisonment is probed. It was up to Marie, who was running a shoestring operation and struggling to support herself and her son on $13,000 a year, to find attorneys for those who were without representation. The state did nothing to help. Increasingly, even talking to prisoners was a hassle. Only attorneys got automatic access from the Department of Corrections, and Marie was not a lawyer.[2]

Earl Washington was twenty-four years old, tall, shy, and as fidgety as a stray pup on the day Marie encountered him at Mecklenburg. According to his record, Washington had been convicted of the rape and murder of a nineteen year old mother of three in Culpeper, a picture postcard town a couple of hundred miles away at the eastern base of the Blue Ridge Mountains. Almost a year passed between the time Rebecca Lynn Williams was found stabbed and bleeding on the sidewalk outside her apartment and the arrest. The break in one of Culpeper's most perplexing unsolved crimes came when Washington, a farmhand and day laborer in the next county, broke into the home of an elderly neighbor. Planning to steal a gun, he beat her over the head with a chair when she confronted him, and soon found himself in a police lockup. One thing led to another during the police questioning, and before the interrogations were done, Washington had confessed to Williams's murder and several other unsolved crimes. Only the Williams confession stuck. By the time the case went to court, Washington was protesting that he was innocent. By then, no one was listening. He was convicted almost solely on the basis of his own confession.[3]

"Tell me about your family," Marie said.

She began the Mecklenburg interview gently. Her strong Swedish features could be commanding, when necessary. But what people usually noticed first were the steady brown eyes and the way her slow, serious drawl erupted in a husky chuckle. The combination could be disarming, even with frightened or jaded prisoners. Washington seemed more nervous than tough.

"Where does your family live?" she repeated. They were seated at a wooden table in a visitor's area at Mecklenburg, Earl at the end, Marie with notebook and pens before her.

"Bealeton," he said tentatively.

"The address?"

Silence.

"Is it route something-or-other?"

"I don't know."

"Does your family live on a particular road?"

"No, they live in a house."

It took Marie Deans about five minutes to conclude that, unless she was very much mistaken, Earl Washington was mentally retarded. She switched to a different topic.

"Tell me about Rebecca Williams."

"I didn't do the crime," Washington mumbled. He was insistent, not budging.

"Okay," said Marie, turning to the prior offense, the break-in to which Washington had admitted. "Tell me about Hazel Weeks. I understand that you broke into her home and that you hit her." As usual, when it came to this part of a prisoner interview, Marie's tone toughened slightly.[4]

"Wheee," Washington said in reply, his eyes widening as he sucked in a breath of air and slowly exhaled. Then an unexpected thing happened. Earl Washington's eyes moistened. "She was a nice lady," he said.

In the year since that interview, Marie had met with Washington several times and she was increasingly skeptical that this simple, good-natured man had committed the acts to which he had confessed. But guilt or innocence would soon be moot. Now Washington had been moved from Mecklenburg to Spring Street in downtown Richmond to await his death in less than three weeks, and he had no lawyer. Marlboros and lighter in hand, Marie penned a quick note to Robert and Hashim, then headed outside into the rising heat. Grateful that the migraine was not progressing, she slid behind the wheel of her stripped-down beige Nova, a $1 purchase from her estranged husband, and headed east on Richmond's leafy Monument Avenue, past the statues of Stonewall Jackson and Robert E. Lee and other Confederate heroes, toward the decaying fortress that was Virginia's penitentiary.

Perched on a knoll overlooking downtown, the prison was inspired by Thomas Jefferson and designed by Benjamin Henry Latrobe, architect for the U.S. Capitol. When it opened in 1800, the penitentiary was supposed to have been a model for a new, more humane way of regarding punishment and rehabilitation. Its open courtyard and individual cells were intended to provide time for contemplation and recreation, leading prisoners to repent of their misdeeds and emerge as reformed citizens. That was the theory.[5]

In fact, from the prison's inception the reality had been far harsher. The isolation cells, instead of stimulating introspection, were torturous for those left for long periods in solitary confinement. By the 1820s ordinary twelve- by fourteen-foot cells housed an average of twelve inmates each. The prison could be suffocating in summer, damp and cold in the winter. Raw sewage was piped to a nearby ravine and dumped.[6]

The original Latrobe building was razed in 1928, and a replacement was constructed. A newer cell block, Building A, built at the turn of the century to handle overcrowding, was still operating in 1985. Death row and the execution chamber were housed side by side in the basement of Building A.

The state's electric chair held its first occupant on October 13, 1908. Between then and 1962, when Virginia temporarily halted executions due to growing concern about racial disparities, 236 individuals died in Building A—201 black men, 1 black woman, and 34 white men. Of the fifty-five prisoners executed for rape or attempted rape, every one was black.[7] In a four-day period in 1951, seven black men from Martinsville—known nationally as the Martinsville Seven—died in Building A for the rape of a white woman who survived the attack.

For twenty years, Virginia's electric chair had sat empty. But now the death chamber was back in business. Four men had been executed in the previous three years. James and Linwood Briley, brothers who loosed a murderous spree on Richmond and who later masterminded a mass escape from the Mecklenburg prison, were gone. The night of Linwood's execution brought out Confederate flags and chants of "Burn, Briley, burn," side by side with a candlelight vigil by death penalty foes. James's death that past April prompted a brief, bloody riot in which nine guards were stabbed by prisoners with homemade knives. Indictments were due to be handed down any day by a Richmond grand jury.[8] Morris O'Dell Mason, a paranoid schizophrenic whose illness went untended until his brutal acts shocked Virginia's quiet Eastern Shore, was dead too.[9]

Earl Washington and several others had taken their places at Spring Street. The purpose of Marie's daily visits was to show them a steady face, to let them know that she was working day and night to find lawyers, to reassure them that they were not forgotten. Still, the visits were one of the hardest parts of the job for Marie. Passing through the electronic gates at the entrance to the prison, hearing the hum and clang of doors sealing her off from space and air, she sometimes had to fight a rising panic. The basement cell block itself was roomy enough, but there were mice and roaches and constant drips from overhead pipes. The wooden table where she conferred with the condemned men doubled as a cooldown table for the bodies after an execution, and she imagined that stray flecks on its surface were bits of charred flesh. Prisoners told her that they could hear the hum of the electric chair, loud and distinct, as it was being tested in preparation for their deaths.

Earl's fear was quieter, more fatalistic than most. But Marie had never encountered anyone on death row who was unafraid, and Earl was no exception. He was having trouble eating and sleeping, and he greeted her each day with an almost trembling anxiety. He found solace in telephone conversations with his family and her daily presence. "Marie won't let nothing happen to me," he told one visitor. When the words were reported to Marie, they escalated her own anxiety to something approaching terror.

Years later, Washington described his mood during the period with a rote simplicity: "If God is ready for me to go, I go. If he's not, I won't go."[10]

But in August 1985 Marie could not be so nonchalant. How would anyone know what God wanted if there was no attorney to make the case? Backing the Nova into a parking spot outside the prison, she whispered her mantra. "Go through the fear." Much as she hated these visits, she told herself that everyone has things they're afraid of, things they dread. Either you control the fear, or the fear controls you.

"Go through the fear," she repeated, pushing open the car door. By that, she meant don't just experience the anxiety, but shove it aside. Get beyond it. Move on. She headed up the sidewalk toward the prison door.

After Earl Washington was pardoned in the death of Rebecca Williams and freed in February 2001, Virginia officials liked to say that "the system worked." Because Governor Jim Gilmore, a former prosecutor, authorized DNA testing and later granted Washington an absolute pardon, the system was said to have exposed and corrected its flaws. A broken system presumably would have put Washington to death or kept him behind bars for life, rather than seventeen years and nine months.

On closer examination, however, what appears to have worked was not the judicial system but one woman and four men, plus a host of secondary characters, who refused to give up on Washington long after the courts and the politicians had sealed his doom. Had those five not persisted, in large measure out of a growing affection for a man they viewed as the victim of some of the worst excesses of America's system of capital punishment, Earl Washington would have died. No one then would have known of his innocence, and the same people who pointed with pride to Washington's release would have said, with his death, that the system worked. How is it possible for such grievous error to occur in a judicial system that prides itself on scrupulous review when a life is at stake? And if the system failed so miserably for so long to detect the errors in Washington's case, what assurance is there that other innocent men have not been convicted or executed?

Washington's case is a prototype for many of the things that can go wrong in a capital conviction: a false confession elicited by aggressive police officers unschooled in mental retardation; a suspect—poor, black, uneducated—who prompts little in the way of public sympathy and is easily forgotten; a shoddy defense; an appellate review system indisposed to unearth error; crime-fighting politicians loath to risk their reputations by appearing soft on criminals, and intense community pressure for resolution of a crime that has devastated a family and left citizens feeling unsettled and unsafe.

At the same time, Washington's treatment at the hands of the police and the courts was hardly the worst imaginable. There is no indication that he was treated cruelly by his police interrogators or forced to confess. His trial attorney, while astonishingly inept in several particulars of the case, was sufficiently able in his career to later be named a state court judge, as was the associate counsel. Washington's conviction was reviewed by five different courts in a total of eight different actions.

No single piece of the system failed. Instead, at almost every turn, questions that should have been asked, skepticism that ought to have been aired, protective steps that might have been taken, were not. In retrospect, it is easier to see the flimsiness in the case against Washington. But when, at each step of the process, individuals were only doing their jobs—a bit carelessly here, a tad overzealously there—while relying on the trustworthiness of the work that preceded theirs, it was less easy to see that the whole exercise was coalescing in a terrible injustice.

In the rawest sense, Washington was responsible for his own fate. If he had not broken into the home of Hazel Weeks, none of the later events would have occurred. But the law strives to equate the punishment with the offense. Washington's assault of Mrs. Weeks was inconsistent with his previous behavior and prompted remorse. Nonetheless, having made his mistake, Washington was a prime candidate to be engulfed by the judicial system. He fit almost every subcategory of those who are least likely to benefit from the full protections of the law. Racially, economically, and intellectually, Washington lived on life's margins, as his family had for generations. Few would have mourned his death.

With all that went wrong for Washington, however, an even more astounding array of coincidences and unforeseen events had to go right before he walked through the prison gates a free man. At a time when Washington had no lawyer, a fellow death row inmate launched a class action lawsuit that brought one of the nation's premier legal firms to Washington's defense, saving him from execution with only a few days to spare. A temporary appointment in the attorney general's office led to a behind-the-scenes argument over Washington's guilt that culminated in his first DNA test. A high-stakes gamble by Washington's lawyers to drop his final appeals created a timetable by which former Govenor Douglas Wilder, in his final hours in office, reduced Washington's sentence to life in prison. A national television crew working on a documentary stumbled onto a piece of evidence without which the case might never have been revived. Even after a final round of DNA testing was done in 2000, it is entirely possible that Gilmore would not have pardoned Washington except for another extraordinary turn of events involving a DNA "cold hit."

How many other men, similarly imprisoned, could count on equal good fortune?

The circumstances that worked against Washington are far more commonplace than those that produced his release, and therefore likely to have occurred in other cases. There is nothing novel on death row about mental retardation or the sort of adaptive behavior that led Washington to confess. Indigent defendants in capital cases often receive a mediocre to abysmal defense at trial. State and federal appellate courts are disposed by both temperament and procedure to uphold trial decisions that are not flagrantly flawed. This is particularly true of the courts serving Virginia, but it is not uncommon elsewhere.

On the other hand, many of the factors that led to Washington's release are not easily duplicated. While DNA testing has become more routine, evidence suitable for such tests does not exist in most capital cases. Moreover, DNA tests might never have been performed in the Washington case except for extraordinary good luck, involving the attorney general's office in 1993, the television documentary in 2000, and Washington's unusually committed legal team. While a number of other individuals played important—sometimes invaluable—roles, the five were central.

Marie Deans was the nonattorney in the group, the prisoner advocate skilled at making a human connection with condemned men, motivated by moral opposition to the death penalty and her determination to confront and move beyond the violence that had pierced her own life. Eric Freedman, a Manhattan attorney turned Hofstra law professor, brought to the team talents in logic and argument, plus a growing reputation as one of a handful of national experts on habeas appeals in death cases. Robert Hall was a prominent Virginia trial attorney, dignified and even courtly, but passionate about his clients. Barry Weinstein, a Miami whiz kid who came to Virginia to head a capital representation resource center, left discouraged and disillusioned by the impregnability of the Virginia system. For years, he served as Washington's chief link to the outside world, sometimes driving hundreds of miles to remote prisons to assure the condemned man that he had not been forgotten. Finally, Gerald Zerkin acted as the team's man on the scene in Richmond, helping with strategy and offering critical advice about the personalities and procedures that drove the Virginia system.

The team that shepherded Earl Washington through years of hope and discouragement could not have survived that gauntlet without strong egos and stubborn dedication. An unorthodox group, their diverse backgrounds and mix of professional and personal strengths were critical to the eventual outcome. Each contributed key pieces to a puzzle that otherwise might have been left unsolved. Each also, to one degree or another, bore what author Austin Sarat has called "the burden of representing some of the most hated persons in America."[11] For some, like Hall, the commitment to Washington was driven not by opposition to the death penalty but by a fierce belief in every individual's right to a proper legal defense. For others, like Deans, the death penalty abolitionist movement was a cornerstone of life.

From the outside, death penalty attorneys and foes may appear to be a monolithic group, but there are pecking orders and a range of contributions and motivations. Among abolitionists, the most revered positions are reserved for those like Deans who put their own emotional health at risk by staring death in the eye time and again. Often, those whose careers are intricately entwined in legal aspects of the work are attracted by the intensity of the undertaking and by the association with some of the nation's premier legal minds. If the high stakes are an emotional liability for the attorneys, they are also part of the appeal. Processing wills, closing real estate deals, and overseeing divorces, the bread-and-butter of many legal practices, can turn mind-numbing. Death penalty work can sear the soul, but it is not boring.

Despite the differences in temperament and style in Washington's team, the geographic complications of living in five different locations in three different states, and the pressures and conflicts of their individual lives, the group held together for years. Sometimes months would go by without communication, but one member would eventually contact another, and before the conversation ended, there would be the inevitable query: What about Earl?

Take away any one of the three—the DNA, the luck, and the team—and Earl Washington would not be living today in Virginia Beach, working as a handyman in a program for adults who are mentally challenged. Not only is it easy to suppose that some other convicted men have been less fortunate than he. When one considers all the factors that had to come together in order for him to gain his freedom, it is almost impossible to imagine otherwise.

2

Death in Culpeper

MELISSA MARIE WAS LATE for the school bus again.

Her mother, Rebecca Williams, barefoot, tousled, clad in blue jeans and a red-and-white football jersey, flung open the front door of 682 Willis Lane in Culpeper's Village Apartments and signaled to the bus driver. Missy was coming. Moments later, the preschooler straggled out, stopped for a hug, and disappeared onto the bus.

Becky Williams scooped up the baby from the apartment doorstep and headed inside for the next leg of her morning ritual. Once Missy was off to school, there were still Melinda May and Misty Michele to feed and dress. Becky had been little more than a child herself when her oldest was born, and now at just nineteen, she was already a mother of three. The responsibility was more than she had bargained for, but little else in life had given her as much satisfaction as the three girls. She felt a small swell of pride when relatives commented that she was a "good mother."

This morning, however, her mind was less on the girls than on Clifford, her childhood sweetheart, now her husband. There was no question that she loved Clifford, had almost from the moment a mutual friend had brought him by her house six years earlier. She was just thirteen at the time, tall, with lank, shoulder-length blond hair, a full-cheeked face and eyes that looked straight at a camera without flinching. Clifford was fifteen, large for his age, crazy about engines and hot rods. Neither of them cared much for school. Clifford knew how to have a good time, and Becky was interested in learning. Their romance ignited like a firecracker. It wasn't long before Clifford had moved into Becky's family home and Melissa Marie was on the way.

There were plenty of happy memories from those first few years. Becky's passion was baton twirling; Clifford's was motorcycles. When she traveled to parades in Flint Hill or other Piedmont towns, he would hop on his bike, pick her up at the finish, and the pair would speed away. Sometimes they went fishing at Lake Anna. Other times, they joined the parade of young people driving up and down the main streets of Culpeper on a Saturday night. School was a nuisance. Clifford dropped out to work at a gas station, Becky to care for Missy. Once he went back for a while, then gave it up. She never did. The babies kept coming. "I think she could walk past Clifford and get pregnant," Helen Richards, Becky's mother, said ruefully years later.[1]

All was not idyllic, however. There were arguments, driven by financial instability and emotional immaturity. At times, Clifford drank heavily and he dabbled in drugs, more so as the years passed. Becky's older sister, Hilda, added an unstable element as well. Hilda walked on the wild side. "She partied hard, lived a pretty exotic lifestyle," Clifford Williams said of his sister-in-law.[2] Hilda and her friends were in and out of the Williams household at Culpeper's Village Apartments. How much Clifford and Becky veered into their world is a matter of dispute.

Clifford acknowledges his own penchant, at the time, for a good party. But he denies that Becky was a full participant. "She never would use drugs or anything. She would seldom even drink alcohol." After all, he said, "she spent most of her time pregnant."

Bickering between the pair ran in cycles. A year-and-a-half or so before that morning of June 4, 1982, Becky and Clifford seemed to have their problems in check. They took out a marriage license and made their union official. But now, the old troubles were resurfacing. Clifford was drinking too much and he was spending time away from home with his friends. Becky was frustrated and angry, and she was thinking of doing something about it. But first, there was Mindy toddling along in her blue pajamas and Misty still in her playpen. Both girls needed tending, and Clifford would be home from his night job soon.

It was 8:05 A.M. when Missy Williams told her mother goodbye and climbed onto the school bus, according to an account in the next day's Culpeper *Star-Exponent*.[3] Retracing Becky Williams's steps throughout the rest of the morning was not complicated. Most of the time was accounted for. Sometime between 9 A.M. and 10 A.M., she placed the first of two collect calls to her mother, Helen Richards, who managed an apartment complex in the Washington, D.C., suburbs. Becky was angry. Clifford had not come home as expected after work, and for Becky it was the last straw. "She asked me to come pick her up," Richards recalled. "He was drinking, back doing drugs. She did love him, but she was not going to let her babies live like that."[4] Richards told her daughter she would try to come later in the day.

A neighbor saw Becky and her two youngest girls at a nearby 7-Eleven at about 10:30 A.M., according to the *Star-Exponent*.[5] Nothing seemed amiss. Two other witnesses saw the trio as they headed back to the apartment complex. Eleven-month-old Misty was in a stroller. Two-year-old Mindy was walking at her mother's side. Neighbor Doris Campbell, who was on her way to an 11 A.M. job interview, drove past them moments before she was due at her appointment. Jerry Lane, one of Hilda's beaus, was headed out of the complex as well and stopped to chat near the apartment office, a few hundred yards from her home. He figured that it was around 11 A.M.

According to Helen Richards's telephone bill, Becky's second collect call was placed at 11:09 A.M. She was speaking from a neighbor's apartment because the Williams's phone wasn't operating. Again, Becky expressed her frustration with Clifford and her desire to leave once Missy was home from school. Richards promised to be there later in the day. It was the last time she heard her daughter's voice.

Whatever awaited Becky back inside her own apartment occurred quickly and brutally. There was no sign of forced entry through the only door. It is impossible to know whether Becky's attacker followed her into the apartment or was waiting when she and the children returned. But there is no question that Becky Williams met her death in a frenzied spasm of violence. Blood spatterings on the bed and wall suggest that much, if not all, of the attack occurred in a back bedroom. The coroner's report confirms that this was no casual assault, no simple rape.[6] Becky was stabbed thirty-eight times. Twenty-four of the wounds were superficial, piercing only the skin or its underlying tissues. Fourteen were sufficiently deep to penetrate an internal organ, and five—wounds that bore into the spleen, the small and large bowel, the carotid artery in the neck, and the liver—were potentially deadly.

Incredibly, Becky did not die on the spot but made her way, wounded and bleeding, to the front door.

Shortly before noon, a young couple in the process of moving into the Village Apartments saw an object that looked like a mannequin lying in the doorway of 682 Willis Lane. Pulling into a parking spot, Paul Brundage and his wife quickly realized that the "object" was a naked and bleeding woman.[7] She was lying on her side in the doorway and calling softly, "Somebody help me, please, help me." "I ran over to the doorway and I bent over and asked her, you know, what happened and she says, 'Please help me, I've been raped,' and then she . . . her eyes kind of rolled back in her head . . . and that's all I, you know, I heard from her," Brundage later testified.

Moments later, Patrolman J. L. "Scoobie" Jackson of the Culpeper Police Department looked out the front window of his second-floor apartment and saw the Brundages running away from the Williams's apartment.[8] He also saw something that appeared to be a woman lying in a doorway. Jackson rushed to investigate. Halfway across the parking lot, he could see that his impression was correct. "It appeared to be a white female, screaming and hollering, 'Help me. Help me,'" he testified. "I continued on and as I was approaching, getting closer, I could see what appeared at this time to be blood spots and she was crying, hollering, screaming, saying . . . stating that, 'He hurt me. He hurt me.' I approached her and I asked her what happened and she stated that she had been raped. At this time another female threw a sheet over her to cover her up. I turned to the victim again and asked her was anyone still inside and she mumbled something that I couldn't understand."

Jackson's question was quickly answered. Mindy was standing just inside the apartment door. The officer called to the youngster and she walked toward him. He handed her to a woman in the gathering crowd. Peering into the living room, Jackson saw Misty in a playpen. "I just reached in and picked her up and handed her to another one of the females that was outside," he said.

Two other people received scraps of information from Becky about her attacker. Answering the police dispatcher's call, Investigator Kenneth Buraker of the Culpeper Police Department arrived on the scene at 11:57 A.M. He recognized the victim as Becky Williams.[9] "I stood directly over top of her, so she could see me," Buraker testified. "I asked her if she knew who her attacker was. She replied, 'No.' I asked her if the attacker was black or white and she replied, 'Black.' I then asked her if there was more than one and she replied, 'No.' And at this point the Rescue Squad arrived and I didn't do any more questioning at that time."

Clifford also drove up as Becky was lying on the doorstep. Pushing past the array of police cars and neighbors, he knelt by his wife.[10] "I tried to tell her that the ambulance was on the way, that she'd be all right, you know, that everything would be okay, and I asked her, you know, who did it, and the only thing she replied to me was, 'A black man,'" he said, choking back tears from the witness stand.

As Becky was being transferred to the Culpeper County Volunteer Fire Department rescue vehicle, the fifth member of the Williams family arrived home. Missy Williams climbed down from the school bus and began running toward the apartment. Neighbors blocked her path, guiding her instead toward her sisters. Years later, some Culpeper residents remained haunted by the newspaper description of that moment: "Seeing her mother being placed in the ambulance she cried, 'My mommy. My mommy. What's happened to my mommy?'"[11]

At Culpeper Memorial Hospital, there was a gallant effort to save Becky Williams's life. The wounds were too severe. At 2:05 P.M. she was pronounced dead.

Special Agents Reese Wilmore and Frank Lasley, bureau of criminal investigation, Virginia State Police, had just settled into their task at the Village Apartments. Working methodically, the pair first canvassed the area outside the apartment and then moved indoors, measuring, photographing, and preserving clothing, fingerprints, hairs, blood samples, anything that might be of use in tracing the killer. It was 8:30 P.M. before Wilmore and Lasley finished.[12]

Three days after the crime, fifty-eight items—including a plastic rug runner, a wooden match, a table knife, a pocket knife, a light blue baby's blanket, a royal blue blanket, fingernail scrapings from Becky Williams's hands, samples of pubic and head hair from the victim, a floral sheet, a green and white pillowcase, on and on—were shipped to the state Division of Forensic Science lab in Merrifield. Within a few weeks, blood samples, saliva swabs, and hairs from some initial suspects in the case were also showing up at the state lab.

On June 9, Police Chief C. B. Jones assured Culpeper residents that his office was hard at work on the case. But he admitted that numerous interviews with friends, neighbors, and relatives of Becky Williams had brought them no closer to an answer. "If there's a witness, we haven't talked with them yet," he said.[13] Three days later, Commonwealth's attorney John Bennett reported that "there have been developments" and "they are being evaluated." He declined to elaborate. But on June 16, twelve days after the murder, a headline in the local paper summed up the situation: "Murder Remains a Total Mystery."

Becky's parents had established a reward fund at the Second National Bank. Contributions totaled $1,000. Their daughter was laid to rest on a peaceful hillside after a service at the Culpeper Baptist Church. Residential life at the Village Apartments was returning to normal. Neighbors talked in their doorways. Children chased each other through the parking lot. But the witness or "strong suspect" that police often focus on in the immediate aftermath of a crime was nowhere to be found. Over the next eleven months, little changed. Suspects came and went. Leads emerged and evaporated. Clifford Williams and his daughters were trapped in a downward spiral of grief, confusion, and rage.

To stymied investigators, it was as if the murderer had evaporated as quickly and stealthily as he had appeared. Failure to wrap up the case was both inexplicable and embarrassing. And then, out of nowhere, an answer arrived.

3

A Piedmont Son

HISTORY AND A RARE BEAUTY entwine in Virginia's Piedmont, as do the poles of wealth and opportunity. Culpeper County, the home of Rebecca Williams and her family of working-class whites, and neighboring Fauquier County, where Earl Washington came of age, sit west and slightly south of Washington, D.C. Their villages and byways erupt in a confection of pink and white blossoms in springtime and a splash of autumnal hues in the fall, drawing hordes of sight-seers from cities and suburbs to the east.

In colonial times Thomas Jefferson and James Madison, who lived nearby, made their way by horseback and coach along the counties' rutted thoroughfares as they traveled to and from Washington, D.C., forging a nation. Back home, African American slaves labored to keep the planters' fortunes afloat, freeing them and their compatriots for more cerebral pursuits. No region of Virginia was more wedded to the institution of slavery than the Piedmont.[1] In the 1790 census about one-third of the residents were black; by 1840, there were majority black populations in both Culpeper and Fauquier.[2]

According to family lore and the limited records that exist, the roots of Earl Washington Jr.'s family run deep in Fauquier County, extending to before the Civil War. None of his known ancestors appear in an early county register of freed Negroes.[3] Presumably, all were slaves. George Washington, Earl's paternal great-grandfather, was a twenty-three-year-old laborer when he married another county native, Lizzie Haley, in 1872. Over the next decades they produced several children and watched a daughter die from typhoid fever in 1892 and a son of consumption in 1896. Among the surviving offspring was Ross Washington, also a laborer, who was forty-six years old when his tenth child, Earl Washington Sr., was born in 1925.[4]

If the Washingtons knew the hardship of nineteenth-century rural life, the family of Earl Washington Jr.'s paternal grandmother, Alice Tate, was even more intimately acquainted with grief. County records reveal that Alice's grandparents—Earl Jr.'s great-great-grandparents—lost five children in a seven-year span between 1886 and 1893 to typhoid, pneumonia, and fever. Among them was Alice's mother, Phebe, who died of a fever in August 1889 at age twenty-two, leaving behind her five-year-old daughter. Fourteen years later in 1903, Alice married Ross Washington. Over the next two decades, their children—including Earl Jr.'s father—arrived in rapid succession, about two years apart.

The origins of Marie Mudd Washington, Earl Jr.'s mother, are sketchier. As with the Washingtons and Tates, there are no family diaries, no photographs. Even birth, death, and marriage records that mention the Mudds are rare. Memory is the primary record book. According to Marie's sister, Mary Mudd Jones, both their parents—John P. Mudd and Grace Thomas Mudd—were born, lived, and died in the same southern region of Fauquier County in which Earl Sr., Marie, and their children later resided.[5]

Most of the male Washingtons are designated as "laborers" in census records. Otherwise, there are few clues as to the skills and dispositions that accompanied Earl Washington's ancestors out of slavery. Throughout the Piedmont, slave life generally was characterized by the same mix of abuses, day-to-day ordinariness, and occasional enlightenment that broadly defined master-slave society in the American South. Virginia was the first North American colony to introduce and legalize slavery, and until the Civil War its slave population remained larger than that of any other state.[6] A host of ever-changing laws dictated the conditions under which slaves could be freed, traded, disciplined, and educated. The evolution of laws governing the manumission of slaves is reflective. In 1691, Virginia decreed that no citizen could free a slave without paying to transport them outside the colony. By 1723 an even tougher law dictated that slaves could be freed only for meritorious service, a matter to be determined by the governor and the state's governing council. In the wake of the Revolutionary War, a burst of affection for freedom and self-governance resulted in the relaxation of such restrictions. But white fears, spurred by a growing and sometimes restive slave population, resulted in an 1806 law saying that every freed Negro must leave the state within twelve months unless granted special permission to stay.[7]

Fear of black retaliation against whites was as ingrained in the Piedmont as in other regions of the South. After a slave named Eve mixed a poisonous substance into the milk of her owner in August 1745, killing him, she was burned to death at the order of the local court in Orange County, next door to Culpeper.[8] In 1809, according to court records, ninety-four men were paid $428.24—between 6 cents and 6.3 cents per hour—for patrolling Culpeper County. Such "patrollers" were expected to halt all traveling Negroes and ask them for proof of free status or for a travel pass from their master.[9] A local Culpeper history records that on December 15, 1856 the county organized eight, five-man patrols in response to rumors that blacks were planning to massacre whites. "People are very much alarmed," the captain of one patrol wrote. But fears of an insurrection went unrealized.[10]

At the same time there were occasional acts of benevolence toward slaves. Just a few miles from the community in which Earl Jr. grew up, Armistead Blackwell—a prominent white landowner—died in 1836 requesting that his wife, if she so chose, free their slaves and divide the value of their property among them at the time of her death. Blackwell expected that the freed slaves would travel to Ohio or some other locale outside Virginia to reestablish their lives. Twenty-three years later, on the eve of the Civil War, Elizabeth Blackwell complied with her husband's request. But in a locally famous court case, *Washington et al v. Blackwell Estate*, the former slaves won the right to remain on the inherited Fauquier County land. The eight-hundred-thirty-acre Blackwell estate, known as Elk Run Plantation, was divided into thirty-acre farms and a sum of money was apportioned to each adult, with children receiving a smaller amount.[11] The Washington in the lawsuit was Eli Washington, one of the freed slaves. Whether there is a familial link with the family of Earl Washington is unknown.

While Armistead and Elizabeth Blackwell were ahead of their time, most of the white residents of Fauquier and Culpeper counties were deeply invested in the Southern milieu, an attraction that extended well into the twentieth century. During the Civil War, the region became a crossroads for Yankee and Confederate troops, and the white sons and daughters of the Piedmont lamented the Northern invasion of their land and culture. On April 26, 1861 Amanda Virginia Edmonds of upper Fauquier County, wrote in her journal: "Upwards of 15,000 are stationed in and around Harper's Ferry—have been coming in from the extreme Southern states by hundreds and thousands. Brave, gallant men, so we hear, anxious to have a fight. Virginia has volunteered 80,000. Welcome, most gallant soldiers, to our soil. Our own dear Virginia, destined to be the battleground."[12]

P. A. L. Smith was equally rapturous when he wrote about his life in Fauquier County after the Civil War: "There never was but one real war, and that was from 1861 to 1865. The war that tried every heart and soul, and made men and women of the south brave and good, virtuous and noble."[13]

A century later the northward migration of blacks and a dwindling agricultural base had brought subtle changes to the Piedmont, though among whites reverence remained for the Confederate past. Demographically, Culpeper County contained about 22,600 citizens at the 1980 census, one-fifth of them black. Next door in Fauquier, about 13 percent of the 35,889 residents were African American. The wealthier of the two counties and the closer to Washington, D.C., Fauquier was dotted with palatial estates, hunt clubs, and horse farms. Culpeper, in contrast, fit within the economic mainstream of the rural South. In 1983, the year Earl Washington was arrested for the death of Rebecca Williams, twenty of the richest people in America lived either in Fauquier or adjacent Loudoun County.[14] Names such as Mellon, Kluge, and DuPont were staples on area tax roles, and the presence brought an overlay of tasteful affluence to an otherwise rural setting. An article in the local newspaper noted that the Fauquier County seat of Warrenton had been selected for a doctoral dissertation on preretirement plans because it is "a model community" combining the "rustic beauty of a rural area with the delicate sophistication of suburbia."[15]

Marie and Earl "Egg" Washington Sr. and their children—Alfreda, Earl Jr., Linda, Robert, and Donald—were not equal participants in either Fauquier County's wealth or its ambience. Some of the Washingtons in southern Fauquier County achieved a degree of local prominence as stalwart members of a working-class community. The family of Earl Sr. and Marie Washington was not among them. Numerous sources and events confirm that the family was uncommonly poor.

The Washingtons' sixth child, Grace Etta, was less than three months old when she died in December 1963 of undernutrition. The 1980 census put medium household income for blacks in Fauquier County at $11,938, barely half that for whites. But the Washingtons' income was far less. On an application for free school lunches a few years earlier, Marie reported the family earnings as $75 per week—less than

$4,000 annually. When fifteen-year-old Linda enrolled in school several weeks late in September 1976, she blamed her absence on a lack of school clothes. Shortly thereafter, an official recorded: "Linda came in this morning and asked if we could help them get shoes."[16]

An investigator piecing together a social history of the Washington family during Earl Jr.'s incarceration traced a portrait of multigenerational, rural poverty. At the time, the senior Washingtons were living in a dilapidated farmhouse, typical of those in which their son grew up. "It is difficult to determine how many people are living in the house at any one time because uncles, aunts, cousins and other relatives are constantly moving in and out. There is no indoor bathroom, and the house is heated by a wood stove in the living room," the investigator wrote.[17]

"Socio-economically, they were very deprived. Life was really a struggle for that young man," recalled Frances Glaettli, a middle school teacher of Earl Jr.'s.[18] The family "was pretty much the poorest of the poor, a whole group of people living in the house," agreed Don Huffman, a neighboring farmer for whom the Washington boys worked.[19]

The failure of Marie and Earl Washington Sr. to get ahead did not stem from unwillingness to work. Earl Sr., a taciturn, physically fragile man, was regularly employed as a truck driver for local concerns or as a laborer. Marie, who was thirteen years his junior and whose verbal and mental limitations foretold those of her children, did domestic jobs. Neither had the education or the intellectual skills to lift themselves above living conditions only marginally improved from those of their ancestors. Earl Sr. had a second-grade education and was functionally illiterate. Marie went until the eighth grade. There were physical as well as cognitive limitations to advancement. During their childhoods, a high school for black youth in Warrenton served only a small region of the county. Until the early 1950s, the bulk of Fauquier's black teens were bused to the Manassas Industrial School for Colored Youth, a county away. Had Marie and Earl Sr. pursued their studies, long bus rides and segregated facilities would have been part of the bargain.

In addition to poverty, the Washington household had a harsh and sometimes violent edge, worsened by alcohol abuse. Ten days after Linda was born in 1961, Marie was hospitalized at Fauquier County Hospital for a hysterical episode attributed to postpartum depression and acute alcoholism.[20] In June 1980 Earl Sr. was arrested for being drunk in public. In June 1981 Marie took out a warrant against her husband saying that he "beat me with a board." Earl Jr., ever protective of his parents, acknowledged that they sometimes came to blows when they had been drinking. Once, he tried to intervene on his mother's behalf. "I stepped in between 'em. I got hit, but it didn't hurt too bad," he said. The investigator profiling the family for the Washington defense team reported, "The Washingtons have been visited several times over the past two years. On every occasion there has been heavy drinking with at least one family member appearing drunk."[21]

Huffman recalled that the father was "a heavy drinker, you could tell from his appearance." But the farmer also noted, "They were not the kind of people who sat in the house and didn't work. They were poor but they did work."

There are mixed reports from the Washington children about the degree to which they were disciplined for misbehavior, real or perceived. Linda, the most estranged of the children, told a defense-team investigator that all the siblings were routinely beaten well into their teens. However, both Alfreda and Earl Jr. insist that they were not hit without reason. "We seldom got beat," Alfreda said. "You had to do a whole lot to get your tail tore up." Whatever the truth, there is evidence that the elder Washingtons lived by a code that could be breathtaking in its severity. Asked after his release from prison if he would like to have a pet, Earl Jr. mused over the question, shook his head no, and offered the following story. Once, Washington said, he had a kitten that made the mistake of climbing onto the table and eating out of his father's dinner plate. "He'd told us kids, 'Don't you ever let no cat get on there, or I've got a surprise for him.'" The "surprise" was swift and permanent. When Earl Sr. saw the kitten, he picked it up, opened the door to the heating stove and threw the cat into the fire. In telling this story, Earl Jr. did not appear to blame his father. His tone was informational. His father had warned the children not to let the cat on the table.[22]

Another bizarre episode occurred when Earl Jr. was sixteen and was shot by an uncle, Robert Mudd, apparently for not moving quickly enough to bring in firewood. Mudd, who received a twelve-month suspended sentence for assault and battery, told an investigator that he was shooting at Earl Jr. in jest to make him run faster. An already-fired bullet struck when his nephew unexpectedly doubled back, he said. According to hospital records, Earl Jr. was treated for multiple puncture wounds of the liver and a kidney and underwent an appendectomy. He was found at the same time to be suffering from Ascaris, parasitic roundworms found in humans and pigs.

Not everything was bleak for the large rural clan. The oldest daughter, Alfreda, who even as a child fulfilled the role of family matriarch, protested the depiction of her parents as uncaring or brutal toward their children. "Both of them loved to work. I do too," she said. "Both of them had family values, doing what you have to do to take care of a family."[23] Earl Jr.'s most fervent wish, upon his release from prison, was to visit the graves of his parents, who had died during his incarceration, and he recalled them with affection. "I remember mamma being nice. I think that's where I got it from, being nice, honest," he said. "My daddy was shy. I get that way at times around people."[24]

Nor was the family's poverty unbearable, he said. "We got new shoes sometimes." And while "people used to say they [his clothes] was out of style, I used to say, 'I don't wear clothes to make you happy. The way you all talk, you can't be my friends.'" A half-sister, Shirley Cuesenberry, also argues that some of the negative portrayals of the Washingtons are misguided. "I know that they drank, but I never saw them abusive," she said.[25]

Born in 1960, Earl Jr. was the Washingtons' second child and first son, a playful boy at home, retiring and often ill-at-ease in public. As a young adult, he was regarded by neighboring farmers as the most accommodating of the Washington boys, a distinction that made his imprisonment for murder even more perplexing.[26]

During the nine years that he attended an assortment of public schools before dropping out at age fifteen, teacher after teacher described Earl Jr. as a lovable child who tried hard to please but was stymied by frequent absences and difficulties in comprehension. As he grew older, he became less compliant, but even then observers noted a disarming congeniality. In 1975, the year before he left school, psychologist Margaret Meyer captured his restless dissatisfaction and emerging rebellion, as well as his innate good nature. "Earl is an average size Afro-American boy who has been absent on this writer's regular day at Cedar-Lee for months; therefore, I was surprised to find him in attendance on 2–10," Meyer wrote. "In conference he states that he dislikes school and probably won't be back the rest of this week. He likes to stay at home and cut wood, feed cows, do other farm work and go hunting. Earl was very hyperactive throughout the testing session— moved from chair to chair and played with pencils and dice. There were very few moments when he was completely stationary. Earl's speech is not distinct and he works with the speech therapist on Mondays when he is not absent. He had much difficulty with auditory discrimination also. Earl tended to be both overly oppositional and passive-aggressive (i.e., behaved in a fashion in order to 'bait' the examiner). Though he constantly tested the limits, his naiveté and general happy-go-lucky demeanor prevented feelings of anger being elicited from this writer."

Earl Jr. did not enter first grade until 1967 when he was seven years and three months old. A preschool health examination noted that he was emotionally "a little shy—bites fingernails." He received his first childhood vaccinations that fall. A year and a half later when he was eight and repeating first grade, Earl Jr. was referred to a school psychologist for the first time. The referral form noted, "Earl is very retiring—tries hard to melt into the background. He never volunteers any information. . . . He can do a little addition. . . . Does not play much with others." At the conclusion of second grade, the teacher's report was no more positive: "Slow—does not use time wisely—does not concentrate or [sic] to have an inquiring attitude . . . works very slowly and at times seemed to show enthusiasm over being able to read. Needs individual help and teacher encouragement." His report card listed Fs in reading and arithmetic and Cs in citizenship and physical education.

At the end of third grade, Earl Jr. was back in the school psychologist's office. This time he was recommended for transfer to a class for educable mentally retarded students when the new school year began. His third-grade teacher, who described Earl Jr. as "retarded" and his performance as "failing," nonetheless detected a few strengths. "Very lovable, loves to help," she listed under "major personality traits." The boy liked both math and looking at books, and he "tries hard to be buddies, but many times in trying irritates the children." The formal psychological evaluation observed that Earl Jr. appeared to be "a very pleasant boy" who had trouble understanding instructions and verbalizing responses. "Anything requiring verbalizations on his part entailed tremendously long hesitations before attempting responses," she wrote. And in an observation that might have cued his future police interrogators to regard his confessions skeptically, she added, "His particular weakness is in the area of social competence. He has little notion as to what is expected of him in a social setting and cannot deal effectively with interpersonal situations."

In September 1971, Earl Jr. was assigned to special education classes, where he would remain for the next five and a half years before withdrawing from school. His evaluations remained consistent. "Earl has never been a problem and is pleasant to work with. He is very easily led. He tries to do what is asked, but has no idea what is expected of him," wrote his teacher when he was thirteen.

After his arrest and confessions, police and prosecutors challenged the designation of Earl Washington as mentally retarded. But throughout his childhood, the Fauquier County school system had no qualms about applying the label.[27] Glaettli, who taught Earl Jr. during the 1973–74 school year, said she questioned whether some special education students belonged in the class. About Earl Washington, she had no doubts. "Earl struggled. He certainly tried, but he struggled," she said. "He was one of my lower functioning students." Tested on the Wechsler Intelligence Scale shortly after his eleventh birthday, Earl Jr. showed an IQ of 58, in the lowest 1 to 2 percent of the population and indicative of mild-to-moderate retardation. When psychologist Margaret Meyer conducted her evaluation in February 1975, she determined that his IQ was "in the range of mental retardation (mild)" and that, at fourteen, his perceptual-motor skills were poorer than would be expected of a seven-and-a-half to eight-year-old. "He has obviously built up a defense system to help him 'save face' in these difficult situations," she wrote.

External life circumstances—the lack of reading material in the home, the household disorder, and the frequent absenteeism from school—contributed to the academic failing of Washington and his siblings, all of whom were tagged for special education classes within a few years of entering school. Following an evaluation in 1993, Ruth Luckasson, professor of special education at the University of New Mexico and a leading national advocate for the mentally disabled, said that she had no doubt of Washington's retardation. "His disability was first formally recognized when he entered school at the age of 7 and was placed in special education at the age of 9, and it continues to this day," she wrote.[28]

She listed the evidence: limited cognitive ability, limited logical thinking, poor attention span, poor short-term memory, poor ability to differentiate essential information from nonessential information, and impaired adaptive life skills. Luckasson also identified many of the accepted causes of mental retardation in the school and health records of Earl Washington: alcohol consumption by his mother during pregnancy, likely malnourishment of the pregnant mother, lack of prenatal health care, extreme family poverty, absence of adequate parenting skills, family disruption, likely malnourishment of the children, failure to send the children to school, and a lack of preschool or early intervention programs that might have helped Earl Jr. and his siblings overcome their limitations. Even so, Washington's retardation does not erase his positive traits—"he is motivated to do well, he has a kind temperament, and is cheerful and cooperative," Luckasson stressed.

Increasingly, as Earl Jr. aged, he masked his intellectual shortcomings by not showing up at school. By spring 1975 letters were going home questioning his repeated absences. And the following fall, his shaky performance was underscored by a string of minor offenses—tardiness, truancy, failure to dress for gym. On January 27, 1976, at fifteen years and nine months of age, Earl Jr. withdrew from the Fauquier County schools. The form noted that he had been absent for fifteen consecutive days.

With school behind him, Earl Jr. settled into the only life for which he was equipped—working as a day laborer, usually staying close to home. He moved in and out of the Washington household, living at times with Alfreda who had left home by then. The face Earl Jr. presented to the larger Fauquier community was largely anonymous and benign. Jonathan Lynn, a Fauquier County prosecutor, recalled that all three Washington brothers once broke into a house and stole some food that they then ate. The boys had to go to court, but the punishment was minimal. There were a few other adolescent transgressions, but none so serious as to pierce Lynn's radar screen.

Within the family circle, Washington was louder and more assertive. He had a reputation for doling out treats to neighborhood children, but he could lose his temper when provoked. His weakness for alcohol was beginning to show as well. Gradually, Earl Jr. joined in the weekend drinking sprees that were the family norm. In the spring of 1983 he was arrested for driving under the influence of alcohol and being without a driver's license, charges that were later dropped in the midst of the murder investigation.

But that side of Earl Jr. was not on regular display. Various neighboring farmers who called on the Washingtons at haying or crop time expressed surprise and disbelief at the time of his arrest in the death of Rebecca Williams. "He was an excellent worker, never had an attitude problem," said Don Huffman, who recalled Earl Jr.'s pliant amiability.

Huffman would instruct his young worker in one job at a time, never expecting him to remember several. "He was always very mild-mannered, never got excited or upset. I tried never to be abusive or speak harshly to him because of his mentality."

After the arrest, Huffman told state investigators and Washington's attorney that guilt was inconceivable. "I said from Day One, the man did not do it, and I've never changed my mind," Huffman said. "Because of his mentality, he couldn't have gotten to Culpeper and gotten back. There had to have been blood all over the place. Are you going to tell me somebody picked him up (in that bloodied state) and never came forward? How come these people never came forward?"

But in May 1983 the police and the courts were not interested in Huffman's doubts. Criminal justice officials in Fauquier and Culpeper counties were satisfied that they had on their hands a violent sexual predator. They had, after all, the definitive word on the matter—Washington's own.

4

Arrest

MRS. HAZEL NANCY WEEKS had just returned from the bathroom when she heard the crash and sat up in bed.

According to the clock, it was about 3 A.M. Without her glasses, it was hard to tell the exact time. Most likely, a storm was brewing and the wind had knocked a branch into the front of the house. It sounded as if glass had broken.

A more timid or less practical soul might have burrowed under the covers. But Hazel Weeks had not spent her seventy-eight years as the daughter of one farmer and the wife of another for nothing. If there was a broken window, it needed to be covered before the rain started. Two years earlier, her husband James would have done the fixing. Now he was gone, and Hazel had chosen to remain alone in this house where they had made a life for themselves and their four children. Their son, Jimmy, who lived not far down the road, would have taken her in gladly, as would the others. But Hazel preferred her independence. The children had their own lives to lead and she did not want to be a nuisance. Besides, here she could look out a window and see the field that came up almost to the back door, and she could savor the memories of all the crops and seasons there. She loved the long front yard as well, with the magnolia, crepe myrtle, fir, and other trees blocking the sight and sounds of Route 17 as the traffic sped between Fredericksburg and Warrenton.

Hazel lifted the covers and gingerly swung her legs out of bed. After two knee replacements, she was walking well, but she had to be vigilant against falling. She clicked on the bedroom light and, barefoot and without her robe, headed down the hall toward the front door. Almost there, Hazel realized that she was walking on broken glass. She turned back. In the bedroom, she located her tennis shoes and dirty socks from the previous day, put them on and turned back to survey the damage. She was halfway down the hall when she realized that she was not alone.

A man was standing just inside the living room archway.

Hazel could not see him clearly. All she could tell was that he was male and black. Instinctively, she lifted her cane and ordered him away. "Get out of here," she demanded. His response was swift and violent. Whirling, he lifted a wooden armchair from the end of the dining room table. Within seconds, it came crashing into Hazel's head, then again, and again.

Stunned, Hazel felt her grasp slipping and wondered if she was about to die. And then, the prayer that she did not even know she was praying was answered. "Evidently, I was asking the Lord for help and I think that the word 'money' must have been put into my mind by the Lord," she testified a month later.[1] It occurred to her that if she offered the man the money in her purse, he might stop hitting her.

"I don't have very much money, but what money I have, I'll give it to you, if you'll take it and let me alone," she said.

"Where is your money?" the man replied.

"It's back in my bedroom."

"Where is your bedroom?"

"It's back at the end of the hall."

Hazel's memory of reaching the bedroom was blurred. Either she was pushed or dragged, probably pushed—she thought—because she was still standing. The man asked where her pocketbook was and she pointed him toward the double closet.

"That's the wrong door, try the other door," she instructed.

As the man searched for the purse, Hazel edged her hand toward the telephone, thinking that she might be able to signal for help. But the man saw her and knocked her hand down and her with it to the floor.

"Take off your gown," he said.

Hazel Weeks was a small woman, about 5'2", not frail, but not stout. She stood no chance of defending herself against this intruder, but she was not going to be violated without a struggle.

"He told you to take off your gown?" assistant Commonwealth's attorney John Inger asked, replaying the moment in court during a preliminary hearing in the case a month later. "He did, but the money seemed to knock that out of his head, and besides my gown was soaking wet with the blood that was running from the back of my head."

"You didn't take off your gown?"

"I did not take off my gown."

"Did anything happen after . . . so when he told you to take off your gown, what did you do?"

"I didn't do anything. I didn't have any idea of taking my gown off."

"What did he do?"

"He took the money and left and closed the bedroom door behind him as he went out."

Hazel Weeks inched across the floor to the telephone and dialed the number of her son, Jimmy.

"I was home asleep. The telephone rang. She said, 'Please come, there's somebody in the house.'"[2]

James "Jimmy" Weeks III woke his wife and son, scrambled into his clothes, and raced out to the car and down Route 17 to his mother's house. He entered quietly through the kitchen door and went straight to the refrigerator. The .22, nine-shot pistol that was his brother's had been kept there for years, visible to anyone. If the intruder was still in the house, a gun might be useful. His hand rummaged the top of the refrigerator. Nothing. The gun was gone.

Jimmy switched on a light illuminating the living and dining room areas. He stopped in his tracks. Blood seemed to be everywhere. A broken dining room chair lay on the floor. Items were scattered out of place. Hurrying down the hall, Weeks found his mother on the bedroom floor. Hazel Weeks was coherent, but she was unable to get up by herself because of the knee replacements. She had taken some pieces of used bedsheet that she kept for rags and was pressing them against her skull to stop the bleeding. He helped her to the bed. His wife arrived and began tending to his mother. Jimmy went out to wait for the rescue squad and the sheriff.

Earl Washington Jr. had been drinking hard liquor for hours, and now he was mad.

As usual, a crowd had gathered for a party at the small, unpainted tenant house rented by his Aunt Nellie Mudd a few miles outside Bealeton on Route 17. Some Pendleton boys were there, including Mitchell, his sister Alfreda's no-account husband. So were Earl Jr.'s younger brothers, Robert and "Duck." There were a few women also, but in the aftermath no one seemed to remember their names. At first, the gathering had been friendly enough, but the hours of drinking had turned the evening loud and sour. There were taunts, followed by shoves. Earl Jr.'s fury mounted. Pushing through the crowd, he bolted out the door and headed into the night. His destination was the kitchen of Nellie Mudd's nearest neighbor, Mrs. Hazel Weeks. Once when he asked to use the telephone, Washington had seen a pistol there on top of the refrigerator. Now, he wanted it.

Deputy Denny Zeets of the Fauquier County sheriff's department happened to be patrolling nearby when the report came in at about 3:25 A.M. of a break-in at the home of Hazel Weeks. He sped to the site and found Jimmy Weeks waiting. Moments later, the deputy heard a gun go off. The shot seemed to come from across the highway. Racing down the driveway, Zeets saw lights at a ramshackle dwelling across the way and he headed in their direction. Inside the house, the deputy found Robert Washington, Mitchell Pendleton, and "a couple of other (unidentified) subjects."[3] Robert was nursing a gunshot wound to his foot, inflicted— according to the group—by his brother, Earl Jr. Just then, a second shot was fired outside the house, and Zeets dashed back outside. He saw no one, but a brown purse was lying on the ground. Papers inside identified it as Hazel Weeks's. Zeets was sifting through the purse when he heard a third shot, this one from the opposite side of Route 17, back toward the Weeks home.

Reinforcements were arriving as Zeets hurried across the highway. A group of deputies assembled in Mrs. Weeks's yard, and then fanned out to search the area up and down Route 17. According to Sheriff Luther Cox, speaking to the *Fauquier Democrat*, ten sheriff's deputies, two state troopers, and a tracking dog eventually joined the three-hour manhunt.[4] The drama ended peacefully when dawn came and Deputy A. L. Robinson spotted Earl Washington Jr. an estimated forty feet from the road in a field of three-foot grass, just down the highway from Hazel Weeks's home. Service revolver drawn, Robinson ordered Washington to put his hands up and come out of the grass. He did. The suspect was wearing yellow shorts and unlaced brown shoes, no shirt and no socks. "He was a little bit wet, appeared to be a little tired, not extremely tired," Robinson said. Hazel Weeks's gun was nearby. The deputy escorted his prisoner to the car and advised him that he had a right to remain silent. On the trip to Warrenton, Washington said nothing.[5]

■

The full story of what led Earl Washington Jr. to break into the home of Hazel Weeks on May 21, 1983, what occurred between them, and what happened afterward is veiled by Washington's inability—or reluctance—to recall the details and by Mrs. Weeks's death from natural causes four years later. Washington never denied the break-in or that he hit Mrs. Weeks when confronted. "I feel very bad," he said many years later. "I regret that every day since I been locked up."[6]

Mrs. Weeks spent several days in the hospital, after which she continued to live alone. She sustained no long-term physical injuries, but her son believes that her spirit was permanently wounded. "She was always jovial and after that, she didn't laugh much anymore," he said, describing the episode as the most painful experience of his life.

According to police accounts and Washington's recorded statement on the morning of his arrest, the fight that precipitated the break-in at Mrs. Weeks's involved an altercation with Robert over a woman. In later years, Earl Jr. insisted that his anger had been directed not at his brother but at "some Pendletons." Both he and Robert said that the shooting of Robert was an accident. Charges involving it were dropped.

One of the few certainties is that the events were the launchpad for the confession and conviction that put Washington on death row for another crime. When Washington and his escorts arrived at the Fauquier County Sheriff's Department, the officers filed four charges involving Mrs. Weeks: attempted rape, robbery, breaking and entering, and malicious wounding. The first charge was the pivotal piece in all that came later. If the officers had not believed that Earl Washington attempted to rape Mrs. Weeks, a charge that was dropped after she testified otherwise at a preliminary hearing a few weeks later, Washington might never have been asked about a series of sexual crimes to which he readily confessed.

At 8:30 A.M., Deputy Zeets put down on paper the first of several statements and confessions Washington made that day. Taken at face value, the prisoner's words were damning: "I was at Pendleton's house. I found my girlfriend with my brother. We argued. I told him I was going to get a gun and shoot him. I went to Mrs. Weeks house to get gun, broke out the window and opened the door. I went to the kitchen, got gun from over refrigerator and started back to the door. I saw her coming down hall. I hit her with the chair. She fell to the floor. I keep hitting her untell [sic] the chair broke apart. That's when I decided to f— her. I got on top of her but she started to move and then told me to leave her alone. I told her I want your money. She said it was in her purse. I got up [sic] took her purse from a chair in the living room. I went out the door and back to Pendletons house. I went around back and stopped for a time. I went in the house and shot my brother. I got scared and ran away."

Like other statements and confessions attributed to Washington that day, the words—and the questions that prompted them—were not recorded or videotaped. There were some curious discrepancies. The house was not the home of the Pendletons. It was the home of Nellie Mudd. In his statement, Washington asked for money. According to Mrs. Weeks, she introduced the idea. According to the confession, Washington picked up the purse off a living room chair and fled; in Mrs. Weeks's account, the purse was in a bedroom closet and they went to get it. In Washington's account, a sexual encounter occurred in the hall. In Mrs. Weeks's, they had gone to the bedroom to get the purse when Washington told her to take off her gown. He went no further and the money "seemed to knock that out of his head."

The most benign explanation of the inconsistencies, from Washington's standpoint, would be that white, Southern police officers investigating a break-in by a black man at the home of a white woman erroneously assumed that it involved sex and tailored a confession to match. Unquestionably, the story of the violent black male taking sexual advantage of the helpless white female is an enduring theme of Southern culture.[7] The intersection of that storied myth and the criminal justice system has long worked to the disadvantage of black males, particularly poor ones. Prior to the Civil War, a Virginia Negro—slave or free—who raped or attempted to rape a white woman could be executed at the discretion of the jury. A white man who raped a black woman, however, could only be sentenced to a ten- to twenty-year prison term. Moreover, Negroes could not testify against whites in court, reducing the likelihood of a black woman's getting her story before a judge.[8] After the passage of the Fourteenth Amendment to the Constitution, laws applied equally to blacks and whites. But the discretion afforded judges and juries still tilted justice against blacks in rape cases.[9]

Mrs. Weeks's testimony that Washington told her to "take off your gown" pointed to something more concrete than a police blunder, however: an actual impropriety, albeit at a level well shy of attempted rape. Jimmy Weeks offered one detail not included in his mother's testimony.

On the night of the assault, he said, Mrs. Weeks told his wife that Washington pulled her gown up to her head. As far as Jimmy Weeks knew, nothing else happened. Over the years, some observers have argued that Mrs. Weeks—an otherwise forthright witness—downplayed the extent of the encounter because of embarrassment. She could not have done so with the assurance that Washington was going to prison for another crime. The preliminary hearing was held six months before the Rebecca Williams trial.

The hint of sexual misconduct made Washington an instant suspect in the region's unsolved rapes, and it drove subsequent interrogations. Even after his pardon almost two decades later, confusion about the nature of the Weeks assault continued to plague him. This was due in part to an unnoticed shift in the account of Deputy Zeets about what occurred on the night of the break-in. At the preliminary hearing in June 1983, Zeets said that he answered a dispatcher's call and arrived at the home of Hazel Weeks at about 3:30 A.M. He found the wooden front door standing open. The storm door was closed, and a window at the entrance to the house had been shattered. Zeets rounded the outside of the house, looking for further signs of an intruder. He entered through the kitchen door and met Jimmy Weeks. Hazel Weeks, Zeets said, "was in the bathroom of the house being attended to by her daughter[-in-law]."

Ten months later when the Fauquier County charges were finally resolved, Deputy Zeets again recalled the episode for a presentence investigative report. This time, a critical detail in his story changed. "I was patrolling that area of Route 17 and I received a call of a breaking and entering at the Weeks residence," Zeets said the second time around. "I arrived at the house just three minutes later and found the front door open and glass broken out of the door. . . . I followed the line of blood back to Mrs. Weeks bedroom. She was partially on the bed and was naked. She was bleeding very badly from the head and also had lacerations from the arms and shoulders. Her son and daughter-in-law then came in and started caring for Mrs. Weeks."

The first version, consistent with the memory of Jimmy Weeks, is that the son arrived before the police. Mrs. Weeks was wearing her gown. In the second version, Zeets arrived first. He found Mrs. Weeks on the bed, naked.

The discrepancy in Zeets's story had a tangible consequence. Years later, when Washington was granted an absolute pardon in the murder of Rebecca Williams, state officials refused to reduce his thirty-year sentence in the case of Mrs. Weeks, even though experts on parole practices said Washington would have been freed years earlier save for the death sentence. In defending the harsh treatment, a member of the state parole board explained that Mrs. Weeks had been found "naked and lying in a pool of blood."[10]

The Zeets presentence report, written many months after the fact, is the only document describing Mrs. Weeks as naked. The description is at odds with Mrs. Weeks's testimony, her son's recollection, and Zeets's own testimony under oath a month after the break-in. One other detail points to error in the later account. Zeets said that, as the first to arrive, he found Mrs. Weeks lying "partially on the bed" and naked. But Jimmy Weeks recalled that his mother was on the floor when he discovered her. Because of her knee replacements, he said, she was unable to get up by herself.

Whatever Washington did or intended on that fateful night, the turbulent history of his family, with its years of racial and economic slight, its alcoholism, its domestic violence, and mental gaps came spiraling down through time to a single, distilled sentence, heard during a drunken break-in: "Take off your gown." Out of that moment, those words, the misunderstandings and errors and deceptions that brought Washington to within nine days of execution emerged.

5

Confessions

INVESTIGATOR TERRY SCHRUM did not plan to stay when he walked into the Fauquier County sheriff's department that Saturday morning. It was a day off. Summer was fast approaching, and there was plenty to do at home. But the jailhouse was abuzz with news of the break-in the previous night at the home of Mrs. Hazel Weeks. The suspect, Earl Washington Jr., had been captured in a field after a three-hour manhunt. He was here in the county jail. Within moments, Schrum's plans changed.

"I knew Mrs. Weeks, didn't know her personally. I knew her son Jimmy and I knew she was an elderly woman. I was told he had gone in, hit her with a chair, violent, he's looking for the gun, and that he had got on top of her and tried to take her underpants off," Schrum recalled years later.[1] Washington was twenty-three years old. Mrs. Weeks was seventy-eight. Something didn't add up. "So based on that, him being a young guy, it doesn't make sense. I asked 'em, 'Did anybody interview him about any other cases we had outstanding?' And they said, 'No.'"

Big-city violence was rare in Fauquier County and Warrenton in the early 1980s. But lately, there had been a string of assaults on females. Residents were jittery. Now here was a suspect who—according to what Schrum was hearing—had broken into a house, committed an assault and robbery, and tried to rape an elderly woman. Already the details were being embellished, but the officer had no way of knowing. Unlike the other attacks, which occurred in Warrenton, this one took place about twelve miles away in the country outside Bealeton. The other assaults involved young women, this one did not. Still, there might be a connection. The man ought to be asked.

Terry Schrum's questioning of Washington began at 9:40 A.M. The prisoner had spent the previous night drinking heavily, breaking into a neighbor's house, evading police, and hiding in a field. If he had slept at all, it was either on hard ground in an open field or in brief interludes after his arrest. Still, Washington acted more expectant and fidgety than tired. There was a wide-eyed look and a half-smile on his face, nothing belligerent, and a sort of nervous twitching. Over the next couple hours of questioning, "He moved constantly. He never sat still," the officer recalled.

The interview began with a patient recital of Washington's Miranda rights. Terry Schrum was no expert in mental retardation. His police training barely touched on the subject. The beefy lawman was, according to acquaintances, a tough, straight-arrow cop who wanted to see the guilty brought to justice and did not believe in lying on the stand or abusing a prisoner to get there. What his gut told him that morning in the Fauquier County jail was that Earl Washington was slow.

"I knew he was kind of slow, not pathetically slow," Schrum said. "And when I advised him of his rights, I took a lot of time advising him. I recited what we're supposed to recite. Then I'd explain what each one meant to him, like, 'You have the right to remain silent. Now, Earl, we're sitting here talking to you. You don't have to talk to us if you don't want to.'"

Did Washington understand what was said, asked Deputy Zeets, who was also present.

"Yes, sir," the prisoner replied.

"Are you willing to talk to us without a lawyer?"

"Yes, sir."

After reviewing the Weeks' case, Schrum and Zeets turned to the April 12 rape of Lynn Ellen Rawlings, twenty-three, outside the Shadow Lawn Senior Citizens Center on Culpeper Street in downtown Warrenton. This was the most recent of the rapes plaguing the county, and the officers wanted to see if Washington knew anything about it.[2]

Ms. Rawlings was returning to her car at about 11:15 P.M. after visiting a friend when she saw a light in the basement of Shadow Lawn, where she worked. Bending over to check a basement window, she was grabbed from behind, threatened with a knife, and raped. Throughout the attack, according to the preliminary investigative report, "the subject was making obscene gestures toward and about her with obscene language."

Washington denied knowledge of the rape, but Schrum was not convinced. There was something odd about the way Earl was answering questions. The prisoner was pleasant, unusually so under the circumstances. "He was a likable sort of guy to sit down and talk to. He wasn't vulgar. He wasn't cussing or anything. He didn't get wild and scream," the officer recalled. But every time the questions bore in, Washington's agitation grew visibly. He sighed and shook and ducked his head. He wasn't saying much, but guilt seemed to radiate off him. Schrum's notes recorded the effect: "After denying any knowledge (didn't believe because at first he wouldn't deny or admitt [sic] it, hung his head) of it, we told Earl to go back to his cell and think about it. We told Earl that if he wanted to talk to us and changed his mind, to tell the jailer and he would tell us."

That initial interview lasted two hours and ten minutes. It was not recorded or videotaped. Schrum's notes offer an overview but few details about what was said, when, and by whom.

About an hour later, as Schrum recalled, he was at a downstairs counter in the jail, drinking a cup of coffee, when Jailer Robert Turner rounded the corner, accompanied by Washington. "And he said, 'Earl wants to talk to you,' so we went back upstairs." Yet again, the prisoner was advised of his rights and asked if he was ready to talk about the Shadow Lawn rape. "He said, 'I don't know anything about it,' and smiled," Schrum said. The officer was so struck by the inappropriateness of the smile that he underlined the word three times in his notes.

Schrum's own irritation was growing. This was no smiling matter. "OK, Earl, you're not telling us the truth, are you?" he demanded.

The prisoner's face dropped. He shook his head, no. Then he put his forehead in his hands and sat silently for a moment. Schrum sensed that the moment was ripe to push forward. "Earl," he said, "you are the one that raped the girl over here on Culpeper St., aren't you?"

Earl was quiet, his knee tapping. The officers waited. After a few seconds, the prisoner nodded, yes.

For a while, everyone seemed to relax. But there were more unsolved crimes on Schrum's list, and the officer noticed that Washington was starting to look nervous again. Schrum had done many interrogations over the years, and the anxiety was a signal to him that Washington still had something festering inside.

The left side of Washington's face and head were resting in the thumb and fingers of his left hand, and Schrum observed that the palm and little finger were shaking uncontrollably. The sight bolstered his belief in Washington's guilt.

Schrum knew that the police department over in Culpeper had been wrestling for almost a year with the unsolved murder of a young woman. He was sketchy on the details, but the thought struck him that the prisoner might have been involved in that, too. This was the time to ask.

"Because I felt that he was still hiding something, being nervous, and due to the nature of his crimes that he was already charged with and would be charged with, we decided to ask him about the murder which occurred in Culpeper in 1982," Schrum wrote in his notes on the interview.

"We told Earl that we now wanted to talk to him about an incident in Culpeper in which a girl was stabbed. Earl didn't look at us, but was still very nervous. Asked Earl if he knew anything about it. Earl sat there and didn't reply just as he did in the other cases prior to admitting them."

Schrum had been patient long enough. Boring in, eyes fixed on the prisoner, his voice heavy with the weight of the moment, he asked: "Earl, did you kill that girl in Culpeper?"

For about five seconds, the prisoner was quiet. His shaking was the only movement in the room. Then his head moved up and down, yes, and he began to cry.

Schrum felt the tension release. He took a deep breath, told Washington to compose himself, and waited a moment before continuing. The officer wanted to get some details of the murder, but he knew little about the case himself, not even the woman's name, Rebecca Williams.

"To clarify things a little, I told him that I was talking about the one found laying [sic] outside the apartment or townhouse with no clothes on in Culpeper and asked him if that was the one. Earl said yes," Schrum wrote.

The officers asked a few more questions and the interview ended. No one mentioned rape because the Fauquier deputies were not sure that a rape had occurred. The next step was to get the Culpeper officers to Warrenton for a full interrogation. Schrum also wanted to bring in the Warrenton town police to question Washington about some other unsolved crimes.

As for the prisoner, his confession appeared to have boosted his spirits. The shaking stopped. "Earl stated that he felt better after admitting that he killed the girl," Schrum wrote. "I asked him if it had been eating at his insides." Washington replied, yes.

Once Washington had confessed, events were set in motion from which there was no turning back. A week earlier, Washington's most serious adult charge had been driving-under-the-influence in a borrowed car within range of his home. Before the interrogations ended over a couple of days, he had confessed to three break-ins, two malicious woundings, one attempted rape, two actual rapes, two robberies, burglary, and capital murder—every crime about which he was asked.

The Fauquier County sheriff's department telephoned the Culpeper police department with the news of the Williams confession, and in the late afternoon, Lt. Harlan Lee Hart of the Culpeper police and Special Agent Reese Wilmore of the Virginia State Police arrived in Warrenton. They found the prisoner sleeping and decided to return the next day. Arriving a bit after 9 A.M. Sunday morning, they met with Schrum and Zeets, who had already interrogated Washington again that morning. Their questioning of Earl Washington began at about 10 A.M.[3]

After introducing himself, Agent Wilmore handed Washington a form listing his Miranda rights, but the prisoner seemed to stumble over the reading.

"Can you read?" Wilmore asked.

"Some," Washington replied.

Hart took the form and read it in its entirety. "Do you understand?" he asked.

Washington nodded, yes, and signed the form. The questioning began.

"I understand that you made some statements about stabbing a woman in Culpeper," Wilmore said. "Did you stab the woman? Did you tell the truth?"

The question was greeted with silence. Washington hung his head and pressed his hand to his forehead.

Wilmore switched to more general questions to get the prisoner talking. What was his birth date? Where did he go to school? Who did he work for? Then the officer asked again, "Did you stab a woman in Culpeper?"

This time Washington nodded. "Yes."

"Where did the stabbing occur?" Wilmore asked.

"I don't know," Washington said.

"Could you show us?"

"I don't know. I think I can," he said.

The questioning continued for about an hour. The only written description of the episode is the transcript of Wilmore's trial testimony. If notes were taken, they were never made public. At 11 A.M., Wilmore took out paper and pen and sat facing Washington. Writing as quickly as he could, he recorded an official confession. It began:

> Wilmore: What is your name?
> Washington: Earl Junior Washington.
> Wilmore: Where do you live?
> Washington: Bealeton.
> Wilmore: How old are you?
> Washington: Twenty-three.
> Wilmore: Do you realize you're about to be questioned about a
> crime?
> Washington: Yes.

After a lunch break, Earl Washington found himself with a police escort en route to Culpeper where he was asked to re-create his steps on the day that Rebecca Williams was slain eleven months earlier. Once again, hours of interrogation occurred for which no police notes exist. Washington rode with Hart and Wilmore. Schrum and Investigator S. Allen Cubbage brought up the rear in another car.

The re-creation began on a bridge along a state road not far from Bealeton. Washington said he was picked up by a couple of men whom he had met the previous day. One was named Billy. He did not know the name of the other. (Neither man surfaced during the course of Washington's trial and incarceration.) Arriving in Culpeper, the police entourage met an unexpected snag. Asked to lead the group to the place where the murder occurred, Washington obligingly directed them to the Culpeper Town House Apartments, the wrong place. Washington was said to have recognized his mistake and, noting the prisoner's confusion, Lt. Hart offered to drive the group to every apartment complex in the town. Washington was instructed to speak up if anything looked familiar.

At Catalpa Hill Apartments, Mountain View Apartments, Stuckner's Apartments, Redbud Apartments, and Westminster Square townhouses, nothing did. Finally, the procession drove into the Village Apartments. After a swing through the parking lot outside Rebecca Williams's former home, Washington again indicated that he recognized nothing. On the way out, however, he hesitated, according to Agent Wilmore's later testimony. The group turned back. After another swing through the small complex, Washington again said, no. But once more, on the way out, he noted that Route 29—which runs beside the complex, separated from it by a strip of land and a wire fence—looked familiar. This time, Wilmore decided to act. Returning to the parking lot outside Rebecca Williams's house, Wilmore asked if Washington could point to the apartment where the assault had occurred. "He pointed to an apartment on the exact opposite end from where the Williams girl was killed," Wilmore testified, even though the arrangement of the apartments is not symmetrical and there is no "exact opposite end."

Wilmore responded by pointing directly at Williams's door. "Is that the one?" he said.

Washington replied, "Yes."

Driving up behind, Officer Schrum saw Washington drop his head, then lift it. It was the same gesture the prisoner had made each time he confessed to a crime back in Warrenton. "I told Cubby, this is where it happened at," Schrum recalled.

Were there subtle, even unintentional suggestions to Washington that he had arrived at the correct destination? Jonathan Lynn, who was Washington's attorney in the Hazel Weeks case and later became Fauquier County's chief prosecutor, recalled his own trepidation in trusting Washington's answers during interviews. "Earl was like a little child or anyone who wants to please. . . . I realized early on in talking to Earl I had to be very careful as to how I phrased my questions. If he felt my question was begging a particular answer, I may well get that answer."[4]

To the contrary, Washington's identification of the Village Apartments cemented the belief of police officers that they had found Rebecca Williams's rapist and murderer. Washington had not been beaten or consciously tricked. He seemed to recognize the site of the crime. And his propensity for violence was established by the break-in at Mrs. Weeks's.

No one noted the differences between the assaults on Hazel Weeks and Rebecca Williams. Washington's intent in breaking into the home of Mrs. Weeks was to steal a gun. Rape and murder were the only apparent intentions in the attack on Rebecca Williams. Given every opportunity to rape and murder Mrs. Weeks, Washington did neither. But some details of Washington's confession seemed to match in the Williams case. And why, the officers asked, would an innocent man confess to such a horrific crime?

The next day the confessions continued, with Washington admitting to the malicious wounding on November 12, 1982 of Eugina Hecker during a nighttime attack outside her home, and two separate break-ins at a house on Winchester Street in Warrenton, during which the would-be assailant ran away before attacking his intended victims. None of those interviews or confessions was recorded or videotaped either.

The final confessions were described by Investigator Cubbage of the Warrenton town police in notes dated May 23.

"All right Earl we want to ask you about another case. Do you know where Winchester St. is?" Cubbage began.

"Yes, sir."

"We want to ask you about a girl that lives on Winchester St."

"OK."

"Did you try to have sex with this girl?"

"Yes, sir."

"OK, Earl, tell us about it."

"I just wanted to have sex with her."

"What happened?"

"She had a gun and said she'd shoot me so I ran."

"Do you remember anything else?"

"No, sir."

"OK Earl, back in Sept. of last year, did you go to the same house to have sex with a girl?"

"I don't remember."

"Come on, Earl."

"Yes, sir."

"OK, that's better. Now tell us about it."

"I think I went in through the bedroom window. She was asleep."

"Go on."

"She woke up and started yelling so I ran out."

"What else?"

"I don't remember anything else."

Reviewing the confessions years later, Schrum once again saw their tone and the memory of Washington's demeanor as compelling evidence of guilt.

"See, right here," he said, reading from Cubbage's notes. "'I don't remember.' 'Come on, Earl.' That's all it took with Earl. Once you got him talking to you, that's all it would take. . . . He'd say, 'No,' and then it wouldn't take much to get him to change."

But the same malleability that Schrum saw as proof of guilt is for experts on mental retardation a warning.[5] No one at the Fauquier County sheriff's department was assigned to advocate for the mentally disabled during an interrogation, and none of the principal interrogators had been schooled in a growing body of literature on the psychology of false confessions. At the time of Washington's arrest, the police had no way of knowing that the prisoner had been designated since early childhood as mentally retarded. Their professional training in the subject was slight.[6]

Even so, it might have been obvious that something was awry. One clue was in Washington's most basic expression of identity, his signature. All the police documents and his confession are signed Earl Jr. Washington.

The preliminary hearing in the Hazel Weeks case held one month and two days after the break-in at her home, began with an unusual request from the prosecutor: "Your honor, before we go any further, I'd like to make sure that we clear up any problems on the defendant's name. It is my understanding that his name is Earl Junior Washington, but I'm not sure if it's Earl Junior Washington or Earl Washington Junior."

The judge turned to Washington's attorney, Jonathan Lynn, for clarification.

"Your honor, my understanding is that his name is Earl J. Washington Jr., his father being Earl J. Washington Sr.," replied Lynn. "He is commonly referred to as Junior. Mr. Washington himself is not sure what the J. stands for. I think at this juncture, your honor, we would stipulate that we are talking about the same individual and clear this up at the circuit court level."

In fact, the defendant's name was neither Earl J. Washington Jr., as he told his attorney, nor Earl Jr. Washington, as he signed his confession to the rape and murder of Rebecca Williams. For good reason the defendant did not know what the "J" stood for because neither he nor his father has a middle name. Nor did the fact that his family regularly referred to him as "Earl Jr." make him Earl Jr. Washington, as he may have supposed.

At the time of his arrest and multiple confessions, Earl Washington Jr., as he is identified on his birth certificate, was twenty-three years old, and either he willingly acquiesced in using the wrong signature or he did not know his name.

The hope of Warrenton and Fauquier County police that they had solved the local rape problem with the arrest of Earl Washington was short-lived. On July 21, less than a month after charges were certified against Washington, the *Fauquier Democrat* reported that a twenty-four-year-old woman parked at 4:30 A.M. with her boyfriend on a street in downtown Warrenton was raped after the pair got into an argument and he left. About three weeks later, a nineteen-year-old woman was raped as she walked alone on her way to a friend's house in downtown Warrenton. The September 22 edition of the paper reported the "fourth and fifth assaults of Fauquier County women since August." And on January 19, 1984, the day that testimony began in the Culpeper trial of Earl Washington Jr., the Fauquier newspaper reported that from July to September, five women were raped or assaulted in the Broadview Avenue vicinity of Warrenton. None of those crimes could have been committed by Washington, who had now retracted all his confessions except the one involving Hazel Weeks. Washington had been under lock and key since May.

6

The Trial

PROSPECTIVE JURORS SHED overcoats and stamped snow from their boots as they filed into the Culpeper County courthouse for the opening of the Rebecca Williams murder trial. The county was experiencing the nastiest weather of the winter. A morning snowstorm had slowed traffic to a creep, but highway conditions did not impede the turnout for the long-awaited trial. Nineteen months had passed since the young mother's death, and in a county of about twenty-three thousand souls almost everyone appeared to know something about the upcoming event.

By the end of that day, January 18, 1984, lawyers questioned thirty-eight potential jurors; thirty-seven of them knew about the case before they arrived at the courthouse. Most had read about Rebecca Williams's murder or Earl Washington Jr.'s arrest in the *Star-Exponent* or the *Culpeper News*. Some had heard radio accounts. Many had discussed the events with neighbors or friends. "Well, I know that . . . just from what people talk about and what you've read in the paper, that this girl was murdered. She was stabbed brutally and she was killed and this was done in front of her children," testified Linda Marie Bache, whose general awareness of the case was typical. "It was just a horrible tragedy that this girl had been killed and it was such a terrible thing for Culpeper."[1]

The judge dismissed seven potential jurors because they had formed an opinion about Washington's guilt. As one woman noted, "[It's] been in the newspaper over and over again. . . . Seems to me he was guilty from what I read." A notable number had some personal knowledge of the situation. One of those dismissed was a nurse on duty in the Fauquier County hospital when Mrs. Hazel Weeks was admitted. Another had directed Rebecca Williams's funeral. Another worked with Clifford Williams, and yet another lived across the street from

Helen Richards, the victim's mother. One man was dismissed after describing himself as a family friend of the Washingtons. Another potential juror knew Washington's sister, Alfreda. "I've been hearing that he wasn't . . . he didn't do it or anything," said the woman. She too was dismissed. Only one potential juror said she would have difficulty imposing a death sentence if Washington was found guilty.[2]

Detailed knowledge of the case was not a bar to serving on the panel. Mrs. Janice Inskeep Willis, a pharmacist selected for the jury, knew that Washington's break-in at the home of Mrs. Weeks had triggered his arrest in the Williams case. Later, Judge David F. Berry ruled against admitting evidence of Washington's alleged crimes in Fauquier County, but at least one juror, Willis, knew the connection.

As morning stretched into late afternoon, Earl Washington sat quietly to one side of the witness stand, which faced the empty jury box. The elevated panel behind the jury chairs held space for three judges. That day, Judge Berry sat alone. Watching the proceedings, Washington looked alternately detached and nervous. He wore a slight beard and his hair stood in a high cut that made him look taller and thinner than usual. For long stretches, his chin rested on his hand.[3]

Court observers could not recall another case in which jury selection took all day. But caution was in order. Washington was the first person in three decades to go on trial in Culpeper County facing a possible death sentence. Dusk fell as the panel of ten whites and two blacks, seven of them women and five men, dispersed into the night. The roads were likely to be icy the next morning, Judge Berry warned. Jurors should get an early start or telephone the sheriff's department if they needed a ride.

From the start, Culpeper police entertained two possibilities about the Williams murder: either that a stranger killed Rebecca Williams, as she said, or that she did not want to identify her slayer. It was curious that there was no sign of forced entry. Spouses almost always fall under a degree of suspicion in an unsolved murder. But Clifford Williams was not the culprit; otherwise Becky Williams would not have described her assailant as a sole black man. Police were less sure that the crime was unrelated to Clifford's drug habits or to some other personal problem. Along with more stable families, a host of unsavory characters came and went through the Village Apartments, where rents were tied to income through a government-support program. When new management took over a decade later, there were wholesale evictions based on drug connections and nonpayment of rent.[4] A next-door neighbor of the Williams's, James Pendleton, ran with what was reputed to be a violent crowd. He was known for involvement with hard drugs. The man fell under suspicion for a time, but evidence later cleared him. Nor were investigators quite sure what to make of Rebecca herself. On the one hand, relatives and friends portrayed her as a sweet girl, a good and loving mother. On the other, she was rumored to mix with some of the low-life thugs who passed through the complex. Was one of them repaying her for some perceived sexual slight? The viciousness of the attack—thirty-eight stab wounds—suggested a measure of personal venom. But the brutality might also accompany a murder that was a purely random event, the product of a crazed mind. While it seemed unlikely, the police did not entirely discount the possibility that two individuals were involved. A blood-stained, plastic runner in the hallway contained two partial shoe impressions, one typical of dress-style shoes, the other indicative of sneakers or sports shoes. The footprints might suggest the presence of two men, but one of the prints could have been left by law enforcement officials during the early search of the apartment.

The confession of Earl Washington, combined with his apparent identification of the Williams apartment, ended conjecture. The police were confident they had their man. Commonwealth's attorney John Bennett set about making the case. During the months after the break-in at Hazel Weeks's house, deputies shuttled Washington back and forth between Culpeper and Warrenton for one hearing or another. His lawyers succeeded in delaying the Fauquier County prosecutions until the murder trial was over. If Washington had a string of convictions on his record, the evidence of "future dangerousness" would make a death sentence more likely.

Lawyers who interviewed Washington during the period found him pleasant, cooperative, and intellectually deficient. "He was clearly uneducated, clearly what we call today retarded and not able to really communicate. He spoke in terms of 'yes' and 'no,'" said John Scott, a Fredericksburg attorney and Washington's chief counsel in the murder trial. "We came to realize over the first couple of months that you could ultimately get Earl Washington to agree to anything."[5]

Scott's introduction to the case was not ideal. Two court-appointed attorneys represented the defendant in a preliminary hearing, an event at which a defense team typically learns where the prosecution is headed. Scott missed that critical first step. Worried that appointed attorneys would mount a lackluster defense, the Washington family pooled its meager resources after the preliminary hearing and asked the Culpeper branch of the NAACP to help find a paid lawyer. John Scott came to mind. Years earlier, Scott had gained prominence in the region as one of four black students who were plaintiffs in a federal lawsuit that desegregated the Fredericksburg public schools. In February 1963, the four entered the all-white James Monroe High School under court order. Later, Scott was among the first several dozen black graduates of the University of Virginia law school. In September 1974, he moved back to Fredericksburg to open a local office of Hill, Tucker and Marsh, a Richmond firm that was one of the South's premier practitioners of civil rights law. Scott agreed to take the Washington case, and he assigned a young associate, Gary Hicks, to do much of the legwork.

Scott recalled his first meeting with Washington in the Fauquier County jail. "I had no idea what we were going to find. I knew we had problems, because one of the first things a Fauquier County investigator told me was, 'We've got a confession.'" Two decades later, what Scott most remembered from the encounter was a question: "How could this gentleman, how could Earl confess? There was no way, in my opinion, that he could give a knowing, intelligent confession to anyone about anything. Then I saw the confession and I understood. The written confession is a yes, no document. 'Did you do x?' 'Yassir.' 'Did you do y?' 'Yassir.'"

In its July 1983 term, the grand jury handed down a two-count indictment. A month later, on August 23, Scott made his first court appearance on Washington's behalf to ask for a psychiatric evaluation of his client's competence to stand trial.[6] The judge granted the request, naming a three-person team from the Culpeper Mental Health Clinic to evaluate the prisoner. Two weeks later, the team reported a stalemate. After three and a half hours of clinical interviews with Washington and a review of his confession, members were "unable to determine with reasonable professional certainty" Washington's competence to stand trial, to understand the proceedings against him, and to assist in his own defense. The team asked that Washington be admitted to a state mental health facility for further evaluation. On November 2, the players came back to court to hear the results. Dr. Arthur Centor, a clinical psychologist at the Central State Hospital in Petersburg, reported that he had administered the Wechsler Adult Intelligence Scale R test, which measures intelligence; the Bender-Gestalt, which looks for brain damage affecting intellectual functioning, and the Rorschach ink-blot test, which seeks to determine whether mental illness might be affecting intellectual functioning.

Centor, who evaluated Washington in conjunction with psychiatrist James Dimitris, head of the forensic unit at Central State, determined that Washington had a verbal IQ of 69, a performance IQ of 71, and a full-scale IQ of 69. The scores placed him in a category "between mild mental retardation and low average intelligence," in the lowest 2 percent of the population, Centor said.[7] (Another expert later equated Washington's IQ of 69 to a mental age of 10.3 years.) He found no sign of mental illness or organic brain damage in the other tests. Washington was mentally competent to stand trial and to help with his defense, Centor concluded.

Then, the prosecutor went further. "Are you able to form a conclusion with reasonable medical certainty as to the defendant's ability to, first of all, understand, and then second of all, to waive his rights as required under the Miranda decisions?"

Over Scott's objection, the judge allowed Centor to answer: "Yes, I do have an opinion that he does have the capacity to understand the Miranda rights as read to him."

Did Washington have the mental capacity to make a knowing and intelligent waiver of those rights?

"In my opinion he would have that capacity," Centor said.[8]

Scott countered that earlier testing in the Fauquier public schools showed Washington, at age eleven, with an IQ of only 57. His client was functionally illiterate and undergoing "great mental anguish and physical discomfort" at the time of his confession, Scott said. Unmoved, the judge ruled that the trial could go forward.

No one asked—and hence Centor and Dimitris did not say— whether Washington might have made a false confession.

When the court reconvened on November 29, Scott was blocked as well in seeking a change in the location of the trial. His assistant, Gary Hicks, gamely argued that the Culpeper press had treated Washington's arrest with "great notoriety and sensationalism," including printing details of the charges pending against Washington in Fauquier. The prosecutor countered that the articles were factual, and the judge agreed. "I find nothing of an inflammatory nature in themselves in these news releases," he concluded.[9]

Returning to the courtroom on the morning of January 19, the jurors heard Washington's plea, "not guilty." The opening statements began. Commonwealth's attorney John Bennett went first.

Shrewd and self-assured, Bennett was a member of one of Culpeper's most prestigious law firms. A partner, D. French Slaughter, would be elected to Congress the autumn after the Washington trial. After several years in the part-time post of Commonwealth's attorney, Bennett had just survived an unexpected election scare. His independent opponent in an election two months earlier alleged that Bennett was not taking the job seriously enough and was plea bargaining his way out of too many cases. Bennett won by just 216 votes out of the 4,416 cast.[10] The message was not lost on the prosecutor. He showed no intention of being soft on Washington.

Prosecutor Bennett dominated the trial from its opening moment. And from the start, as well, Scott let pass comments that created an air of inevitability about Washington's guilt and conviction. Describing Washington's confession in his opening statement, Bennett observed that while at the Fauquier County jail the prisoner summoned officers, and "Mr. Washington, the person who is on trial today, stated that he had killed a woman some time ago in Culpeper County." Bennett's wording implied that Washington had raised the matter unprompted. The jury never heard a more accurate version from Scott. Then Bennett uttered the phrase that became the rallying cry of those insisting on Washington's guilt: "You'll also hear the defendant told them a number of different things that could only have been known by someone who had actually committed the offense."[11] Scott did not challenge the assertion, either in his own opening statement or later.

In his first address to the jury, Scott took the tack that he would follow for the duration of the trial. He urged jurors to "observe Earl Washington," and asked them to "listen to the circumstances surrounding the interrogation of Earl Washington Jr. by the law enforcement officers of this county." Scott found Washington's incapacity to make a legitimate confession or to understand his legal rights so obvious that he believed the jury would as well. It was a risky strategy for the attorney's first capital murder trial.

Bennett's opening statement took up eleven pages of the transcript; Scott's required three. Bennett called fourteen witnesses, and their testimony and cross-examination was 162 pages long. Scott called two, Earl Washington and his sister, Alfreda, and their remarks filled twenty-seven pages. Bennett's closing statement covered nine pages of the transcript; Scott's, two. Then Bennett made an almost four-page rebuttal. In virtually every aspect of the trial, from understanding of the forensic evidence to a dissection of the arguments, Earl Washington's side of the story was inadequately told or never told at all. Even his defenders seemed overwhelmed by the weight of a confession that no one had forced Washington to make.

The first six witnesses confirmed that the murder of Rebecca Williams occurred and that it had been brutal. Paul Brundage, who along with his wife first discovered the victim, repeated her words: "I've been raped."[12] Officer J. L. Jackson told how he rushed outside his apartment to check out the commotion and was also told by Williams that she had been raped. "He hurt me. He hurt me," he quoted the victim saying.[13] Investigator Kenny Buraker reported Williams's answers to three questions. Did she know her attacker? No. Was he black or white? Black. Was there more than one? No.[14] Clifford Williams recalled his wife's three-word answer to his question, who did it? "A black man." Clifford also testified that he last had sex with his wife three days before the murder.[15]

Dr. James C. Beyer, deputy chief medical examiner for the state in charge of the northern Virginia office, testified that his autopsy identified thirty-eight stab wounds, fourteen of which involved "significant penetration" of internal organs.[16] Smears taken from vaginal secretions and surrounding body areas tested positive for sperm. Many of the sperm were complete, with both heads and tails, suggesting that they were less than twelve hours old when taken from Williams's body. The sperm could not have come from sexual intercourse with her husband the previous Tuesday, Beyer said.

The next eight prosecution witnesses were a mixed bag of police officers, neighbors, and family. The group illuminated various aspects of the morning that preceded Williams's death and the investigation that followed it. Neighbor Doris Campbell saw Becky and her children walking back toward the apartment complex at about 10:50 A.M.[17] Another neighbor, Beverly Deal, looked out her window sometime between 11 A.M. and noon and saw a black man who appeared to be crossing the wire fence that separated the Village Apartments from Route 29, a major thoroughfare.[18] Under cross-examination, Deal said she saw the man for no more than a couple of seconds. Neither Bennett nor Scott asked whether Washington was that man.

Someone had helped police prepare a composite drawing of a stranger who might be the killer, but that person (or persons) was not called to testify. Presumably either Washington was not the man they saw or they were unsure.

One tantalizing glimpse into Rebecca Williams's life appeared and was as rapidly yanked from view. Helen Richards, the victim's mother, confirmed that Rebecca called her at 11:09 A.M. But when Richards started to veer into the purpose of the call, Bennett silenced her.[19]

"I spoke with her twice on that day," Richards began. "She made two collect calls to me, one sometime around 9 or 10 in the morning, concerning that her husband hadn't come home from work and she was angry and. . . ."

Bennett interrupted. "Okay, just . . . without going into the. . . ."

"She wanted me to pick her up."

"Okay."

"Okay, and then I said, well, I'll come down around three. . . ."

"Not . . . if you wouldn't go into the contents of the conversation, but if you'd tell the court what time it was when you spoke with your daughter, please."

The hint of conflict between husband and wife was not revisited.

The central trio of law enforcement witnesses were Fauquier County Investigator Terry Schrum; Lt. Harlan Lee Hart of the Culpeper police department, who headed the investigation into Becky Williams's death; and Special Agent Reese Wilmore, who assisted that investigation on behalf of the Virginia state police. It was Hart and Wilmore who traveled to Warrenton to flesh out Washington's confession on May 22, 1983 and who escorted him through Culpeper.

Schrum began by recounting how, on May 21 at 12:40 P.M., he and Deputy Zeets were told by the Fauquier County jailer that Washington wanted to talk to them.[20] "We told him that we wanted to talk to him about an incident which occurred in Culpeper in which a girl was stabbed," Schrum testified. He went on to describe Washington's nervousness, his silence, and then his positive response to the outright question: "Earl, did you kill that girl in Culpeper?" Schrum noted that Washington supplied a few other details. Asked to describe the victim, he said she was "kind of short, young, wasn't fat, but was a little on the heavy side." Washington also said that he "stuck her with a knife a few times . . . more than once."

Lt. Lee Hart took the witness stand next, describing how he was called by the Fauquier County sheriff's department on the afternoon of May 21 and advised of a possible break in the 1982 murder case.[21] He contacted Wilmore and the pair drove to Warrenton for an interview. When they arrived, Washington was asleep, and the officers decided that it would be prudent to return the next day. Following Hart to the stand, Wilmore told how he and the lieutenant retraced their steps on Sunday—Mother's Day—and questioned Washington at length.[22] He took down Washington's confession by asking a question and then rapidly recording both the query and the prisoner's response. No tape recorder was used.

One piece of evidence damaging to the prosecution would never have been revealed if Wilmore had not voluntarily brought it up. When first asked whether the victim was white or black, Washington erroneously said black, Wilmore testified. Later, when the officer repeated the question about race, Washington amended his answer to correctly say white. Police notes did not mention the gaffe.

The prisoner also gave Wilmore and Hart a revised and more accurate description of Rebecca Williams. "He said that she was 5'6", she had brown hair, she may weigh as much as 170 and as he put it, she was a little heavy," Wilmore testified. According to court records, Becky was five feet, eight inches tall and weighed 180 pounds.

Then Wilmore read into the court record the full transcript of Washington's signed confession.

Wilmore: What is your name?
Washington: Earl Junior Washington.
Wilmore: Where do you live?
Washington: Bealeton.
Wilmore: How old are you?
Washington: Twenty-three.
Wilmore: Do you realize you're about to be questioned about a
    crime?
Washington: Yes.
Wilmore: Have you been advised of your rights?
Washington: Yes, sir.
Wilmore: Have these rights been read to you?
Washington: Yes, sir.

Wilmore: Do you understand them?

Washington: Yes.

Wilmore: Do you wish to talk with us about the stabbing and rape of Rebecca Williams?

Washington: Yes.

Wilmore: What grade did you complete in school?

Washington: Ninth.

Wilmore: Where?

Washington: Bealeton.

Wilmore: Who do you work for or with?

Washington: Farming with Giles Early.

Wilmore: Last June did you go to Culpeper?

Washington: Yes.

Wilmore: Who did you go with?

Washington: A friend named Billy.

Wilmore: Was he white or black?

Washington: Black.

Wilmore: Who else was along?

Washington: I don't know him.

Wilmore: Was he white or black?

Washington: Black.

Wilmore: Whose car was it?

Washington: The boy Billy and I were riding with.

Wilmore: What kind of car was it?

Washington: A Ford.

Wilmore: What color was it?

Washington: Blue.

Wilmore: Where had you met Billy before?

Washington: Warrenton, at the Hilltop.

Wilmore: How long have you known him?

Washington: Three or four days.

Wilmore: Where did they pick you up?

Washington: A mile from where I was living.

Wilmore: Where was that?

Washington: I was living in Bealeton with my sister.

Wilmore: Who were you living with?

Washington: My sister, Linda Washington.

Wilmore: Where was she living?

Washington: With Will Shumake . . . taking care of him.

Hart: Where did you go?

Washington: Went to the Hilltop in Warrenton.

Hart: Where did you go from the Hilltop?

Washington: Rode around.

Hart: Did you go to Culpeper?

Washington: Yes, sir.

Wilmore: Whose idea was it?

Washington: The dude the car belonged to.

Hart: Where did you go in Culpeper?

Washington: Rode around for a while.

Hart: Where did you go after that?

Washington: Went to a set of apartments.

Hart: Whose idea was it to go to the apartments?

Washington: The dude the car belonged to.

Hart: Can you show us where these apartments are?

Washington: I think I can.

Wilmore: Why did you go to the apartments?

Washington: I don't know for sure.

Wilmore: What occurred when you got to the apartments?

Washington: They parked in the parking lot and stayed in the car.

Wilmore: What did you do?

Washington: Got out of the car.

Wilmore: What did you do then?

Washington: I went into an apartment.

Hart: How did you get in the apartment?

Washington: Kicked the door open.

Hart: Did you know whose apartment it was?

Washington: No, sir.

Hart: Was the door locked?

Washington: I don't think so.

Hart: Was anyone inside?

Washington: A white woman.

Hart: What happened then?

Washington: I took out my knife.

Wilmore: What kind of knife was it?

Washington: A pocketknife that I carried on my side in a case.

Hart: What happened then?

Washington: She told me to get out.

Hart: What did you do then?

Washington: I stuck her.

Hart: Did you stick her more than one time?

Washington: One time in the stomach.

Hart: What happened then?

Washington: I took her to the bedroom. (Washington's actual signed confession says: "I took her to bedroom.")

Hart: What were you planning on doing in the bedroom?

Washington: Make love to her.

Hart: Did she want to make love?

Washington: No.

Hart: Did she resist?

Washington: Yes, I was holding a knife on her.

Wilmore: Did she undress or did you make her undress?

Washington: I made her undress.

Hart: Did you make her undress completely?

Washington: Yes, sir.

Hart: Did you remove any of her clothes?

Washington: Yes, sir.

Hart: What clothing?

Washington: The halter top.

Wilmore: Did you have sex with her on the bed?

Washington: Yes, sir.

Wilmore: How many times?

Washington: Once.

Hart: Did you stab her after you had sex?

Washington: Yes, sir.

Hart: How many times?

Washington: Once or twice.

Hart: While you were stabbing her, did you injure or cut yourself?

Washington: Yes.

Hart: Where?

Washington: In my left hand.

Hart: Did you bleed?

Washington: A little bit.

At this point, Bennett interrupted to say that the upcoming language might be offensive. The judge instructed Wilmore to read on.

Wilmore: What do you mean when you say you wanted to make love to her?

Washington: I mean fucking her.

Hart: Was the radio in the apartment on or off?

Washington: On, but it wasn't too loud.

Wilmore: Was there anyone else in the apartment?

Washington: I didn't see anyone.

Hart: Did you remove any of your own clothes while having sex with her?

Washington: No more than pulling my pants down.

Hart: Did you leave any of your clothing in the apartment?

Washington: My shirt.

Hart: The shirt that has been shown you, is it the one you left in the apartment?

Washington: Yes, sir.

Wilmore: How do you know it is yours?

Washington: That is the shirt I wore.

Hart: What makes it stand out?

Washington: A patch had been removed from the top of the pocket.

Wilmore: Why did you leave the shirt in the apartment?

Washington: It had blood on it and I didn't want to wear it back out.

Wilmore: Where did you put it when you left?

Washington: Laid it on top of the dresser drawer in the bedroom.

Wilmore: Was the dresser drawer open or closed?

Washington: Open.

Wilmore: What time did this occur?

Washington: Near the middle of the day.

Wilmore: Where was Williams when you left the apartment?

Washington: I left her in the bedroom on her back.

Wilmore: Was she conscious when you left?

Washington: No, sir.

Hart: What type of shoes were you wearing that day?

Washington: Tennis shoes.

Hart: Where are they now?

Washington: I don't know.

Wilmore: Did you know the Williams girl?

Washington: No, sir.

Wilmore: Had you been in the apartment before?

Washington: Yes, one time with a friend.

Hart: Who were you with?

Washington: I don't remember.

Hart: Did you go in the house?

Washington: No, I stayed on the outside.

Hart: What did he go there for?

Washington: I don't know, but he said he knew them.

Hart: How long was this before the stabbing happened?

Washington: About a month.

Wilmore: Where did you go after leaving the apartment?

Washington: I walked to the highway and was thumbing. A white guy in a car picked me up.

Wilmore: What did you do with the knife?

Washington: Threw it away.

Wilmore: Where?

Washington: On the side of the road coming from Culpeper.

Wilmore: What kind of knife was it?

Washington: A folding type in a case.

Wilmore: Where did the white man let you out of the car?

Washington: Route 29.

Wilmore: Where on Route 29?

Washington: I don't know, but I can show you.

Hart: Did you tell anyone that you had stabbed and raped a white woman?

Washington: No, sir.

Wilmore: Why are you telling us?

Washington: Because it is the truth.

Hart: Have you been made any promises for your cooperation?

Washington: No, sir.

Hart: Have you been threatened in any way?

Washington: No, sir.

Hart: Are you making this statement on your own free will?

Washington: Yes, sir.

Wilmore: Is there anything else you want to say, Mr. Washington?

Washington: No, sir.

The document was signed, Earl Jr. Washington.

Wilmore elaborated on two critical points. First, he supplied details of the odyssey to Culpeper during which Washington identified the Village Apartments. A day or so after the confession, the officer said, seven town officers and seven state police officers returned to the rural site between Culpeper and Warrenton where Washington claimed to have thrown the murder weapon out the window of the car in which he was hitchhiking. In places the honeysuckle was almost knee deep. In one spot, water had backed up through a highway culvert, causing flooding. The officers scoured the roadway, up and down, for about a mile. No knife was found.

Wilmore also produced the blue shirt that was the only piece of physical evidence introduced at the trial. Mention of the clothing item surfaced earlier, briefly, in the testimony of Gladys Williams, Clifford Williams's mother. Shortly after the murder, the dresser from the couple's bedroom was delivered to her home, Mrs. Williams said. While sorting and cleaning her son's clothes, she came across a shirt that appeared too small for him. Clifford did not recognize the item, and Mrs. Williams washed it and laid it aside. A couple of weeks later, her husband wore the shirt while draining oil from his truck. He, too, thought nothing of it. Shortly afterwards, however, Lt. Hart asked the Williamses if they had found anything in the dresser that did not belong to Becky or Clifford. Mrs. Williams mentioned the shirt.

When the officers saw what appeared to be several small blood stains on the shirt, they sent the item to the state forensic lab for testing, Wilmore testified.

Later, he continued, during their initial interview with Washington in Warrenton, he and Hart asked the prisoner if he had left anything at Becky Williams's apartment, to which Washington replied, "A shirt." (In Washington's signed confession, the question reads somewhat differently: "Did you leave any of your *clothing* in the apartment?")

Wilmore described how he and Hart then produced the shirt discovered by Gladys Williams. "I took the shirt out and held it in front of Mr. Washington and asked him if it was his shirt," Wilmore said. "He said yes, it was his. I asked him how did he know that it was his and he continued, that was the shirt I had on that day. I then asked him what makes it different or what makes it outstanding. He said, there's a patch on the pocket . . . had been ripped off."

On cross-examination, Scott argued that the Commonwealth had not properly established that the shirt being presented in court was the shirt found by Gladys Williams. Argument on the point consumed several pages of testimony, and Scott was sustained on the technicality. The lawyer did not address several larger issues involving the shirt, however. He did not, for instance, tell the jurors that Negroid hairs and hair fragments recovered from the shirt pocket were never compared with Earl Washington's hair. Nor did Scott mention a report in which a forensic investigator reminded local police officers that the state lab could make such a comparison if more of Washington's hairs were submitted. The hairs never were.

Scott did not question either the logic of Washington's confession on the blue shirt. For instance, how was it possible that a state police team searched the Williams apartment from 1:50 P.M. to 8:30 P.M. and missed a blood-stained shirt lying on the top of an open drawer in the bedroom where Williams was killed? And did it make sense that—according to his confession—Washington left the shirt at the scene but continued to wear the jacket that had been covering it while he raped and murdered Rebecca Williams?

As for Washington's identification of the shirt by a missing patch, how hard was it to describe the shirt when Washington was looking straight at it?

As Wilmore testified, "Well, sir, I was holding the shirt . . . I was holding the shirt up several ways so he could see it. I was holding it in front of him and I asked him, is this your shirt, and he said, yes, that is my shirt." Washington gave no description of the shirt prior to looking at it.

At 4:10 P.M., after four hours of testimony, the Commonwealth rested. Forty minutes later, the defense finished as well.

Only two witnesses took the stand on Washington's behalf—the prisoner himself and his sister. Alfreda Pendleton testified that she regularly did her brother's laundry when he lived with her for a while and that the blue shirt was not his. "He never owned any like that," she repeated several times. Bennett refuted the testimony with just two questions:

Bennett: Ma'am, you're a sister to the defendant by blood?
Pendleton: Yes.

Bennett: You love your brother?

Pendleton: Sure, I love all my sisters and brothers.[23]

If Pendleton's testimony was of marginal help, Washington's most likely was of no help at all. Through twenty-three pages of the transcript, he denied almost everything about his confession, down to the fact that he gave it.[24] Seated uncomfortably on the witness stand, directly facing the jury panel and the judge behind them, Washington appeared tense and defiant. His answers were ludicrous.

"Did you hear Mr. Wilmore read to you what purports to be your confession," Scott began.

Washington: Yes, sir . . .

Scott: Do you recall giving this statement to Investigator Wilmore on May 22, 1982 [*sic*]?

Washington: No, sir.

Scott: According to the evidence presented here, on May 21, 1982 you were questioned by Investigator Schrum. Do you know Investigator Schrum?

Washington: Yes, sir.

Scott: And according to Investigator Schrum he asked you, did you kill that girl in Culpeper?

Washington: No, sir.

Scott: Do you recall him asking you that?

Washington: Yes, sir.

Scott: And what did tell him?

Washington: I told him, no sir.

Moments later in the testimony:

Scott: Do you recall a time that morning (at the Fauquier County jail) when Investigator Hart and Investigator Wilmore came to see you?

Washington: No, sir.

Scott: Did you hear Investigator Hart and Investigator Wilmore say they questioned you?

Washington: Yes, sir.

> Scott: And that you admitted to having sex with or forcing a young lady to have sex here in Culpeper County and then you stabbed her? According to them you said, once or twice.
>
> Washington: Yes, sir, I heard him when he said that.
>
> Scott: Did you tell them that?
>
> Washington: No, sir.

Elsewhere:

> Scott: Investigator Wilmore testified that when he first questioned you in Warrenton on the morning of May 22, 1983, that you told him that you had raped a black woman.
>
> Washington: No, sir.
>
> Scott: Did you tell him that?
>
> Washington: No, sir.
>
> Scott: Did you rape anybody?
>
> Washington: No, sir.
>
> Scott: Do you know what it means by the word rape?
>
> Washington: No, sir.
>
> Scott: Did you murder anybody, Mr. Washington?
>
> Washington: No, sir.

Adopting an air of incredulity, Bennett within moments made mincemeat of the defense strategy. He pressed Washington on his claim never to have seen the confession.

> Bennett: Have or haven't you seen it before?
>
> Washington: I think I seen it when I . . . at . . . I seen it when I first came over, when I went to court, came up . . . came to court the first time.
>
> Bennett: That's when you signed your name to it?
>
> Washington: No, sir.
>
> Bennett: When did you sign your name to it?
>
> Washington: I don't really know.
>
> Bennett: That is your name at the end of the statement?
>
> Washington: Yes, sir.
>
> Bennett: But you just told the members of the jury and the Court that you didn't say any of the things that were in here.

Washington: No, sir.

Bennett: Not a single one?

Washington: No, sir.

Bennett: Nothing in here you've ever said to the investigator that testified, Investigator Wilmore, or to Lt. Hart that was . . . testified after him?

Washington: No, sir.

Bennett: How did they know how old you were?

Washington: I told them how old I was and I told them my name and that was about it that I told them.

Bennett: That's all you told them?

Washington: Yes, sir.

Bennett: Are you sure about that?

Washington: Yes, sir.

Bennett: That's not going to change?

Washington: No, sir.

Bennett: How did they know that you used to work for Giles Early?

Washington: I don't know.

Bennett: Okay. How did they know that your sister's name was Linda or even that you had a sister?

Washington: I don't know.

Bennett: You do have a sister named Linda?

Washington: Yes, sir.

Bennett: How did they know that your sister was working with . . . for Will Shumake?

Washington: I don't know.

Bennett: She was working as a practical nurse, wasn't she? Isn't that true?

Washington: No, sir.

Bennett: She didn't work for Will Shumake?

Washington: No, sir.

Bennett: Do you know who Will Shumake is?

Washington: Yes, sir.

Bennett: So you're telling the members of the jury here in this Court that they just made everything up in this statement?

Washington: I don't . . . the only thing I understand . . . I didn't see it.

Bennett: Do you know Investigator Wilmore?

Washington: No, sir.

Bennett: Do you know why Investigator Wilmore, who has worked with the State Police for twenty-five years, would want to sit down and write out something like this that's how many pages long . . . twelve pages long, and have you sign it at the end and say that you said all those things when you didn't say a single one of them? Do you know why he would do something like that?

Washington: No, sir.

It was a devastating exchange for Washington.

Scott's defense hinged on the jury's determining, through observation, that Washington was mentally incapable of comprehending what had happened to him during the police interrogation. But a state psychologist had testified that Washington was competent to stand trial, and no one disputed the officers' claim that they had taken care to make sure Washington understood his Miranda warnings.

Meanwhile, Scott offered no countertestimony about the tendency of individuals with retardation to agree with their interrogators. Nor did he press for an independent psychological evaluation of his client's mental prowess. The attorney—who was earning only a couple of thousand dollars for his work—did not have the financial resources for such an examination, and not until some years later did the Virginia courts begin funding separate mental evaluations for defendants in capital cases. A pro bono evaluation would have been available through the Institute for Law and Psychiatry at the University of Virginia, but Scott did not ask for it.

In his closing statement, Bennett offered four items known by Washington "that could only have been known by someone who committed the offense."[25] There were possible explanations or defenses for all these claims, but Scott did not offer them. He elected instead to make a more general response.

First, according to Bennett, Washington said that he gained entrance to Becky Williams's house when he "kicked on the door, but the door was open." Dramatically, Bennett continued: "What's the testimony of Special Agent Wilmore who was there at the scene? There was no damage to the door. It apparently was, in fact, open. If the door had been *locked or closed* (italics added) there would have been some damage to the lock," Bennett said.

The prosecutor's rendition of Washington's confession was not precisely accurate. Asked how he got into the apartment, the prisoner said in his formal confession that he "kicked the door open." Asked if the door was locked, he said, "I don't think so." Washington did not say, as Bennett claimed, that the door was open, a subtle distinction. In fact, Washington's statement is just as consistent with the door having been shut. And as Bennett acknowledged, a closed door that was kicked open might well show some damage. There was none.

Second, Bennett noted, the officers asked Washington if the radio was on or off. He said on. That was correct, but he had a fifty-fifty chance of getting the answer right.

Third, according to the prosecutor, "they asked the defendant to describe how it happened and what did the defendant say? That he took Rebecca Lynn Williams into the back bedroom and you'll recall the diagram of the house, the bedroom was all the way at the end of the hall, the back bedroom in the apartment. How could anyone know that, except the person who was there and the person who did it?"

Washington's signed confession says nothing about a "back bedroom," however. It says only "I took her to bedroom." In his testimony about Washington's confession, Wilmore quoted the prisoner as saying that he had taken Williams to a back bedroom. Without a tape of the interrogation, it is impossible to know which version is correct.

Fourth, Bennett cited the blue shirt. "They asked him, did you take anything with you? 'No, didn't take anything with me.' Did you leave anything there? 'Yes, I left a shirt.' Why did you leave the shirt there? 'Because it had blood on it,'" Bennett told the jury. "You heard the testimony of Kenny Buraker from the town police department that when that shirt was handed over to him it had red spots on it that appeared to be bloodstains. You've heard the testimony that when they took that shirt back and held it up in front of the defendant he said, yes, that was the shirt I was wearing. They asked him, how do you know that was your shirt? Because the patch was missing over the left top pocket. Now, how does somebody make all that up, unless they were actually there and actually did it?"

Scott offered none of the possible counterarguments, including the fact that a long police search did not turn up the shirt and that Washington did not describe the shirt until it was held up in front of him. In fact, Washington never supplied any detail of the case that police did not know in advance.

Nor did the attorney list the many inconsistencies and errors: Washington misidentified the race of the victim. He did not recall seeing anyone inside the apartment, although Williams's youngest daughter was in a playpen just inside the front door, and her middle daughter was walking around the apartment. Washington claimed to have stabbed Williams a couple of times rather than three dozen. The initial description of Williams as "kind of short, young and . . . a little on the heavy side," did not jibe with her 180 pounds and tall frame. Asked if he had removed any of Williams's clothing, Washington replied: "The halter top." But in a series of clothing items tested by the state lab, there is no mention of anything resembling a halter top. Questioned as to whether he injured himself while stabbing his victim, Washington replied that he cut his left hand and bled "a little bit." Yet no evidence of Washington's blood was found at the crime scene.

Nor did Scott cultivate any doubt about Washington's alleged departure from the apartment. If the prisoner's story was correct, he stabbed a woman thirty-eight times, stripped off a bloody shirt from underneath a jacket that somehow avoided getting soiled, and was picked up by a stranger who was not put off by Washington's appearance and did not think it worth reporting when he tossed a bloody knife out the car window. Neither of the men who allegedly dropped Washington off at the Village Apartments ever surfaced.

Except for a couple of opening sentences about the jury system and a few closing remarks, the sum total of Scott's parting defense—as jurors returned on the morning of January 20 for the third day of the Washington trial—consisted of fifteen sentences.[26] They included almost nothing about the facts of the case.

"There is no question, none, that a serious crime was committed in this county, no question," the attorney began. "The primary thing for you to decide is whether or not this gentleman, this man, Earl Washington, did it, and whether the proof has been presented as to his guilt beyond a reasonable doubt. The legal definition of reasonable doubt is set forth in the instructions. Now, you observed the evidence as it was presented. You observed the testimony or heard the testimony of the police officers who allegedly took Mr. Washington's statement, and you observed and heard Mr. Washington. Now one of the instructions that you will have with you, or the instructions read to you by the Court this morning, has to do with the weight to be given Earl Washington's statement, his confession, and it has to do with whether or not you believe that confession was given freely and willfully and on the basis of that consideration you are entitled, as jurors to give that statement as much weight or as little weight as you deem appropriate."

"You saw Earl Washington. You heard him. I respectfully submit, and this is argument, that the Commonwealth's assertion that Earl Washington claims that a conspiracy took place among law enforcement officers is misplaced. Earl Washington doesn't probably know what a conspiracy is. That's argument. Those aren't facts. That's my presentation to you. You heard the evidence, but you must consider all that you heard and all that you observed in making your decision. This case is in your hands where it properly belongs."

That was all.

The jurors began their deliberations at 10:35 A.M. It took them just fifty minutes to reach a verdict. Earl Washington was guilty of capital murder, as charged. Several jurors later said that there was never any dissent.

After a lunch break, the court moved directly into a second, penalty phase of the trial to determine whether Washington's punishment would be death or life in prison. To order an execution, the jurors were required under Virginia law to find one of two conditions: either the crime must have been "outrageously or wantonly vile, horrible, or inhuman" in that it involved torture, depravity of mind, or aggravated battery, or there must be clear evidence of future dangerousness in the defendant, based on prior criminal conduct or psychological disposition. It was hard to dispute that Becky Williams's death from thirty-eight stab wounds involved aggravated battery.

As mitigating witnesses, Alfreda Pendleton testified that her brother had always done his share of work around the house, such as chopping wood and carrying water,[27] and Centor—the Central State psychologist—presented school records showing that "from earliest grades (Washington) was noted to be functioning on a retarded level." Any good that Centor's testimony might have done Washington was likely outweighed by the psychologist's response to a prosecution question during cross-examination, however.

"Does the defendant possess sufficient intelligence to appreciate the prohibition against murder?"

Over Scott's objection, Centor was allowed to answer: "It's my opinion that he does have the capacity to appreciate the nature, character and consequences of his acts, and the difference between right and wrong I might add."[28] For Washington, it was a damning moment.

Neither Alfreda Pendleton nor Dr. Centor were any match for Helen Richards, who took the stand for the defense with an emotional description of the effect of Becky Williams's death on her children.[29] Victim impact statements in such cases later became the norm in Virginia, but in 1984 they were not yet allowed. Scott's failure to object was a misstep that Washington's postconviction attorneys found puzzling.

When Richards gained custody of the three girls from their father in May 1983, a year after their mother's death, the middle daughter Mindy had not grown in size for almost a year, Richards said. Mindy was shy and withdrawn and afraid of people. The older daughter, Missy, who arrived home from school to see her mother being carried away, had been tested as emotionally disturbed and learning disabled. Both children were receiving psychiatric help and had shown improvement, she said. "They have a telephone that is just used for talking to their mama in heaven and this is the way they talk about their problems. They sit down on the phone and they take turns talking to mama in heaven, to let her know how things are going, especially if they're very, very upset," she said.

Only one member of the jury, Debera Ann Holmes, had qualms about sentencing Washington to death. One of two black jurors, Holmes thought the prisoner's mental incapacity should perhaps save him from execution. The other jurors were unwavering, and Holmes eventually bowed. A single holdout would have netted Washington a life term. After ninety minutes of deliberation, members filed back into the courtroom. Foreman Patricia L. Barratt read the verdict: "We the jury . . . having unanimously found that his conduct in committing the offense is outrageously or wantonly vile, horrible or inhuman . . . unanimously fix his punishment at death."

Seated behind the defense table, Earl Washington blinked rapidly and rubbed with a finger at one eye. His glance darted around the courtroom. He said nothing. In handcuffs and leg irons, surrounded by a phalanx of sheriff's deputies, the first man to be condemned to death in Culpeper County in thirty years headed back to his jail cell.

7

Prisoner

DEATH ROW WAS a cauldron stoked to boil when Earl Washington Jr. arrived there, deep in the piney woods of the Southside, a few miles from the North Carolina border, on May 9, 1984. Three weeks later, the rural farmhand sat paralyzed in front of a television screen as a group of his fellow inmates outwitted their captors at the Mecklenburg Correctional Center and staged one of the most brazen prison escapes in American history. Armed with metal shanks, the prisoners seized control of the death pod and, masquerading as a bomb squad handling live ordinance, duped their way out of a prison that was one of the most modern and supposedly most impenetrable in the nation. All six who fled were recaptured, but two—Linwood and James Briley, murderous brothers from Richmond who masterminded the plot—were free for nineteen days.[1]

Washington, who was just getting settled at Mecklenburg, knew nothing of the escape plan. When it began to unfold, he was petrified.

Joe Giarratano, a death row inmate who elected not to flee, saw Washington frozen in a chair about five feet away from the television set and took pity. All around him "there was a flurry. Other prisoners were getting the hell out of the way. Poor Earl couldn't move," Giarratano recalled. "I finally was able to walk over to him—this was probably the first time I ever told him not to worry—told him that it would be best if he went to his cell. He literally was paralyzed with fear. He couldn't get up. I put my arm around him to help him get up and when he stood, his whole body began to shake, and he couldn't move. I spent a couple of fast minutes trying to calm him. Gave him a cigarette (he was shaking so hard he couldn't light it). I lit the smoke for him and after . . . the first couple of drags, I was able to walk him to his cell."[2]

It was a year and one week since Washington's arrest for the break-in at the home of Hazel Weeks, a few days less since police charged him

with the murder of Rebecca Williams. He had spent the last year shut-
tling between jails and courtrooms in Culpeper and Fauquier counties.
His family was never more than a few miles away. Visits and telephone
calls with Alfreda, his mother, and the rest were frequent. Now, the
nightmare had evolved into a grim reality. In 1984, Virginia's execution
chamber remained at the Spring Street penitentiary in Richmond, but a
prisoner spent the months and years leading up to an execution at
Mecklenburg. Alone, stripped of everything familiar and of all support,
Earl had to thread his way past the tough, the coldly brilliant, the mentally ill denizens of death row. He was not prepared or equipped for
such a setting. That his arrival coincided with the great escape may
have worked to his advantage. The most dominant of his fellow prisoners were occupied elsewhere.

Washington's death sentence had been confirmed by Judge Berry in
March 1984. The prisoner's final months in a local jail were consumed
in resolving the charges against him in Fauquier—the robbery and rape
of Lynn Ellen Rawlings, the malicious wounding of Eugina Hecker, and
the robbery and wounding of Mrs. Weeks, as well as the break-in at her
home. In a plea arrangement, prosecutors and the defense agreed that
Washington would receive consecutive, fifteen-year sentences for the
breaking-and-entering and the malicious wounding of Mrs. Weeks,
crimes he had never denied. The remainder of the charges would be
dropped.

Washington had long since recanted the earlier confessions, and
there was little or no evidence to support them. In the Hecker assault his
statement said nothing about a major detail of the case, the fact that a
light bulb had been removed from Hecker's front porch as a way of
shielding the crime.[3] There was no weapon, no forensic evidence, no
eye-witness identification. In contrast, Ms. Rawlings picked Washington out of a photo lineup, but her identification was suspect. For one
thing, Rawlings had previously identified another man as her assailant.
According to police notes, on April 28, 1983—sixteen days after her attack—Lynn Rawlings was driving with police through Warrenton
when she pointed to a man walking down the street and said, "I can't
be positive, but if that's not him, it's his twin brother."[4] An investigation
was dropped after the man passed a lie detector test. Defense attorney
Jonathan Lynn also had conducted an experiment pointing to Washington's innocence. Ms. Rawlings said that her attacker wore a distinctive,
large square gold ring with a black stone in the middle of it on his right

hand ring finger. In an attempt to confirm Washington's innocence, Lynn called in several family members, one at a time, and falsely told them that the rapist wore no jewelry. If they could come up with a piece of jewelry worn by Earl, it might clear him of the charge, Lynn said. Even with such a strong incentive, the only jewelry anyone could recall Washington ever wearing was a wrist watch owned by one of his sisters. For Lynn, that was proof of Washington's innocence.[5]

The belief was further strengthened on the morning of May 1, 1984 when the attorneys were scheduled to appear in court to seal the plea agreement. Arriving at the courthouse, Lynn was dismayed to find that prosecutors wanted to change the terms. Prodded by the Rawlings family, they suggested that Washington plead guilty to the attack on Lynn Rawlings. The charges involving Hazel Weeks would be dropped. The penalty would still be thirty years.

"I was not happy. I'd spent time with Earl. I felt he had made his own decision," recalled Lynn. However, he agreed to present the offer to his client. "If anything, I tried to suggest that it was to his benefit to go ahead and make the change. If he did, he's still getting the same time. If he didn't, we could wind up going to trial." This time, Earl Washington, who had compliantly confessed to a whole string of crimes when he was arrested eleven months earlier, refused. "He said something on the line of, 'I didn't do it. I'm not going to plead guilty to something I didn't do.'"[6] The prosecution agreed to let the Weeks plea stand.

The episode stayed with Lynn for years because it seemed in such contrast to Washington's earlier compliance.

Arriving at Mecklenburg, Washington joined a long line of Virginians tapped for the ultimate punishment. No state has a lengthier, more intimate relationship with executions. That is in part a matter of historical coincidence, in part a product of temperament and philosophy. Virginia, which over time has performed more executions than any other state, also conducted the New World's first—the death by hanging in the early 1600s of George Kendall, a colonist accused of sowing discord.[7]

When the first colonists arrived at Jamestown, they brought with them a royal charter and various articles prescribing the death penalty for murder, manslaughter, incest, rape and adultery, as well as a number of treasonable offenses such as tumults and rebellions. All except manslaughter were non-clergyable, which meant that a conviction made the death penalty mandatory.[8] At various points over the next two hundred years, dozens of crimes were punishable by death, among them, bigamy, boat stealing, cursing, hog stealing, horse stealing, man stealing, price gouging, and Sabbath breaking, along with the more common violations.[9]

The racial double standard in the law was pervasive. In 1691, the House of Burgesses passed legislation allowing designated individuals to kill any runaway slave proclaimed to have no intention of returning. Thirty years later, responding to a growing fear of insurrection, the legislature set a mandatory death sentence for any group of five or more slaves who conspired to rebel or make insurrection. In the 1856 edition of *A Sketch of the Laws Related to Slavery*, George M. Straud cited more than sixty instances in which African Americans could be condemned to death in the Commonwealth, while a white person committing the same crime would net only prison time.[10] Historian Daniel J. Flanigan concludes that the Old Dominion's antebellum penal system for slaves was perhaps the most repressive in all the slave South, largely because Virginia had one of North America's oldest criminal slave codes.[11]

In the last quarter of the eighteenth century Thomas Jefferson led a movement to abolish the death penalty in Virginia for all crimes except murder and treason. After a twenty-year debate, the movement prevailed. Executions were abolished for free men in 1796, except for murder in the first degree.[12] The construction of a penitentiary in Richmond aided the cause by making imprisonment a more viable alternative. An elated George Keith Taylor, the chief patron of the death penalty reform, wrote to an acquaintance hours after the bill passed: "I have great pleasure in announcing to you that the bill to amend the penal laws of this Commonwealth, passed the House of Delegates yesterday, by a majority of twenty nine votes. This is a consolatory proof that deep-rooted prejudices may be eradicated by reason and truth."[13]

Within ten years, the death penalty was restored for the crimes of treason and arson, although no further capital offenses were added for free men prior to the Civil War. For slaves, it was a different matter. Slaves continued to be tried in segregated courts before judges who held life-and-death sway over them. As of 1848, a slave could be executed for any crime that netted a free man a sentence of three or more years in prison, crimes including burglary, armed robbery, and kidnapping, as well as murder, arson, and treason.[14] Under an 1849 law, a black man—slave or free—who raped a white woman could be executed. Until the end of the Civil War, the attempted rape of a white woman by a black man was also punishable by death, whereas a white man who raped a black woman could receive no more than a ten-to-twenty-year prison term.[15]

After the Civil War, the death penalty was restored for burglary, armed robbery, and rape. Distinctions between blacks and whites under the law were theoretically eliminated with the adoption of the Fourteenth Amendment, but in practice the discretion afforded judges and juries still resulted in racially skewed justice. Eighty-five percent of individuals executed in Virginia between 1908 and 1962 were black, as were all those executed for rape, attempted rape, and armed robbery.[16]

In 1908 the state passed what was considered a progressive death law, substituting electrocution for hanging and moving all executions to a central place, the state penitentiary. However, race was never far from the minds of those instituting reform. In an effort to reduce maudlin voyeurism, the law stated that only a dozen "respectable citizens" could attend an execution and details of the event could not be printed in the newspaper. The creation of such a "private execution" was "well calculated to inspire terror in the heart of the superstitious African," observed an editorial in the *Richmond Times-Dispatch*.[17]

Despite second-class status, Virginia blacks in both colonial times and later held an advantage over those in some other states because of the Old Dominion's insistence on adherence to the rule of law. Across time, this enduring sentiment has been a mixed blessing for Virginia's powerless. It has protected them from the worst excesses, such as lynchings. On the other hand, it has contributed to a veneer of civility that all too often has allowed the powerful to ignore systemic injustice.

Before 1865 slaves accused of crimes were protected by the fact that Virginia insisted on trying major slave crimes in courts of law. After the Civil War a similar mind-set continued to benefit black Virginians. Between 1885 and 1930, fewer black people were lynched in older slave societies such as Virginia and South Carolina than in younger ones such as Georgia and Mississippi. Even so, "white authorities still maintained white supremacy through the semblance of the rule of law and the use of the criminal courts, just as slave owners had ultimately done before 1865. The racist and deadly 'efficiency' of the courts is apparent."[18]

When Virginia passed an antilynching statute in 1928, it was not at the urging of humanitarian reformers, but "at the insistence of law-and-order conservatives who promoted modern law enforcement as the most effective method of preserving racial stability."[19] While Virginia had fewer lynchings, it also joined Texas and North Carolina at the top of the list of states executing blacks for rape. The Virginia Way was to enforce the subordination of blacks through the legal system.

Two Virginia death penalty cases that gained national notoriety in the mid-twentieth century combine with the Earl Washington case to demonstrate the prideful faith of Virginia's powered elite in the superiority of its institutions. To their credit, in the cases of Odell Waller in 1942 and the Martinsville Seven in 1951, state officials went to considerable pains to ensure that justice was done. But their adherence to procedure did not erase their inability to acknowledge and address substantial evidence of racial disparities within the legal system.

Odell Waller was a black sharecropper in Pittsylvania County who was executed in July 1942 for the killing two years earlier of Oscar Weldon Davis, a white tenant farmer with whom Waller had a crop-sharing agreement. According to an account by historian Richard B. Sherman, Waller, his wife, and aunt were to get one-fourth of the corn and wheat crops and one-half of the tobacco crop that both families worked. In 1940 Davis's tobacco acreage was cut in half by the government, creating a financial bind for the Wallers (and undoubtedly for Davis as well). From April to July 1940, Waller went north to Maryland to secure a steady income by working on the construction of an electric power line. His aunt and wife continued to work the crops. On July 11 and 12, using Annie's binder and with help from cousin Robert Waller, the family threshed the wheat in Odell's absence. However, when it came time for a division, Davis took all 208 bags of wheat, presumably because Odell Waller had not contributed.[20]

On July 14 Odell Waller, home from Maryland, drove to Davis's home to collect his wheat. He had a .32 pistol in his pocket and a shotgun under wraps in his truck. A few minutes into their discussion, Waller pulled out the pistol and fired several shots at Davis before fleeing across a cornfield. Three days later, following surgery, the white farmer died of a collapsed lung. Waller was captured in Columbus, Ohio, on July 24 and brought back to Pittsylvania County for trial.[21]

No one disputed that Waller had committed the crime, but there was considerable difference at trial over whether the shooting was premeditated, whether Davis appeared to be armed, and whether Waller intentionally shot him in the back. Waller's defense was limited by the fact that his attorneys had two days' notice of the trial, although the presiding judge did grant them an extra week for preparation when the court convened on September 19, 1940. "In retrospect," Sherman writes, "it was apparent that the defense could have done much more on several key points," among them, problems with jury selection, medical evidence, and the inconsistent testimony of prosecution witnesses. Waller's attorneys also "could have done more to explore Waller's status as a black sharecropper in a white-dominated world."[22] The attorneys did file a motion asking that the grand jury be quashed because its members were selected from a list of poll tax payers and, therefore, largely excluded Waller's peers. However, given the time constraints under which the lawyers were operating, they did not document the claim.[23] After a fifty-two-minute deliberation, the jury returned a verdict of first-degree murder, punishable by death.

A major thrust of the postconviction defense was to prove that racial economics played a role in Waller's conviction. It was true that Southside Virginia was a less threatening place for African American residents than many other portions of the South. "It was not a region characterized by violent confrontation, and there were even some examples of interracial cooperation, such as the recent erection (in Pittsylvania County) of a community center to provide a place of recreation for black children."[24] However, it was also true that only about two hundred blacks out of a voting age population of more than eight thousand were registered to vote in the county in 1940.[25]

The Virginia Code in 1940 did not specifically bar individuals who had not paid their poll taxes from serving on grand juries. (In order to vote, a $1.50 annual poll tax had to be paid in each of the three preceding years.) However, an investigation by Waller's local appeals attorneys—Martin A. Martin of Danville and Hilliard Bernstein of Richmond—disclosed that of the seven persons on the special grand jury that indicted Waller, all but one had paid their poll taxes for three years. Every member of Waller's trial jury had paid his poll tax for 1938, 1939, and 1940. Martin and Bernstein argued that this systematic reliance on poll tax payers to create juries meant that many of Waller's peers were excluded from the jury pool.[26]

Such an argument held sway with prominent individuals from outside Virginia, including First Lady Eleanor Roosevelt, educator-philosopher John Dewey, author Pearl Buck, and others who supported the commutation of Waller's sentence to life in prison. But those whose opinions mattered most—the Virginia judges and Governor Colgate Darden—were not persuaded. Darden granted Waller several reprieves and even took the remarkable step of traveling incognito to Pittsylvania County to interview principals in the case, but in the end he allowed the execution to stand. To have done otherwise, Sherman writes, would have been to acknowledge failings in the Virginia judicial system that neither the governor nor his associates was prepared to admit. "The forms of the judicial process had, presumably, been followed. Therefore Waller must die."[27]

In the case of the Martinsville Seven a decade later, clear evidence of racial bias in the execution of black Virginians for nonhomicidal rape failed to persuade jurists that the sentences were constitutionally flawed. The Martinsville Seven were seven black residents of Martinsville, Virginia, who—according to their own admission—attacked Ruby Stroud Floyd on January 8, 1949 and raped her. Mrs. Floyd was a white homemaker who had traveled alone in the late evening through a black section of town known as Cherrytown in order to collect money that was owed her. On her way home, she was accosted by several men who had been drinking throughout the afternoon. They were later joined by several curious acquaintances who also either raped or attempted to rape the victim. There was no evidence of homicidal intent.[28] After the seven were arrested, public officials in Martinsville took care to protect the seven defendants from mob violence. The men were dispersed to jails throughout the region and secretly transported into the city on the morning of the preliminary hearing, an event for which no public notice was given. The grand jury that indicted the defendants was composed of four white men and three African Americans.

"In stark contrast to stereotypical notions of southern justice, the community did not rely on crude methods of racial control, such as mob violence or kangaroo courts," writes historian Eric Rise in chronicling the story. And yet, "the legal system continued to enforce codes of racial behavior, but through modern police methods and legal processes."[29] In the end, despite widely varying degrees of culpability, each of the seven was sentenced to death.

During the appeals, the NAACP and attorney Martin A. Martin abandoned due process arguments in favor of an assault on racial discrimination in the application of the death penalty. The Martinsville Seven case was the first in which attorneys attacked the death penalty by using statistical data to prove systemic discrimination.[30] In the course of preparing the appeals, attorneys Samuel Tucker and Roland Ealey of Richmond asked the superintendent of the Virginia State Penitentiary to give them a complete list of all death row prisoners who had been convicted of rape. They also asked for the race of the prisoner, the race of the victim, and whether the sentence had been carried out.

Ealey later recalled that it struck them "like a bolt of lightning" when they realized that between 1908 and 1950, forty-five black men—and no whites—had been executed in Virginia for the sole crime of rape.[31] Responding in Hustings Court in September 1950 to the NAACP claim that blacks were being put to death without due process, attorney general Lindsay Almond railed: "There's not a word of truth in it, and they know it."[32] The court and subsequent appeals courts deemed that the statistics did not warrant overturning the death convictions. Governor John Battle also proved unwilling to acknowledge systemic failings in Virginia's criminal justice system when the clemency plea for the Martinsville Seven reached his desk. On January 30, 1951, as about four hundred demonstrators from more than fifteen states arrived in Richmond, Battle met with three representatives of the group. Arguing that the rape of Ruby Floyd "may well have been the most atrocious crime ever committed in America," Battle made plain that he did not intend to intervene in the executions.[33] During the first week of February 1951, all seven died in the electric chair at the Virginia State Penitentiary in Richmond. Never before or since has a state executed so many men for a single rape incident.

Over the next decade, awareness of discrimination grew, and mounting concern about racial bias led to an unofficial moratorium on executions in Virginia between 1964 and 1972, when capital punishment halted nationwide as a result of *Furman v. Georgia*. That U.S. Supreme Court ruling found the death penalty to be cruel and unusual because of its arbitrary application. Four years later, in *Gregg v. Georgia* and two companion cases, the court let stand state statutes that met more stringent guidelines of uniformity.

In the wake of *Furman*, latent support for capital punishment grew in Virginia. In 1977 following *Gregg*, former Governor Mills Godwin Jr. signed a new death penalty law, established under the strict guidelines set down by the high court. On August 10, 1982, "Old Sparky"—as the death chair was dubbed—came out of mothballs for the execution of Frank Coppola, a former Portsmouth policeman who was the first Virginian and the fifth American executed post-*Furman*.

By the time the case of Earl Washington Jr. came to the fore, much had changed in Virginia. Race and economics no longer determined jury pools. Racial disparities in sentencing were far less pronounced.[34] But the suspicion that race and economics had worked to the detriment of a poor, black, mentally challenged farmhand from Fauquier County in his quest for justice was unavoidable. The same refusal to see systemic flaws in the Virginia criminal justice system continued to cloud the vision of prominent officials. As signs of the weaknesses of Virginia's system of capital punishment mounted in the late twentieth century, a spokesman for the state attorney general's office proclaimed, "Virginia has the most fair, balanced and carefully implemented death penalty system in the country."[35]

Washington's death sentence in the spring of 1984 did not, of course, mean that he was immediately going to die. First came a series of appeals and reviews (see figure facing p. 83). The first, granted automatically to every individual sentenced to death in Virginia, is conducted by the state Supreme Court. At that stage, it is the court's job to look for significant trial errors; to determine whether there was passion, prejudice, or arbitrariness in the sentence; and to consider whether the sentence was proportional to sentences in other similar crimes. The decision can be appealed to the U.S. Supreme Court. If that fails, a death row inmate may file a petition for a state writ of habeas corpus with the state court that originally convicted him. A habeas petition is a civil action challenging the legality of an imprisonment. Typically, such issues as ineffective assistance of counsel or prosecutorial misconduct are explored. Also known as the "Great Writ" of liberty, habeas corpus has for centuries stood in Anglo-American jurisprudence as a bulwark against state tyranny.[36]

A state habeas denial can be appealed to the Virginia Supreme Court and, from there, the U.S. Supreme Court. If that fails, a petition for a federal writ of habeas corpus can be filed with the U.S. district court. Again, the focus is on unconstitutional or illegal imprisonment. The ruling can be appealed to the 4th Circuit Court of Appeals serving Virginia and, from there, to the U.S. Supreme Court. If a prisoner loses in all those venues, the only remaining hope is for the governor to step in and block the execution.

What Washington and his attorneys could not have known, so soon after the resumption of executions, was how rarely any of those venues would lead to a reversal of a Virginia death verdict. Since 1977 the Old Dominion has been, far and away, the least likely state in the nation to second-guess verdicts rendered at trial in death cases. That is in part a matter of legal procedure, in part a reflection of judicial temperament on both state and federal appeals courts serving the state.

Procedurally, two rules are most cumbersome when it comes to getting a verdict overturned at the state level. One is the Twenty-One-Day Rule, which holds that new evidence—even evidence of innocence—cannot be introduced more than twenty-one days after the trial court certifies the judgment order. In 2001 the Assembly approved a procedure by which exceptions could be made for certain DNA evidence, but there is no DNA evidence in the bulk of death cases. The twenty-one day period was amended to ninety days by the 2003 General Assembly. Second is the rule of "procedural default." Except in rare instances, it bars criminal defense attorneys from raising an issue on appeal that was not brought up during the original trial. Moreover, in order for a complaint to be raised at any point in the appeals process, it must have been raised at every previous stage in the process. While most states have similar rules, Virginia exceeds others in both the strictness of its language and the rigidity of its application.[37]

Strict procedural rules are only one indication of official confidence in Virginia's judicial system, however. Again to a degree unparalleled in any other state, the Virginia Supreme Court is unlikely to find error in the way juries are picked, defense attorneys are assigned, evidence is presented, and rulings are made in capital cases. A massive Columbia University study conducted by James Liebman and released in 2000 found that the Virginia Supreme Court, when reviewing direct appeals of capital verdicts between 1973 and 1995, found error requiring a new trial or lesser sentence just 10 percent of the time. Nationwide, state supreme courts on average found error 41 percent of the time. In Texas, number one among the states in executions in the last quarter of the twentieth century, the figure was 31 percent. In Florida, number three behind Virginia, it was 49 percent.[38]

At the federal district court level, defendants initially meet a slightly more sympathetic audience. But when those cases move on to the 4th Circuit Court of Appeals, any advantage is erased. All told, according to Liebman, when state and federal actions are combined, only 18 percent of the Commonwealth's death sentences were overturned in the period studied in the Columbia University report, compared with 68 percent nationally.[39] "Virginia is a distinct outlier here, falling almost literally 'off the charts' on the low side of error detection. Virginia's overall rate of detected error is barely half that of the next closest state (Missouri, which itself is much lower than all the other states), and barely a quarter the national rate," Liebman writes.[40]

A January 2002 report of the Joint Legislative Audit and Review Commission, a watchdog agency of the Virginia General Assembly, confirmed the daunting odds for inmates and attorneys who look to post-conviction appeals as an avenue for relief in Virginia death cases. JLARC found that between 1977 and 2001 the Virginia Supreme Court affirmed 93 percent of all death sentence verdicts considered on direct review, the first stage of the appeals process. (The court did not find a single death sentence excessive or disproportionate.)[41] When death row prisoners move on to habeas appeals, their prospects remain bleak. Between 1995 and 2001, out of 56 state habeas cases considered, the Virginia Supreme Court granted relief once, for an error rate of 2 percent. During federal habeas between 1977 and 2001, 15 of 111 petitions were granted at the district court level, but only 2 of those decisions were sustained by the 4th Circuit Court of Appeals.[42] Given the climate, Virginia was second only to Texas in the number of executions carried out by the state between 1977 and 2001. On a per capita basis, Virginia exceeded Texas.[43]

None of that was known to Earl Washington when he arrived at Mecklenburg in May 1984, however. All Washington knew was that he was far from home in a setting unlike any in his experience. Giarratano, who became Washington's friend and defender on death row, recalled a naiveté that set the former farmhand apart. The lack of sophistication could render Washington trembling and speechless at a moment such as the great escape. At other times, it was an advantage. "He was probably the most easiest [sic] going guy on the row. Always had that big Earl smile," Giarratano wrote. "If someone would ask him for his last cigarette he'd give it to them without hesitation. Not out of fear, just because he wanted to please them. Everyone, prisoner or guard, liked Earl. He would give anyone the shirt off his back. I don't recall Earl ever having an argument with anyone, and there was always bickering and arguing going on."[44]

Washington's evaluation, years later, of his fellow death row prisoners reflected the accommodation and simplicity with which he viewed the world. "The way I looked at it, some of 'em were very nice people," he said.

While Washington adjusted to Mecklenburg, elsewhere the wheels of justice were turning. On November 30, 1984 the Virginia Supreme Court rejected Washington's motions on direct appeal. Having considered the arguments of counselor John Scott and the counterarguments of assistant attorney general Linwood T. Wells Jr., the justices sided with the state. The trial record furnished "strong factual support" for the defendant's having made an intelligent waiver of his Miranda rights and a voluntary confession; a change of venue was not warranted; no additional notification of his rights was necessary when Washington was taken to the crime scene in Culpeper; the "unique characteristic of (the) shirt" together with testimony connecting the shirt to the crime scene "was sufficient proof of its authenticity"; and so on.[45] Moreover, the court held that the crime was proportional to others netting a death sentence, and the sentence was not imposed with undue passion or prejudice.

"Without provocation, Washington picked out his victim, a stranger, on the street, stalked her to her home, broke in, forcibly raped her, stabbed her 38 times, and left her to bleed to death, all in the presence of her two helpless children," concluded the formal opinion.

Five months later on May 13, 1985, the U.S. Supreme Court rejected Washington's plea for a review of the state court action, and on June 30, 1985, Judge Lloyd Sullenberger of the Culpeper Circuit Court set a September 5 execution date. The only way to block that rendezvous would be to extend the legal process through the filing of state and federal habeas claims. The fact that such relief was available to Washington did not mean that he had automatic access to it, however. There was a catch. John Scott had continued to represent Washington through his direct appeal to the Virginia Supreme Court, but now Scott was gone. The state did not provide attorneys for habeas filings, and the Washington family was too poor to hire one. The official expectation was that Earl Washington, through his access to the prison law library and to a couple of attorneys who were sporadically at Mecklenburg, would set in motion his own habeas claims.

To Joe Giarratano and Marie Deans, whose friendships with Washington deepened during his first year at Mecklenburg, the idea was preposterous. If Earl Washington was to live, there were only two options: he could start his own habeas appeals or they could find someone to do it for him. It did not help their morale to know that Washington appeared to have total confidence in their ability to rescue him.

"Back then, Earl was compliant and really trusting," Giarratano recalled. "I don't think he had a clue what was happening. If I said it was
okay, then that was okay with him. If a guard would have said, 'Earl,
see that chair over there? Do us a favor. Go sit in it. We'll be there in a
minute to strap you in,' Earl would have said, 'Okay,' and went to sit in
the chair to wait. At least back then."[46]

Earl Washington Jr. in the late 1980s while on death row at the Mecklenburg Correctional Center.

SEP 27, 199:

Dear MR. BARRY,
How are you doing?? Fine
I hope. I am doing just fine okay. NO I
did not think you would forget ME. I am
doing just fine to. I have not have a visitors
in 3 years to. what is going on with the
my family, I have not hear from my family
in some times now. But by my book mi
is die now to me. But the only
family that I do hear from is my
niece's to. I have some people's want to
talk about my care to. I hope that
Marie Dean is doing very well to. Tell
her that I said hello to. And that
I am doing just fine. But I am doing
EXERCISE now. But I am letting you
know what I need to, Becouse you ask
me if I need anything. YES. But I will
be very glad to go home to. But they
move me to KEEN mountain CORRECTional
CENTER on August 5, 1999 to, I am going
to close for now. I hope to hear
From You soon.

Earl Washington

Earl Washington Jr.'s letters from prison.

3/26/2000

Dear MR. BARRY WEINSTEIN,
How are Yo do Fine I hope. I am doing Just fine. But I have not hear from my sister's and brother's in a long time now. But my niece Rosemary in the only family that do write to me too. I Just don't Know why my family don't write me anymore at all now. But at time I do get mad with my family too. But Vince Carter them lost today to. I am staying out of trouble to. I Just want to go home Right soon too. Well I am going to close for now okay.

Earl Washington

Marie Deans and Earl Washington Jr. entering the press conference in Virginia Beach on February 12, 2001, the day of Washington's release. *Courtesy of the Richmond Times-Dispatch Library.*

Press conference in Virginia Beach on the day of Earl Washington Jr.'s release from prison.

Barry Weinstein with Earl Washington Jr., soon after Washington's release from prison, at his new apartment in Virginia Beach.

Earl Washington Jr. and Pam Edwards shortly before their wedding on May 4, 2002.

Earl Washington Jr. with defense team members (from left to right)
Bob Hall, Eric Freedman, Barry Weinstein, Jerry Zerkin, and private investigator
Kevin Walsh, after Washington's wedding in Virginia Beach.

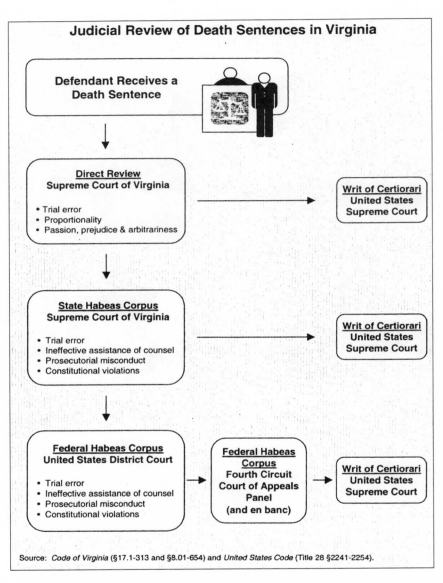

Judicial Review of Death Sentences in Virginia

Defendant Receives a Death Sentence

Direct Review
Supreme Court of Virginia

- Trial error
- Proportionality
- Passion, prejudice & arbitrariness

Writ of Certiorari
United States
Supreme Court

State Habeas Corpus
Supreme Court of Virginia

- Trial error
- Ineffective assistance of counsel
- Prosecutorial misconduct
- Constitutional violations

Writ of Certiorari
United States
Supreme Court

Federal Habeas Corpus
United States District Court

- Trial error
- Ineffective assistance of counsel
- Prosecutorial misconduct
- Constitutional violations

Federal Habeas Corpus
Fourth Circuit Court of Appeals Panel
(and en banc)

Writ of Certiorari
United States
Supreme Court

Source: *Code of Virginia* (§17.1-313 and §8.01-654) and *United States Code* (Title 28 §2241-2254).

(Chart) *Courtesy of the Virginia Joint Legislative Audit and Review Commission.*

8

Deadline

ERIC FREEDMAN was still at his desk in the 345 Park Avenue offices of Paul, Weiss, Rifkind, Wharton & Garrison when the telephone rang at 10 P.M.

On the line was a young associate, Marty Geer, who had flown from New York to Virginia that morning—August 14, 1985—to identify possible representatives for a class action lawsuit. Their prestigious Manhattan law firm had decided to provide legal support for a complaint filed pro se (without attorney) the previous month by a Virginia death row prisoner named Joe Giarratano. Giarratano was attacking as unconstitutional the failure of the state of Virginia to provide lawyers for death-sentenced prisoners during habeas appeals. While the petition had Joe's name on it, he had filed it on behalf of a fellow prisoner, a mentally retarded man assigned a September 5 execution date. The man's appeals had not run out, but he had no attorney to file for a stay of the execution. His name was Earl Washington Jr. Unless something happened quickly, he would die.

Marty Geer first heard Earl Washington's name and story when she arrived at the Mecklenburg Correctional Center on August 14 to interview Giarratano about the class action.[1] Walking into a central visiting room accompanied by her escort, Marie Deans, Geer was startled by the intensity of the prisoner's greeting. "Earl Washington has an IQ of 69, an execution date three weeks away and no lawyer. What the hell are you going to do about it?" Giarratano asked, skipping the formality of a "hello."

What Giarratano wanted was for Paul, Weiss not only to pick up the class action but to try to block Washington's execution by filing a state habeas petition on his behalf as quickly as possible. Now Geer was seeking advice from Eric Freedman, who was as close as Paul, Weiss came to an expert on the death penalty. "I've got the perfect plaintiff for the class action," she told Eric when he answered the telephone. "He's retarded. He's probably innocent. There's only one problem. They can't find him a lawyer. He's going to be executed on September 5."

Should Paul, Weiss agree to prepare the state habeas petition? she asked.

Freedman listened carefully, made some mental calculations about the steps that would be necessary to get this case before a federal judge who might stay the execution, or—worst case—to the U.S. Supreme Court. The timetable was tight, but not impossible. "Find out all you can from Washington tomorrow, about his life, his trial, his lawyer," he urged. He agreed to approach Jay Topkis, a senior partner in Paul, Weiss and an inspirational force behind much of the firm's pro bono litigation, about the possibility of taking on the Earl Washington state habeas petition.[2]

If Geer had any doubt about Washington's inability to spearhead his own legal defense, it was erased within moments of their meeting the next day. Neatly groomed and muscular from working out, Washington might have seemed intimidating because of his size, Geer thought. But his childlike demeanor and obvious distress at the interview made him seem more sympathetic than frightening.

"What do your parents do?" she asked, hoping to set him at ease.

Washington was silent. Looking first confused, then agitated, he began rubbing his hands nervously up and down on his face.

Marie Deans, who for the second day was accompanying Geer, asked gently, "Earl, are they farmers?"

A smile of recognition engulfed his face as he nodded, "Yes."

An unusual convergence of events brought Marty Geer to this remote spot for her first prison visit. The daughter of educators and a 1983 graduate of the University of North Carolina law school at Chapel Hill, Geer had been at Paul, Weiss for only two years, but she was already highly regarded. Under the guidance of Topkis, the law firm had been searching for a class action lawsuit that would have a broader impact on death penalty litigation than the individual cases its attorneys had been handling pro bono. The discussion, held in conjunction with the NAACP Legal Defense Fund, was coalescing around the idea of attacking inadequate trial counsel in capital cases.[3] The strategists believed that there would be far fewer death sentences if defendants were better represented at trial. Geer was assigned to research a possible lawsuit. Her attention was directed to Virginia because its trial counsel system in capital cases seemed almost obscene. No special training or expertise was required, and the average amount paid trial counsel in capital cases involving indigent defendants was $649.[4]

The law firm's plans had taken a detour earlier in the summer, however. While the brain trust of the death penalty abolitionist movement was charting strategy in Manhattan, Joe Giarratano was doing his own thinking on death row at Mecklenburg. A ninth grade dropout who was living in a drug-induced haze when he was arrested for the 1979 murder of a Norfolk woman and her daughter, Giarratano had undergone a prison transformation, schooling himself—with the support of Marie Deans—in literature, spirituality, philosophy, and the law.[5] It struck him as both unfair and unconstitutional that, once the first round of direct appeals was over in a capital case, the state of Virginia did nothing more than supply prisoners with paper, pen, stamps, access to a law library, and a minimal bit of legal advice about what came next.

During the mandatory, direct appeals of capital convictions, the state provided indigent prisoners an attorney. But once that stage was finished, the state considered its obligation largely over. If an inmate wanted to push his case further by raising state and federal habeas claims, he was expected to file legal papers outlining basic claims and requesting assistance with volunteer help or on his own. The state post-conviction petition is among the most critical documents in the capital litigation process.[6] To expect self-representation by a man such as Washington, who could barely read and appeared to have only cursory understanding of what had happened to him, was ludicrous.

Nor was it right, Giarratano thought, that Marie was spending sleepless nights, even jeopardizing her health, scouring the country for volunteer legal help.[7] So far, she had succeeded in finding pro bono attorneys, but as more and more men approached their execution dates, the need for assistance was accelerating.

Aided by the prison law library, his own inquisitive mind, and a handful of books—*Legal Research in a Nutshell* and *How to Find the Law*—also supplied by Deans, Giarratano developed a legal theory: an indigent man's First Amendment right of access to the courts was violated if he was not assigned legal counsel for the full range of appeals in a capital case. This differed from the more common argument that lack of an attorney might violate the Fourteenth Amendment right to due process of the law. Giarratano and Deans shopped out the idea to several prominent law firms. None bit, although John C. "Jack" Boger—a former Paul, Weiss attorney who was heading up the Legal Defense Fund's death penalty work and was considered one of the nation's premier abolitionist attorneys—was intrigued.

The failure to find legal support for Giarratano's idea stemmed in large measure from the fear that any such case would be lost, making matters worse. The U.S. Supreme Court held in a landmark 1962 ruling, *Gideon v. Wainwright*, that indigent prisoners had a right to counsel in state criminal cases and on direct appeal.[8] But the court later ruled, in *Ross v. Moffitt,* that there was no constitutional right to court-appointed counsel for petitions to the U.S. Supreme Court for writs of certiorari, which are formal requests for the court to consider an appeal. Legal scholars generally believed the *Ross* decision meant that there was no right to counsel for habeas appeals, even when a death sentence was involved. Some states, although not Virginia, were choosing to provide attorneys for the later stages of appeals. Law firms that reviewed the Giarratano proposal feared that a defeat in court would prompt states that were cooperative to become less so.[9]

That rationale might also have sufficed for Giarratano, had not the case of Earl Washington so dramatically highlighted the system's flaws. With the U.S. Supreme Court's refusal to review Virginia's confirmation of the trial court action and the state's setting of a September 5 execution date for Washington, Giarratano abandoned his effort to recruit a law firm to structure a class action. He began putting together the document himself. His vehicle was a civil lawsuit filed against state officials asserting deprivation of federal constitutional rights, known as a Section 1983 complaint. If he could get the matter before a court, Giarratano thought, perhaps he could save Washington. During visits to the prison law library, Giarratano sat in a locked cage honing his language, while a designated prisoner or guard retrieved books from the stacks. He scratched out the document first in long hand, then copied it on an electric typewriter supplied by Deans. On July 3, with the execution two months away, the complaint that later would become styled *Giarratano v. Murray,* was received by the U.S. District Court for the Eastern District of Virginia. The essence of the request was laid out in the first cause of action: "Plaintiff's First Amendment rights of access to the courts are violated when indigent capitally sentenced individuals are not afforded legal counsel to prefect [*sic*] collateral challenges evolving from their conviction and death sentence; and can be executed by State authorities,

under existing policy or practice, if the individual cannot initiate proceedings." Earl Washington embodied Giarratano's claim.[10]

"Without Earl as the plaintiff, all the case law from the U.S.
Supreme Court down was fully against us," Giarratano explained years
later after his own death sentence was commuted to life in prison as the
result of an international campaign casting doubt on his guilt. "There
was not another man on the row who could have been the plaintiff in
that case and the case survive summary dismissal. Earl was the constitutional dilemma that could not be rationalized around. 'Yes, Mr. Washington, you are free to appeal your case. Go to the law library and learn
how to draft your petition. If you have questions, you can contact the
institutional attorney; and, oh, if you don't get filed, we will kill you in
thirty days.'"

Informed of Giarratano's filing, the national network of death
penalty attorneys spun into action. If the prisoner was going forward,
then the best course was to back him up with expert legal representation. Jack Boger of the Legal Defense Fund wanted the complaint
turned into a class action. He contacted Jay Topkis, his old colleague at
Paul, Weiss, and urged him to take the case. Topkis agreed to do so, putting aside the planned assault on inadequate trial counsel. On August
14—a day when the thermometer hit a hundred degrees in Richmond—
Marty Geer arrived in Virginia to identify representatives for the revised class action.

What Giarratano hoped was that Paul, Weiss would push immediately for a temporary restraining order from the federal judge handling
the Section 1983 complaint in order to block Washington's execution.
Geer thought that was a risky course, unlikely to succeed, while divert-
ing attention from efforts to find a different attorney to file Washington's state habeas appeal. The telephone conversation with Freedman
led to a compromise. Giarratano would write a letter about Washington
to the judge; the Paul, Weiss attorneys would proceed as planned.

Giarratano's subsequent letter, which became part of the permanent record in the class action, laid out the refusal of the Virginia courts
to appoint Washington an attorney and noted the prisoner's mental incapacity. At the time of his arrest six years earlier, Giarratano had appeared psychologically crippled and barely communicative. Now he
wrote: "I feel an enormous sense of responsibility with Mr. Washington's life at stake. It appears to me that if Mr. Washington is executed

that fundamental principles of Due Process and Equal Protection would, literally, be thrown out the window."

The prisoner went on to say that he had spent most of the previous twenty-four hours doing legal research. He identified more than half a dozen cases supporting his claim.[11]

After meeting with Giarratano and then Washington, Geer returned to New York, just as her star plaintiff was about to be transferred to the state penitentiary in Richmond for his September 5 execution. Back in Manhattan, Eric Freedman's suggestion that Paul, Weiss pick up Washington's habeas appeal had been greeted skeptically by Topkis, who feared complicating the right-to-counsel class action. The partner authorized Freedman and Geer to begin researching a habeas appeal that might stop the execution. But he urged them to find another law firm to take over the filing. Working backward from September 5, Eric developed a time line that would allow the case to reach the U.S. Supreme Court, if necessary, before the execution date. To meet that schedule, a full petition had to be submitted to Judge Sullenberger in Culpeper no later than August 27. When Geer returned from Richmond with only cursory knowledge of Washington's case and without any trial files, twelve days remained.

Six years out of the public-spirited environment of Yale Law School, Eric Freedman was already something of a legend among young Paul, Weiss associates interested in using the law for public service. They had watched him on national television defending Texan Charlie Brooks, who in 1982 became the first man executed in the United States by lethal injection, and they were aware that the attorney had played important roles in a number of other death penalty cases handled by the firm. The summer of 1985 was only eight years removed from the point at which the nation had resumed executions following a ten-year hiatus. From 1977 to 1983, there were only eleven executions nationwide, but the pace was quickening. In 1984 alone, the number grew to twenty-one.[12]

Bespectacled, brilliant, frequently disheveled, a font of ideas, Freedman already had the aura of the kind of person he aspired to be: a law professor doing public interest work on the side. With a father who had been a foreign editor and later assistant managing editor of the *New York Times* and a maternal grandfather who had been a prominent Jewish banker and pre-World War II leader of the parliamentary opposition in Hungary, Freedman had the pedigree as well as the intellectual acuity to rise at a major law firm. He had no interest in doing so. "I didn't want to be a partner in a Wall Street firm," he said.

His introduction to death penalty work came about largely by accident. Shortly after the young attorney arrived at the firm, Topkis circulated a memo to the litigation associates asking if anyone wanted to take on a death penalty case. "If he'd said, 'We have this environmental case' or 'We have this school desegregation case,' I probably would have done that. In a general way I opposed the death penalty. But it was not at the top of my list of issues." The first time Eric attended the annual gathering of antideath penalty litigators and activists at the Airlie Conference Center, ironically at Warrenton, he found many of those he met intensely ideological. Their zeal made him vaguely uncomfortable. But as he handled more and more death cases, each in his view more troubling than the last, his own commitment to the abolitionist cause grew.

Despite the tight time frame, encompassing one work week and two weekends, the Earl Washington habeas petition could not be a slipshod job. An execution was pending. If a stay was granted, mistakes in the filing might preclude raising an important issue in Washington's defense at a later time. Because of "procedural default," omitting an allegation might prevent that issue from being raised in later proceedings. The first step was to secure a copy of the trial record from Washington's former attorney, John Scott. Sometimes, obtaining such a record can be difficult because habeas appeals typically point to inadequacies of the trial attorney. Scott proved to be remarkably cooperative, however. He directed his secretary to pack up the entire case file and ship it to New York by express mail. He also provided the telephone number of the hospital room where his wife lay ill and where he could be reached.

With those materials in hand, Eric Freedman began crafting legal claims while Marty Geer researched the case law that would support them. Both were trying to keep up with their regular work during the day, while reserving nights—usually until 2:00 or 2:30 A.M.—for Washington. Geer had just ended a five-year romantic relationship, which reduced her outside commitments. Eric's girlfriend at the time lived in Washington, D.C., freeing him for round-the-clock work as well. Poring over the trial records, both attorneys were astonished by the degree to which Washington's confessions, not only to the Williams rape-murder but to several other crimes, either seemed guided by his police interrogators or concocted on the spot.

Girded by the growing feeling that Washington was innocent of all those crimes, save for the Weeks assault, Freedman turned to Marie Deans for help with lining up expert witnesses on mental retardation. At her request, John Follansbee, an associate professor of clinical psychiatry at Georgetown Medical School and a former chief psychiatrist for the U.S. Army in Europe, agreed to travel to Richmond free of charge to interview Washington on Thursday, August 22, five days before the habeas petition was due in Culpeper and fourteen days before the scheduled execution. Follansbee arranged for a clinical psychologist to administer a battery of intelligence and achievement tests two days later, also without charge. Meanwhile, Edward J. Bronson, a pixyish professor of political science at California State University at Chico and an expert on juries and pretrial publicity, flew crosscountry to analyze Culpeper newspaper articles and radio reports following Washington's arrest. The law firm picked up his plane fare and Bronson catnapped on a conference room floor as he too worked without fee through the final weekend.

By Thursday, the day Follansbee was interviewing Washington, it was clear that no other law firm was going to take over the filing. Topkis agreed that Paul, Weiss would have to complete the habeas petition and plead for a stay of the execution. On Friday, several other associates agreed to devote their weekend to helping out. A larger team had become essential. At about 2:00 A.M. that night, Geer thought she saw a law firm partner running down the hall and, as a joke, jumping on the back of a major client. Thinking that she must be hallucinating from a lack of sleep, she went home. She returned at 10 A.M. Saturday and worked until 9:00 P.M. Monday with one hour of sleep on an office couch. Eric too had been working almost nonstop, taking only forty-five-minute naps most of the week.

The mounting assemblage of arguments and documents propelled the legal team toward its self-imposed Tuesday deadline. "Here was this group of people all working together to save someone's life—someone who even then we believed might well be innocent and someone who, but for our efforts, would have been killed because he had no lawyer to help him," recalled Geer. The sense of mission was exhilarating.

As the senior associate on the case, Eric Freedman wrote the bulk of the prose. The younger attorneys fed him legal citations, identified useful language from previous filings, and pulled together affidavits and exhibits. Eric, stripped to his T-shirt at night, wandered through the offices trailing tea bags, pontificating, marshaling his troops. Exhaustion and camaraderie flavored the mediocre food that was carted in from nearby delicatessens. Geer mediated for Eric with the typists who grumbled about his incomprehensible penmanship. In his script, the word "beginning" appeared to have three letters.

By Monday, August 26 the team was operating in a daze. They had not showered or changed their clothes and had barely slept since Saturday morning. But the petition was taking form. It outlined fourteen arguments against the legality of Washington's confinement and death sentence, among them, that he was not properly informed prior to the police interrogation of his right to remain silent and to consult an attorney, that he was not appointed a psychological expert for his defense, that the pretrial publicity was prejudicial, and that he received ineffective assistance from counsel.[13] John Follansbee, the psychiatrist, submitted an affidavit describing the inmate as "a calm, even cheerful, young man . . . (who) is easily led. Out of his need to please and his relative incapacity to determine the socially and personally appropriate behavior, he relies on cues given by others and a reflexive affability. . . . [I]t was my impression that if on the evening of his execution the electric chair were to fail to function, he would agree to assist in its repair." The further examination by Richard Saunders, the president of the Maryland Psychological Association, confirmed earlier testing showing that Washington had an IQ of 69. Saunders concluded that Washington probably suffered organic brain damage of long standing. Bronson, the jury expert, analyzed forty-three newspaper articles, thirty-seven of them pretrial, and six radio broadcasts involving the Williams murder and Washington's arrest. He observed that of thirty-eight persons interviewed for the Washington jury, thirty-seven—or 97.4 percent—were aware of the case. He called that "an extraordinary percentage," and said he had never seen anything like it.

At the close of the business day on Monday the document was complete. It filled two volumes four inches thick. Cheryl Matthews, a paralegal who had graduated from college that spring and come east from Michigan, was designated to hand-deliver the massive petition to Richmond, where it would be signed off on by the attorney general's office the next morning. Then she would drive to Charlottesville to get the signature of the Virginia attorney of record in the case, Lloyd Snook, and would proceed to Judge Sullenberger's office in Culpeper, where Eric would meet her later in the day. If, as expected, Sullenberger denied the stay, the team would appeal to the Virginia Supreme Court, which famously issued its refusals in one- or two-sentence orders. Then, it would be on to federal district court where Eric hoped for a sympathetic hearing. If all the rulings were against them, the team would reach the U.S. Supreme Court just before the execution, with no time to spare. That meant the papers had to be in Culpeper the next day.

Leaving for LaGuardia where she was supposed to catch the last flight of the evening to Richmond, Matthews was in tears. She was cutting the time too close. Geer hurried her to the car service, trying to offer reassurance. "If you miss the flight, figure out another way to get there," Geer urged her young colleague. Later that night, the attorney was almost asleep when the telephone rang. The phone lines were crossed and there was a bizarre mixing of conversations, but the message came through. Matthews had made the flight; she was in her hotel room in Richmond. She would meet Eric Freedman in Culpeper Tuesday afternoon.

It was nearly 4:00 P.M. when Freedman, Matthews, and an attorney from the local prosecutor's office assembled in Sullenberger's office in Culpeper's steepled, white-columned courts building. Freedman outlined the key issues in the petition, hoping that Sullenberger would issue his rejection quickly and they could move on to the next court. Instead, to his amazement, the judge surveyed the documents and said simply, "Fine. I'll sign a stay."[14]

"I was in complete shock," Freedman recalled. "I had not the slightest thought in the world that this was going to happen."

Nine days before Earl Washington's date with the electric chair, the execution was off, at least for a while. Two days later, the Virginia Department of Corrections transferred Washington from the Spring Street penitentiary back to Mecklenburg. He had been in a cell adjacent to the death chamber for fourteen days.

In addition to the five individuals who eventually formed the core of Earl Washington's defense team, a number of others played critical roles in the prisoner's ultimate release. Among those, none surpassed death row inmate Giarratano in ingenuity and persistence on Washington's behalf. The civil rights complaint that he filed in July 1985, primarily as a ploy to stop Washington's execution, became the broader class action lawsuit envisioned by Paul, Weiss when Marty Geer was sent to Richmond and first met Washington.

As Giarratano's case progressed, it provided a startling picture of the nonchalance with which Virginia regarded legal representation for those on death row. Both U.S. District Court Judge Robert Merhige Jr., who first heard the case, and the 4th Circuit Court of Appeals sided with Giarratano in saying that the legal tools provided by the state were inadequate. According to testimony, Virginia had seven institutional attorneys who, in addition to running private law practices, worked part-time to meet the needs of over two thousand prisoners, including the men on death row. If prisoners needed any direction in launching their own complex habeas appeals, those lawyers and the prison law library were their only guaranteed resources. "The scope of assistance these attorneys provide is simply too limited," wrote Merhige in his December 1986 opinion. "For death row inmates, more than the sporadic assistance of a 'talking law book' is needed to enable them to file meaningful legal papers."

When *Murray v. Giarratano* reached the U.S. Supreme Court, the 5 to 4 decision overrode the lower courts and tilted in favor of the state. But in a separate opinion, Justice Anthony Kennedy observed that he had joined the majority because no one had died without a lawyer. If anyone had, Justice Kennedy would be voting the other way, it appeared. Virginia understood the message. Soon thereafter, the state began automatically appointing attorneys for the habeas appeals of indigent prisoners in capital cases.[15]

What would have happened to Washington if Giarratano had not filed his lawsuit and if Paul, Weiss had not come forward to produce a habeas petition on Washington's behalf? Would Marie Deans have been able to find an attorney to take the case? And if not, would Washington have been executed on September 5, 1985?

Senior assistant attorney general James Kulp provided an answer of sorts during questioning by attorney Jon Sasser in a hearing before Judge Merhige on Giarratano's lawsuit.[16]

Sasser: (I)f there is an inmate that somehow makes his way to the death house here in Richmond and still doesn't have counsel, do you do any motions for stay on his behalf?
Kulp: No, we have no right to intervene on behalf of the inmate. . . .
Judge Merhige: As I understand your testimony, and I hope I understand it correctly, the short answer to Mr. Sasser is, you

all don't—I am not being critical of it—you don't affirmatively do anything.

Kulp: No, sir. Well, I will take it back, your Honor. I don't think
that that has been true in the past, when I say we don't do
anything affirmatively, because for example, in the Washington case I was on the phone with Marie Deans, who was assuring me they were going to have someone to file. And I kept
saying, let's have them file, please have them file so we don't
get down to the last minute. So I think although we can't go
to court on his behalf, I think we were trying to tell them,
look, do something. That we are not going to oppose a stay.

Sasser: You did something in the Earl Washington case?

Kulp: No, I said except talking to Marie Deans and trying to get
her, she kept advising me that somebody was going to file on
his behalf.

Sasser: Did she tell you who?

Kulp: No, she did not.

Sasser: You are absolutely convinced someone was going to file
on his behalf?

Kulp: No question in my mind; somebody was going to file.

Sasser: If somebody had not, what would have happened say
two days before the execution? Nobody filed yet. What were
you all going to do?

Kulp: If he had made any indication to anyone that he wanted
to file a petition, we would have advised the people at the
penitentiary to have him write it out in a letter and send it
down to Judge Merhige, or anybody else.

Sasser: Would you have sent someone from your office to talk
to him and ask?

Kulp: No.

Sasser: You would have sat and waited for him to come to you?

Kulp: I don't think we have any obligation or any way we can
go in and represent the inmate.

Sasser: If you didn't hear from Mr. Washington, you were going
to execute him whether he had a lawyer or not, isn't that correct?

Kulp: The order would have been carried out I am sure.

Sasser: The order of execution?

Kulp: That is correct.

Literate or not, mentally capable or not, condemned men were expected to launch their constitutional appeals on their own. The state's belief was that nonlawyer Marie Deans, battling migraines and anxiety, armed with little more than an iron will, would come up with a lawyer to help. The state might encourage Deans to press on, but it would do nothing affirmatively to help her.

In 1985 in Virginia, when Earl Washington came within nine days of execution, that was the system.

9

A Discovery

THE AUGUST STAY of Earl Washington's execution released tension that had been building for months. With Judge Sullenberger's order, Marie Deans, Eric Freedman, and other advocates took a collective breath and settled into what would be the second phase of the prisoner's defense. Two years, three months, and seven days separated Washington's arrest from the order to halt his death. It would be another eight years before his habeas appeals worked their way through the state and federal courts. Washington was twenty-three when he was arrested, twenty-five when he was almost executed in 1985, and thirty-three when the appeals ended. By then, he had spent almost one-third of his life within the narrow confines of death row.

When Earl climbed into a Department of Correction's van for the trip from the Spring Street penitentiary back to Mecklenburg on August 29, Marie Deans allowed herself only momentary relief. Paul, Weiss was clear that the firm's commitment ended with the execution stay. Now someone else had to take over the case. Once again, it was up to Marie to find that person.

Just two years after her arrival in Virginia, Deans was already at the hub of the state's fledgling death penalty abolitionist movement. Growing up in the 1950s in Charleston, South Carolina, as the only living child of a father who was a master watchmaker and jeweler and a mother who worked in administration at the Citadel, she might have gravitated to the city's social swirl. Instead, the lanky tomboy cherished books and ideas, and by the time she was a teenager, the soul of an iconoclast was budding. Sitting one day at the lunch counter at the downtown Woolworth's, Marie gradually realized that something odd was happening. She had never seen a racial sit-in, but once she recognized that one was under way, she decided not to budge. "I'll call your daddy," the manager threatened. Not until her father arrived did she move.

Her family's social awareness steered her toward political activism throughout her undergrad days at the College of Charleston and young adulthood. But it was only when personal tragedy struck that she began to focus on capital punishment. The journey began in 1972 in the flashing blue lights and police tape guarding the house where her mother-in-law lay dead. Marie was thirty-two at the time, pregnant with her second child. She and her husband lived in Mt. Pleasant, South Carolina, just around the corner from Penny Deans, who was unpacking her car after a trip to North Carolina when her murderer attacked. He was from Maine, an escaped convict who picked a random victim. The family was devastated.

Sent back to Maine to stand trial on an earlier murder charge, the man was convicted and sentenced to life in prison. Marie and her husband were satisfied. Her husband asked the local prosecutor, a friend, that the killer not be returned to South Carolina for the trauma of a trial. The couple had not focused previously on the death penalty. But when each realized that the other was opposed, they began speaking out publicly, Marie's husband first and then, when the public reliving of his mother's death proved too wrenching, Marie. One day, she was contacted by a prison support group concerning a death row inmate who had decided to drop his appeals. The activists wanted her to try to persuade J. C. Shaw to reconsider. Would she? She had never been on a death row and she was terrified, but she went.

"Do you know why I'm here?" Marie asked as she nervously faced Shaw.

"No, why?" he replied.

Searching for an answer, she let go of pretense and, as she would with dozens of other prisoners in the years that followed, spoke as truthfully as she could.

"I don't know why either," she said. "But I know you are a human being, and I don't want you to die." Eventually, Shaw agreed to renew his appeals.

The experience of her mother-in-law's death was the one Deans shared when asked what brought her to death penalty work. But in truth, the events that steeled her to confront individuals who had committed horrible acts were embedded earlier in life. In part, her resolve was a function of her upbringing in the socially conscious Lutheran

Church, the church of Sweden. "It's a liturgical church, and one of the lessons that is repeated every year is when the adulteress is brought to Jesus," she said. In the lesson, Jesus focuses not on the adultery or the adulteress, but on his listeners. "He turned to us and said, 'Who are you?'" The message for Deans was that eternal judgments are not man's to make.

It was a lesson enhanced by the struggle to understand her mother, a woman whose sometimes bizarre behaviors were eventually diagnosed as schizophrenia. Grappling to reconcile the better nature of a mother who had been intelligent and productive in healthier times with the cruelties of mental illness, the daughter developed, over time, an ability to separate the act from the actor. "I had to reach the point where I could look back at my mom from her perspective, not mine," she said. That hard-earned understanding, enhanced by the crush of her mother-in-law's death, gave her a rare degree of empathy in the face of violence. "I've never been an 'us' and 'them' person. I wasn't raised that way. My church, my family washed it out of me," she said.[1]

After Penny Deans's death, one step led to another. Marie became a liaison to death row in South Carolina, work that connected her to Joe Ingle, head of the Southern Coalition on Jails and Prisons. With her marriage dissolving, she decided to launch a coalition office in Virginia. Her first mission was to find out if what Frank Coppola—the first man executed in Virginia after the *Gregg* decision—had told Ingle was true. Coppola had said there were men on the row who didn't know their execution dates and had no lawyers. He was right.

Now, in September 1985, Deans was—as she had countless times in the previous two years—searching for a lawyer who could slow the pace to an execution. The effort to find an attorney willing to take over the complicated state habeas argument led her to Fairfax attorney Robert Hall. "How did I recruit Bob?" she asked with a husky chuckle. "Probably just pestered the hell out of him. That was my usual method."

Meanwhile in New York, Eric Freedman heard that Peter Huber, an accomplished young conservative who was passionately opposed to the death penalty and had recently completed clerking for U.S. Supreme Court Justice Sandra Day O'Connor, might be willing to help. He was. The state habeas team was set.

Bob Hall, who in time would become the third permanent member of Washington's defense team, along with Deans and Freedman, was known by peers for a vigorous courtroom style and a thoughtful nature, qualities that had boosted him earlier that year into the presidency of the Virginia Trial Lawyers' Association. At six feet, three inches and approaching two hundred fifty pounds, Hall was physically imposing. His size was coupled with a calm demeanor that would be a steadying influence for the Washington team. Of the team members, Hall had spent the least time in death work, and he was the only one who retained a shred of ambivalence about the punishment. "I'm 99.5 percent opposed. . . . If people have a right to retribution, that's about all there is," he said.[2]

Hall's sense of responsibility to the legal profession led him to accept cases such as Washington's. The attorney never forgot the admonition of Chester Antieau, a constitutional law professor at Georgetown: "You have a duty to be skeptical that they got the right guy or the right result for the right guy because of the level of representation that court-appointed counsel can bring to these cases." The fact that capital, postconviction work was not central to Hall's law practice did not diminish his commitment to Washington. Asked her husband's most defining trait, Sally Hall—who married him when they were both students at Georgetown University—answered without hesitation. "Tenacity," she said, "tenacity in the face of total opposition and disbelief. He locks onto an idea. From the time he saw the initial chemical reports, he was convinced Earl was innocent."[3]

An Ohio native, Hall came East at age fourteen after his parents separated and his mother took a job in Washington, D.C. A Rockefeller Republican in his college days, Hall turned down a position in the tax section of Arnold, Fortas and Porter after graduating from night law school at Georgetown, opting instead to become minority (GOP) counsel to the Senate District of Columbia Committee. His goal was to practice trial law. But with a young family, financial stability came first.

In 1966, Bob Hall hung out his shingle. His general practice included court-appointed criminal work, but his only death penalty appellate case prior to Washington's was that of James T. "Jimmy" Clark. Clark was convicted of capital murder and sentenced to death in a murder-for-hire case in Fairfax County. Acting through an intermediary, the wife of the victim allegedly hired Clark and a second man to murder her husband. The Commonwealth's attorney struck a deal with both Clark's accomplice and with the intermediary. Each received a reduced sentence in exchange for testifying against the wife, who eventually was acquitted anyway. Once all the bargaining was over, Clark—who had been willing to testify—was the only one sentenced to die. The outcome struck Hall as a real-life version of Russian roulette.[4]

Hall and a law partner were appointed to defend Clark on his direct appeal to the Virginia Supreme Court. When the conviction and sentence were affirmed, the lawyers filed a habeas petition alleging ineffectiveness of counsel. Hall and his partner argued that Clark's attorney had failed to introduce mitigating evidence in the penalty phase of the trial that might have made the jury more sympathetic to Clark. The U.S. 4th Circuit Court of Appeals agreed, remanding the case to the Fairfax circuit court where Clark's death sentence was commuted to life in prison. That rare victory placed Hall in an elite group of lawyers who could point to success in a capital case within the appellate system serving Virginia. As late as April 2000, Clark's was the only Virginia capital case in which the 4th Circuit had upheld an ineffective assistance of counsel claim.[5]

Bowing to Deans's entreaties, Bob Hall expected that Huber's knowledge of the appellate process and the work of Paul, Weiss would make his own outlay of time and energy minimal. Hall's nonchalance evaporated on the morning when he set the Washington case file on his desk and began to read. Before long, any thought of scant involvement evaporated. He was drawn in by his own competitive instinct and by the thrill of budding moral outrage. A host of attorneys had handled the Washington files, but none of them—at least, none of the defense attorneys—had recognized what Hall saw almost immediately: one of the laboratory reports contained forensic evidence that might be exculpatory. That evidence had not been mentioned to Washington's jury. Hall was hooked.[6]

Bending his large frame over the documents piling his desk on the morning of his discovery, Hall gravitated first to the laboratory reports. His curiosity about them came naturally. Some three decades earlier, he had started his undergraduate studies in the electrical engineering college at Cornell University. He might have finished there had he not run up against the mysteries of thermodynamics and the realization that he would rather be sitting in a session on classical poetry than one on ion exchange. Hall switched to Georgetown and later to law, but scientific matters still intrigued him. Reviewing the Washington trial transcript, Hall was curious that no forensic evidence was presented linking his client to the crime. In fact, no scientific evidence was presented at all in the trial, other than reports about the condition of Rebecca Williams. Surely some tests had been done. What did they show? He was confident that if the information had pointed to Washington's guilt, jurors would have heard about it from Bennett.

In fact, the Northern Virginia office of the state Division of Forensic Science in Merrifield had been active in the Williams murder case starting soon after Rebecca's death. Numerous reports throughout 1982 and 1983 traced the police investigation.[7] Although there was never any public acknowledgment, the police clearly were curious about the victim's activities prior to her death. There was a drug screen on her blood sample, as well as a test for alcohol. Both were negative. A red balloon fragment taken from the house tested negative for controlled substances as well. An August 19, 1982 analysis listed the results of tests on eighty-four items, ranging from cigarette butts to fingernail scrapings. Tests were conducted as well on head, face, and pubic hair samples from five suspects. Similar evidence from a sixth suspect was added in late August, and two other individuals joined the suspect list in November. A ninth was included on a February fingerprint analysis. Then, the forensic tracks stopped cold. No other evidence was submitted to the state lab until May 23 when fingerprints, palm prints, and hair and saliva sample kits from Earl Washington arrived.

Scanning the reports, Hall noted an oddity. On May 26, 1983—three days after Washington's samples reached Merrifield—the lab reported that his fingerprints and palm prints did not match those preserved from the crime scene. However, the report said nothing about Washington's hair samples. Why not? Two and a half months elapsed before the lab reported on August 12 that no comparison had been made between Washington's hairs and the hairs recovered from the pocket of the shirt that the police picked up from Clifford Williams's mother. The explanation on the report was vague. The comparison was not made "per a telephone discussion with Inv. K. H. Buraker on 5–27–83," said the report by Deanne Dabbs of the state lab. What sort of discussion? The report did not say.

As a defense attorney, Bob Hall was trained to be suspicious. Had the Culpeper police investigator instructed the lab not to test the hairs? And if so, why? Comparisons had been made between the shirt hairs and the hairs of the other suspects. Why not Washington's? Picking up the chain, he noted that on September 8 another analysis referred to the hairs. This time, there was an instruction from Dabbs. The nine hairs and hair fragments recovered from the shirt "can be compared to the hair samples of Earl Junior Washington if additional head and facial hair samples from him are submitted to the laboratory," she wrote. That was the last of the matter. The hairs apparently were never submitted, because there were no subsequent analyses. Why was the invitation ignored? Perhaps, Hall speculated, the police did not want any evidence that would interfere with their airtight case.

He read on. The August 12, 1983 report listed eleven components found in Washington's blood. Two particularly interested Hall: first, the ABO blood type, in Washington's case, O; second, the PGM type, 2–1. Hall knew that human blood is classified into one of four ABO types— A, B, AB, and O—determined by which antigens are present on the surface of the red blood cells. A person is labeled a secretor or a nonsecretor, depending on whether those blood antigens also show up in bodily fluids such as saliva and semen. Along with about 80 percent of humans, Washington was a secretor, which meant that an analyst could determine his blood type from his bodily fluids. From previous rape cases, Hall recalled the name of another key biological marker found in blood, the enzyme phosphoglucomutase, PGM for short. When it comes to PGMs, humans are divided into three major categories or phenotypes: a PGM type 1, type 2, or type 2–1. Washington was the latter. Hall took note of his client's blood type and continued.

Switching to the lengthy August 19, 1982 report and an updated 1983 version, he started down the list of analyzed items. He read slowly and carefully. Item #1: a Marlboro cigarette. No saliva had been found on the cigarette butt, the report said. Item #3: child's pajamas. Human blood matching that of Rebecca Williams was found on the clothing, along with several Caucasian hairs. There was a "double overhand type knot" in the garment. Item #4: a hand towel. No hairs were found on the hand towel. Hall yawned, lifted his glasses, and rubbed his eyes. He continued down the list. At item #25, a royal blue blanket containing five small, human blood stains, he paused. Switching over to Item #48, pretransfusion blood samples from the victim, he compared Rebecca Williams's blood type with that on the blanket and saw that they were the same. There were also five other stains on the blanket, each of them containing spermatazoa and/or spermatozoa heads. Hall's attention focused. So, there had been seminal stains on the blanket as well. What did they show? The next sentence stopped him cold: "Further test results on four (4) of these stains indicate that the secretions in each are type A, PGM 1." The fifth stain was insufficient for typing in the PGM system, but the ABO type was A.

Steadying himself, Bob Hall reread the words to see if there was any mistake. Sifting back through the reams of paper, he pulled out the August 12, 1983 report. "Earl Junior Washington's blood type is O . . . PGM 2–1." He laid the paper alongside the August 19, 1982 report, and read the words about the semen stains again: ". . . these stains indicate that the secretions in each are type A, PGM 1." The blood types did not match. Unless there was some mistake, Earl Washington had not deposited semen found on the blanket on the bed where Rebecca Williams was presumably stabbed and raped.

Quickly, questions surfaced. The semen did not belong to Washington, but what of Clifford Williams? This was, after all, the bed of a married couple. Hall scanned the report, his eyes settling on Item #59. Clifford Williams, the report read, was a PGM 1, but his blood type was O. If the semen on the bed was pure, it was not Clifford's either.

Elated, Hall picked up the telephone receiver and dialed Marie Deans. He figured it was about time she got some good news. "You'll never guess what I just found," he said.

"I wanted to cry out of relief, frustration, gratitude to Bob," recalled Deans. "I wanted to walk to Fairfax and give him a hug." Finally there was tangible evidence that her suspicions about Earl's innocence were correct. But her elation was tempered. Nothing had been said about the seminal stains during the trial; now it might be too late.

Discovering the nonmatch between the semen and Earl Washington's blood type was easy for Bob Hall. Figuring out what to do with the new information, now that the trial and the direct appeal to the Virginia Supreme Court were over, was more tricky. It was not as simple as going into court and saying, "Look what got missed at trial." Under Virginia's Twenty-One-Day Rule, which prohibits the introduction of new evidence once a verdict is twenty-one days old, no procedure existed for going directly back to a state court for an audience. Further complicating the matter, the problem was not that the evidence did not exist during the trial; it was that no one thought to introduce it.

At the habeas stage, the point at which Hall made his discovery, strict rules govern the introduction of evidence and arguments. The purpose of the tight control—ensuring that cases are not retried—is a practical one. For attorneys and defendants with legitimate complaints, however, the result can be a procedural nightmare. The conundrum facing habeas attorneys is summed up by two Virginia cases, *Hawks v. Cox*, 211 Va. 92 (1970), and *Slayton v. Parrigan*, 215 Va. 27 (1974). *Hawks* instructs that if a matter was raised and rejected at trial or on direct appeal, it cannot be reconsidered during habeas, even if there is a new twist to the argument. *Slayton* counters that if the matter was *not* raised at trial or on direct appeal, but could have been, then it may not be considered either. Assistant attorney general Linwood T. Wells condensed the matter at a habeas hearing in the Washington case: "You can't raise issues now in habeas corpus that weren't raised at trial and on appeal; if you did raise them at trial and on appeal, then you can't raise them now because it's repetitious."

One of the few ways for defense attorneys to get around that damned-if-you-did, damned-if-you-didn't dilemma is to argue that the trial attorney was ineffective for failing to take certain actions or raise certain motions. As a result, many habeas debates hinge on the defense counsel's performance. But proving that the trial counsel was ineffective is not easy either. A third case, *Strickland v. Washington*, 466 U.S. 668, 104 S. Ct. 2052 (1984), sets a high, two-part hurdle.[8] First, the defendant must show that his lawyer's performance fell below prevailing professional norms of effectiveness. Next, the petitioner must show that, minus the errors, there is "a reasonable probability" that the outcome of the trial would have been different. In Washington's case, that meant demonstrating that if Scott had used all the evidence and arguments available to him, the jury probably would have had a reasonable doubt about his guilt or, at least, about sentencing him to death. If Hall and Huber wanted a judge to consider the unexposed blood-type evidence, it would probably have to be as part of a broader complaint about the way Scott handled the overall case.

Invigorated by his discovery, Bob Hall threw himself into a fuller investigation. He was struck, as Marty Geer and Eric Freedman had been earlier, by Scott's willingness to cooperate and by his lack of defensiveness in reviewing the earlier proceedings. Scott willingly submitted a statement acknowledging his lack of familiarity with several pertinent federal court rulings. At the same time, Hall increasingly suspected that the Culpeper Commonwealth's attorney's office had not done everything it could—or should—have done to explore evidence in the case and to share information with Scott. Why had no one made sure that Scott understood the blue blanket test results? And why had Washington's hairs never been tested?

The transcript of a preliminary hearing held about a month after Washington's arrest underscored the sense that the Commonwealth had deliberately kept information from Earl Washington's attorney. At the hearing, Scott had not yet entered the case and a court-appointed lawyer, Thomas J. Province, was representing Washington.

"Do you know if any lab tests were performed on this blue shirt that you've described?" Province asked Special Agent Wilmore, who was then on the witness stand.[9]

> Wilmore: Yes, sir.
> Province: Do you know what tests were performed?
> Wilmore: Some tests for blood.
> Province: Tests for hair?
> Wilmore: I believe a test for hair was conducted on it too.
> Province: Do you have the results of those tests?
> Wilmore: The test for blood, the lab said that—I don't have them with me.
> Bennett: I'm going to object to this.
> Judge: Objection sustained.
> Bennett: As soon as the results come back I'll be happy to furnish those to counsel.

That was the last of the matter. The hair test, which Bennett promised to the defense team, was not mentioned again in court or, apparently, to Scott. Hall could see from Deanne Dabbs's reports that the hair test simply was never done.

Providing Scott with the lab reports was probably all that the law required of Bennett, but the duty of a Commonwealth's attorney's office is not only to win convictions. It is also to see that justice is done.

Hall's regard for Bennett plummeted further during a November visit to Culpeper. The defense attorney wanted to see for himself the shirt that supposedly linked his client to the crime scene. Would it actually fit Washington? Were there any markings that might allow Hall to trace its origins?

Arriving at the circuit clerk's office, he was informed that—on Bennett's orders—no one was to open the sealed bag containing the shirt. "Look, I'm his lawyer. I want to look at the evidence that was used at trial," Hall demanded. The clerk refused. Exasperated, Hall went down the hall to Bennett's office. The message, conveyed through a secretary, was the same: nobody's looking at the shirt without a court order. Now seething, Hall telephoned Judge Berry and explained the problem. The judge was sympathetic. After a flurry of conversations with Bennett and the clerk, the ban was lifted and the bag opened.[10] Armed with labeling information, Hall traced the shirt to a Bedford, Pennsylvania, uniform rental agency, but there the trail stopped. Once an agency shirt became worn, the identifying pocket patch was removed and the shirt was sold to a wholesaler. After that, it could have gone anywhere.

Hall and Huber's first task was to update the massive state habeas petition filed by Paul, Weiss. That document, prepared under an excruciating deadline by attorneys with no background in the case, was invaluable in its focus on basic constitutional questions. Now, Hall's probing into the details of the case had raised new questions about inconsistencies in the forensic evidence and in Washington's confession.

From the outset, Hall and Huber knew that Washington's confession would be their greatest obstacle. Not only the police and jury members, but judges as well, would wonder: "If Washington did not commit the crime, why did he confess?" The lawyers approached the confession from several angles. First, if the confession was true, was it lawfully obtained? Was Washington properly given his Miranda rights? Did Scott raise appropriate challenges?

Yes and no, the attorneys concluded. The Culpeper officers stressed their repeated recital of the Miranda warnings. But by failing to get an independent mental evaluation, Scott may have missed a critical opportunity to demonstrate that Washington could not have understood the larger implications of waiving his right to counsel.

Worried that such arguments might be procedurally defaulted, the lawyers also grappled with the larger question: was the confession valid? Several points made them suspicious. Some of the language in Washington's confession did not strike them as words or rhythms an African American farmhand with an IQ of 69 would have used. Rereading the confession and police notes carefully, they also observed that some of the facts changed from interrogation to interrogation. The evolving physical description of Rebecca Williams was an example. The leading nature of some of the questions raised another flag: "Earl, did you kill that girl . . . the one found laying outside the apartment or townhouse with no clothes on in Culpeper?" The lawyers also recognized that the police notes were far from complete. Hours of interrogation were barely accounted for, and Wilmore showed the limitations of the notes when he acknowledged at trial that Washington had misidentified Williams's race. That gaffe was not mentioned in the notes.

All those problems needed to be highlighted in an updated petition. The attorneys wanted a full hearing on the matters and their hope, a thin one, was that such a hearing might be granted on the basis of Scott's flawed performance. Hall felt that the defense attorney had done a reasonable job raising some issues on the direct appeal to the Virginia Supreme Court, a proceeding for which he was paid a grand total of $550 by the state.[11] But in retrospect, it was easy to see enormous shortcomings in the representation of Washington at trial.

The challenge facing the team in the habeas proceeding was underscored by the government's response to the initial Paul, Weiss petition. Addressing more than a dozen issues raised in the filing, the state's "motion to dismiss" summarily discounted almost all the claims on procedural grounds, citing either *Hawks* or *Slayton*. For instance, the claim that Washington's confession violated *Miranda v. Arizona*, 384 U.S. 436 (1966), because he did not have the capacity to "knowingly and intelligently" waive his right to counsel, could not be reconsidered, the office of the attorney general said. That argument had already been rejected by the Virginia Supreme Court under *Hawks*.[12]

Simultaneously, the Washington team was trying to inject into the record some new reasons as to why it should prevail on *Miranda*, the state complained. Under *Slayton*, "this he may not do."[13] The new arguments could have been raised at trial and on direct appeal, but they were not; therefore, it was too late to raise them now. Numerous other defense arguments were rejected on similar grounds.[14] As for ineffectiveness of counsel, none of the failings were so severe as to have deprived Washington of a fair trial. The overall state response was routine and predictable.

A November 29, 1985 filing by Hall and Huber laid out the revised case.[15] The updated habeas petition described the newly discovered forensic evidence and highlighted inconsistencies in Washington's confession that were inadequately presented to the jury: Washington said the victim was alone although her two children were present; he claimed that the victim was unconscious, when she was found conscious; he confessed that he cut his hand during the attack, but his blood was not found at the scene; he claimed to have removed his shirt because it was bloodied, but investigators did not notice any shirt during an intensive investigation; he said he was wearing a tan windbreaker when he left, while a neighbor reported that a man wearing a white T-shirt had been seen near the crime scene; the language used in Washington's confession did not fit his normal speech patterns, and so on.

The memorandum also asserted that Scott erred in failing to seek an independent psychiatric evaluation or to take advantage of mental health experts in Fauquier County who might have testified on Washington's behalf. The trial attorney did not protest vehemently enough when Dr. Centor, who was instructed only to examine Washington for competency to stand trial, went further and testified that he was capable of knowingly and intelligently waiving his right to counsel. Scott damaged the case by failing to protest the emotional testimony of Helen Richards about her granddaughters "talking" to their mother on a toy telephone. Finally, Scott gave a perfunctory closing argument in the guilt phase. "He simply asked the jury in an off-hand way to give Mr. Washington his day in court," Hall wrote.

Judge Sullenberger sitting in Culpeper conducted the first review of the habeas petition. Any appeal would go to the Virginia Supreme Court. Although Bob Hall had no illusions about the difficulty of persuading a Virginia judge to counteract a trial judgment, he was confident that his arguments were solid. To his mind, there was no question that a judge and jury might have reached a different conclusion if they had heard all the evidence and claims now being presented.

The state's rebuttal was signed by assistant attorney general Wells, a career public servant who sometimes tantalized defense attorneys by hinting that he might have personal reservations about capital punishment. If that was so, there was no sign of it in the documents filed in the Washington case. The office did not deviate from its long-standing presumption that trial court verdicts in capital cases are correct and are to be defended in all but the rarest of instances.[16]

In a December 31 response to the updated Hall-Huber filing, Wells was dismissive, even scornful of the allegation that Scott's failings rose to a level of constitutional ineffectiveness. Hall's much-vaunted discovery that semen on the royal blue blanket was a match for an earlier suspect in the case but not for Washington, did not merit concern. "If petitioner's counsel had been successful in introducing such evidence as this, the jury would have come to the conclusion, of course, that at some time prior to the death of the victim, who was married, sexual relations might have taken place in the room where the blanket on which the stains were found had been discovered."[17] Nowhere did the motion address the unanswered question of whether the semen actually belonged to Clifford Williams.

A contention that Scott should have informed the jury that fingerprints found in the house did not match Washington's was "frivolous," the state asserted. "There can hardly be said to exist an individual who would not expect prints of people other than a victim to be found in a household."[18] The lack of Negroid hairs at the crime scene and the fact that hairs in the shirt pocket were consistent with those of the earlier suspect also were matters of minimal concern. Since the Commonwealth never argued that there *were* Negroid hairs at the crime scene, it was of no moment that there were not. "Failure to argue every conceivable point does not constitute [in]effective assistance of counsel," the state said.[19]

Rather than address the inconsistencies in Washington's testimony point by point, the state's attorneys asserted that collectively they were not worth considering. "It may simply be said that these alleged inconsistencies, whether taken one by one, or as a whole, are not, when judged in the light of common experience, inconsistencies at all, or are ones about which no juror could concern himself."[20] As for the brevity of Scott's closing remarks, "one can only wonder how long an argument to a jury at the sentencing stage of the trial must be before one is judged to be effective rather than ineffective."[21]

At a September 17, 1986 hearing in Culpeper before Sullenberger on the state's motion to dismiss, Wells summed up the state's arguments: most of Washington's claims had been procedurally defaulted; mere mistakes or omissions by trial counsel did not rise to the level of constitutional ineffectiveness, unless the outcome of the trial was altered; an assortment of legal rulings were being incorrectly interpreted by the defense; and many of the complaints about evidence either would not have been admitted into the trial record by a judge or would not have swayed a jury.[22]

In rebuttal, Hall argued that the critical—in fact, only—real piece of evidence supporting Washington's conviction was his confession. "Absent that confession, no conviction of Earl Washington," Hall said. Once Washington had been found guilty, the critical piece mitigating against death was his mental retardation. If the trial attorney had established either substantial doubt about the confession or built a stronger case that

Washington's actions were affected by his mental limitations, then the outcome of the trial might indeed have been different. Scott's failure to secure a psychological evaluation from someone other than a government psychologist, coupled with his failure even to point out the numerous inconsistencies in Washington's confession and the many questions about the forensic evidence, were ample reason for the judge to order a hearing on ineffectiveness of counsel, the attorney said.[23]

Two months later Sullenberger outlined his decision in favor of the state, in a seven-page letter to Hall and Wells. "The court has considered miscellaneous and cumulative claims of petitioner and finds none requiring an evidentiary hearing and none having a basis for granting of a writ," he wrote. Eight of Washington's claims were dismissed under *Hawks* or *Slayton*. The alleged ineffectiveness of counsel must be weighed against the requirement of *Strickland*, Sullenberger said.[24]

Sullenberger dismissed with a single sentence the central allegations that Washington's confession and the blue blanket seminal stains had been insufficiently probed. "The court has reviewed the record and is unable to conclude that there are sufficient factual allegations or assertions that counsel failed to do anything requested by petitioner so far as investigation was concerned," he wrote. The failure to call a psychologist other than Centor to testify on Washington's behalf at the sentencing phase did not constitute ineffectiveness. Review of Scott's perfunctory closing arguments "fails to establish that their content or length showed either deficient performance by counsel or deprivation of a fair trial." All this being the case, the habeas petition was dismissed.

Judicial history in the Commonwealth offered scant reason for Hall and Huber to expect anything else. Even so, the decision was a blow. "I was bitter then. I was really disappointed that we couldn't get a hearing. I felt we had established a prima facie reason to have an evidentiary hearing," Bob Hall said. Arguably, none of Scott's omissions individually rose to the level of ineffective counsel, but the combination seemed indisputably defective. The unexplored forensics gave Hall the greatest hope, but there were other reasons for reconsideration. If a psychologist more sympathetic to Washington had testified to the man's vulnerability to suggestion, if the failure to videotape or record the confessions had been noted, if the lack of forensic evidence linking Washington to the crime had been highlighted, if the multiple inconsistencies in his testimony had been aired, was there not at least "a reasonable probability" that a jury might have reached a different conclusion on either guilt or sentencing?

For Hall, there was no doubt.

Nor was there much doubt that Sullenberger's ruling ended Washington's prospects for receiving a state writ of habeas corpus. The decision would still be appealed to the Virginia Supreme Court, but a court that almost never found error on direct appeals in capital cases was even less likely to overrule a circuit court judge on a habeas decision.

Founded in 1779, the Virginia Supreme Court is one of the oldest continuous judicial bodies in the United States. Throughout its history it has been largely a reflection of the state's dominant political values and culture.[25] In 1986 the court was still the domain of conservative white jurists, as it had been for generations. John Charles Thomas, the first and to that point only black member of the court, had been appointed just three years earlier. Selection of the first female member was still two years away. As chief justice, Harry L. Carrico advocated a rigorous adherence to case law and legislative statutes.[26]

More than a year elapsed between Judge Sullenberger's decision and the ruling of the Virginia Supreme Court. When the order came on February 26, 1988, it was a two-sentence rejection of Washington's appeal. "Upon review of the record in this case and consideration of the arguments submitted in support of and in opposition to the granting of an appeal, the Court is of opinion there is no reversible error in the judgment complained of. Accordingly, the court refuses the petition for appeal."[27] There was no further explanation. The federal courts would be the next stop.

At Mecklenburg, Earl Washington had fallen into a quiet routine. Hampered by illiteracy on all sides, communication with his family trickled to a rarity. Joe Giarratano and a couple of other inmates were helping him a bit with reading and writing, but progress was slow. Penmanship was a painful undertaking. Washington's first letter to Marie Deans consisted of little more than "Thank you for your letter. I am fine. Love, Earl," written in crude block letters. Life, such as it was, revolved around television, cards, chores, and an occasional basketball game. There was horseplay, particularly with Giarratano. Once when the pair were supposed to be painting the cells of the pod, they wound up painting each other as well. Descriptions of Virginia's death row in the 1980s featured stories of sexual predators and violent exchanges among inmates, but none of that trouble touched Earl Washington. His good nature and obvious slowness seemed to serve as a protective shield from guard and prisoner alike. Like others on the row, he was sobered by the slowly accelerating pace of executions, one per year from 1986 through 1989, then three in 1990 and six more in 1991 and 1992 combined. The day when Earl might walk in the footsteps of those condemned men was still a while away, but with every twist in the road it grew closer.

10

Appeals

THE ITALIANATE COURTHOUSE and post office at 10th and Main, even more than the state Capitol rising behind it, was for many years the public forum of downtown Richmond. Secretaries, junior associates, and partners from the city's major banks, its brokerage houses, and law firms rubbed shoulders as they waited to post a letter on the bustling main floor or passed through security to the cloistered courtrooms above. Upstairs, in the cavernous hallway outside the chambers of the 4th U.S. Circuit Court of Appeals, small groups of men and women wearing dark suits and starched shirts spoke in hushed tones as they huddled in conference or, heels clicking like castanets on the polished floors, headed into one of the courtrooms.

There, on June 4, 1990, far from the pastures of Fauquier County and the steel bars of the Mecklenburg Correctional Center, a three-judge panel took up the case of Earl Washington Jr., who was then entering his eighth year in prison. The contrast between the chaos of Washington's life and the decorum of the courtroom was extreme. It was a measure of the American judicial system that even a poor, uneducated farmhand was not beneath the concern of one of the nation's highest courts. Whether the structure or inclination of this particular panel would allow the unearthing of a miscarriage of justice that had gone undetected by a series of lesser courts was another matter.

During the 1960s and 1970s as the federal courts prodded the nation toward racial integration, the 4th Circuit appeals court gained a moderately activist, liberal reputation. By 1990, it was midway in a transition that a decade later would cause it to be labeled "the boldest conservative court in the nation."[1] Serving five Southern and mid-Atlantic states—Virginia, Maryland, West Virginia, and the Carolinas—the court in its later incarnation was the most restrictive in the nation in granting relief in death penalty cases.[2]

In 1990, however, court-watchers believed that the 4th Circuit was relatively moderate in its approach to capital punishment. In part the impression stemmed from its ruling in *Giarratano v. Murray*, later overturned by the U.S. Supreme Court, that Virginia was not providing adequate counsel to death row inmates as they pursued habeas appeals. "My general impression is that it is somewhere between the 5th Circuit (known as a 'killer court') and the 9th Circuit, which still seems to examine the propriety of capital cases," William S. Geimer, the director of the Virginia Capital Case Clearinghouse at the Washington and Lee University School of Law, told a reporter in 1989.[3]

The three-judge panel assigned to consider the Washington case was, as the 4th Circuit went, a lucky draw for the defendant. Two of the three judges—J. Dickson Phillips Jr. and John D. Butzner Jr.—were part of the court's more liberal wing. The third, J. Harvie Wilkinson III, was strongly predisposed to honoring the decisions of state courts in capital cases, but his opinions in various matters were not uniformly predictable.

Phillips, a North Carolinian nominated by President Jimmy Carter to the 4th Circuit seat, was aligned with a school of Southern progressives who coexisted uneasily in the Tar Heel state with the racially charged conservatism epitomized by U.S. Senator Jesse Helms. Butzner, the most liberal member of the court, was a former Fredericksburg attorney and state judge, nominated by President John F. Kennedy for a federal district court seat and by President Lyndon B. Johnson to the appeals court. In senior or semiretired status since 1982, Butzner remained physically fit and carried a full workload. Wilkinson, nominated by President Ronald Reagan, was a spirited conservative who had worked as a law professor, a newspaper editor, and a deputy assistant attorney general in the civil rights division of the U.S. Justice Department. Only forty-six years old in 1990, he had both the intellect and the ambition to rise higher within the judiciary. As former editor of the *Virginian-Pilot* newspaper in Norfolk, Wilkinson wrote the 1979 piece changing the newspaper's editorial position from opposition to support of the death penalty. The switch came in the wake of a horrible series of crimes committed on Virginia's Eastern Shore by Morris Odell Mason, who is cited by death penalty foes as the first severely mentally ill prisoner executed in Virginia post-1976. "Certain persons have so shredded the charter of civilized life, and certain extreme criminal acts must be so resoundingly discouraged and condemned, that death becomes a necessary end. But necessity is ever a street without joy," Wilkinson wrote. Mental illness was not mentioned.[4]

After the Virginia Supreme Court rejected Washington's state habeas petition in February 1988, Bob Hall oversaw the filing at the federal district court level of the next habeas petition. U.S. District Court Judge Claude M. Hilton, sitting in Alexandria, dismissed that petition without a hearing. The appeal to the 4th Circuit came next. Hall's expertise was in forensics and trial law. He preferred that someone else quarterback the effort before the 4th Circuit. Peter Huber, who later gained prominence as an author, had moved on to other endeavors. Hall decided to contact Eric Freedman.

Since filing the 1985 state habeas petition that led to the stay of Washington's execution, Freedman had been busy pursuing his chosen career path. Leaving Paul, Weiss, he took the unusual, backward step of clerking for a federal judge and then used that experience to help secure a teaching position at Hofstra University. "My politics were liberal. My instincts were liberal, and I was not in the least bit at psychic peace with being at a major corporate Wall Street law firm," he explained.[5] With his goal of joining a university faculty achieved, he was able to return to death penalty habeas work in combination with teaching.

"Bob called me up," Freedman recalled. "He said, 'Well, you heard this thing's been dismissed (by Hilton).' I said, 'Yes.' He said, 'Would you mind looking at a draft of my brief in the 4th Circuit?' He sent me a draft that basically consisted of a couple of topic headings: confession was involuntary, lawyer was wildly incompetent. Where the argument was to go, it said, 'Argument to be inserted.' It was his friendly way of proposing that I do the appeal, which at that point I was happy to do."

Along with his expertise in federal habeas proceedings, Freedman also injected a much-needed dose of optimism among Washington's advocates. For those who worked day in, day out within the Virginia court system representing death row prisoners, it was easy to feel beaten. Now, Washington was regaining an advocate who operated largely on intellect, not emotion, and who did not carry the psychic baggage of earlier failures in the Virginia courts. Freedman thought that the blue blanket, blood type discrepancy was compelling evidence of both innocence and ineffective representation, and he looked forward to arguing the case. "I thought he (Washington) had a winning case. Innocence is always a good thing," Freedman said.

Opening the June 4 hearing at the 10th and Main courthouse, Freedman outlined the evolving arguments. Butzner, Phillips, and Wilkinson, seated in high-backed leather chairs, peppered him with questions.

Wilkinson wanted to know about Washington's role during the interrogation. "Was it purely a passive role . . . or did he actually supply concrete details about the perpetration of this crime?" the judge asked.

"It was purely passive," Freedman said, recalling that Washington first wrongly identified Rebecca Williams as a black woman.

"Are you saying he had words put in his mouth?" persisted Wilkinson.

"That's what I'm saying, Judge," Freedman replied, cautioning that he did not believe the Fauquier and Culpeper law enforcement officials tried to railroad Washington. They simply may have believed the prisoner was "holding out on them."

Questioning assistant attorney general Wells, the state's lawyer, Judge Butzner wanted to know if Washington was led to falsely confess. "Did the police say, 'Come on, you know she's white'" when Washington gave the wrong answer about Williams's race?

Wells said that he did not know. Exasperated, the assistant attorney general added, "If we need a hearing on (Washington's) competency in this case, then we need a hearing on every other issue in this case."

Summing up, Freedman urged the judges to remember that "retardation doesn't only mean you don't know things." It also means that you try to conceal your retardation and your ignorance. "Earl Washington is mentally retarded and can't tell you the colors of the flag, or what a thermometer does, but he has been sentenced to death. . . . He is simply innocent."[6]

As the hearing concluded, the judges followed a tradition of civility unique among the federal circuit courts. Rising, the judges came down from the dais and shook hands with each of the opposing attorneys before returning to their seats. "The 4th Circuit is the most polite court in the country," celebrity attorney Alan Dershowitz once joked to a Richmond audience. "Just before they affirm and send your client to prison, they come down and shake your hand and tell you how much they enjoyed your argument."[7]

Walking out of the courtroom, Freedman was mildly optimistic. He knew better than to expect a speedy answer. The 4th Circuit was faster than many of its counterparts in issuing opinions, but the court wrote some two thousand opinions and disposed of more than three thousand cases in a given year.[8] Appellate lawyers were used to waiting.

Eighteen months later, the answer came. It was the first good news for Washington since Sullenberger's 1985 stay. In a unanimous ruling written by Phillips, the panel sent the case back to Judge Hilton for an evidentiary hearing. The sole question the judges wanted answered was whether Scott's failure to present evidence about the blue blanket seminal stains to the jury amounted to ineffectiveness of counsel. Without expert testimony on the meaning of the forensic evidence, it was impossible to know whether there was a "reasonable probability" that the outcome of the trial would have been different had that material been presented.

At the same time, the judges dismissed a host of other arguments surrounding the legality of Washington's confession and the adequacy of Scott's representation. While Scott's failure to point out the inconsistencies in Washington's confession "might be thought to constitute professionally deficient performance," the court could not conclude that the omission altered the outcome of the trial, the panel said. The state court's conclusion that the confession was properly taken is "presumed to be correct." The prosecution had no legal responsibility to make sure that the defense attorney understood the lab reports, only to make sure that he received them. The district court was correct in deciding that the pretrial publicity in the community, while widespread, was not inflammatory. Scott was not obliged to come up with an independent psychiatric evaluation of Washington. And so on.[9]

The decision was less than Freedman, Hall, and Deans wanted, but it was more than might have been expected. Hall was elated that, finally, he would be able to explore the forensic evidence in a courtroom. At a minimum, the decision also meant that Washington would be living a bit longer. Deans telephoned the prisoner with the good news. As usual, he was upbeat. The 4th Circuit action only served to bolster his confidence that his life was in safe hands.

It was also comforting for the defense team that Phillips's opinion laid out so clearly the shortcomings in the case against Washington. No one could read the document, they felt, without realizing that there were serious problems with the conviction. Finally, someone in authority had acknowledged the obvious.

The evidence against Washington was "obviously constitutionally sufficient to convict," Phillips wrote, but it also "was not without its difficulties for any fair-minded jury asked to find guilt of a capital offense."

The judge explained his reasoning. The defense team could hardly have said it better. "The evidence consisted essentially of a confession obtained by interrogation almost a year after the crime, from a mildly retarded person upon whom suspicion had not earlier focussed [sic] during the crime's investigation, and who was not indeed suspected when the critical interrogation which elicited his inculpatory statement was commenced, apparently blindly, while he was in custody in connection with an unrelated crime. The circumstances under which the statements were elicited by police interrogation were such as to raise at least colorable questions of the voluntariness and intelligence with which they were given."[10]

In a footnote, Phillips explained that he was not questioning the constitutional validity of Washington's confession. Rather, in weighing whether introduction of the forensic evidence might have altered the outcome of the case, it was important to know how solid the other evidence against Washington was, Phillips said.

In that vein, he analyzed the confession. "In brief summary, in addition to the conceded fact of Washington's mild retardation and low I.Q., the habeas record revealed the following items: the statements were elicited by a process of interrogation over a period of two days, and came as responses to specific questions and suggestions (later reduced to written form), rather than as volunteered narrative; the responses contained numerous original factual errors—including the race of the victim, the injury inflicted, the non-presence of any others at the crime scene (two children were present), and the location of the victim's apartment—all later corrected by further questions and suggestions."[11]

Phillips cited the Follansbee affidavit, asserting that Washington is "easily led" and highly vulnerable to suggestion, and he saw problems in Washington's identification of a shirt with which he was confronted a year after the Williams murder. "Though facially damning," he said in reference to the shirt, "the circumstances under which this chain of evidence was put together were not without their own special difficulties for a factfinder. In the first place, Washington's admission of ownership was an elicited one in the course of the interrogation whose general difficulties for the factfinder have been earlier noted." In addition, "despite an extensive investigative search of the crime scene soon after the crime's commission, the shirt was not found or, if noted, was not thought significant by any investigator who did see it." Phillips was also disturbed by the failure to compare Washington's hairs with those in the shirt. And the judge noted the discrepancy between Special Agent Reese Wilmore's testimony about Washington's confession and the actual confession. According to the officer, when Washington was asked whether he left anything at Rebecca Williams's apartment, he replied, "My shirt." But according to a transcript of the confession, the actual question was whether he had left any *clothing* at the scene.

While the evidence was sufficient for a constitutional finding of guilt, Phillips repeated, "it is not without real, as opposed to merely fanciful, problems for any fair-minded jury asked on its basis unanimously to find guilt beyond a reasonable doubt." In his opinion, the addition of evidence such as the seminal stains—if they should prove to be exculpatory—"probably" would have precluded a guilty verdict.[12] It was by far the closest any official had come to recognizing the shortcomings in the conviction.

The critical question was whether Judge Hilton agreed. The evidentiary hearing would be conducted without Eric Freedman. Up for tenure, the professor was advised by colleagues to concentrate on law review publications, not pro bono work in a capital case. Freedman concluded that he had no option but to comply. He would be available by telephone, but not in person. Since the evidentiary hearing was to focus on the forensic evidence, Hall would carry the bulk of the load. He and Deans asked Richmond attorney Gerald "Jerry" Zerkin to assist. Zerkin's assent gave Washington's defense team its fourth member.

The newest arrival was slight in stature, with refined features fitting the image of what he had briefly toyed with becoming—an art historian. But he was not diminutive in either tone or temperament. One of Virginia's premier specialists in postconviction capital work, Zerkin could be blunt, forceful, and quick-tempered. Over the next few years, his certitude at times put him at odds with others on the team, but his sure instincts were valued. Despite occasional spats, "there's this connection between us that's never been severed," Deans once observed. "We could probably argue for the rest of our lives and still be friends."[13]

Zerkin's liberal tendencies, fostered by a family with working-class roots and Democratic Party leanings, were reinforced by the student activism that he encountered at Boston College Law School in the mid-1970s. He gravitated toward legal services for the poor, and after graduating, came South in 1976 as a staff attorney for the Richmond Legal Aid Society.

Jerry Zerkin was introduced to death penalty work a few years later after he entered private practice and was asked to serve as local counsel for James Briley, who was being represented in his habeas appeals by a prominent Washington, D.C., firm. Briley, the third Virginian executed after the return of capital punishment, introduced Zerkin to the radical contradictions sometimes found in those on death row. "He did some horrible things, God knows," said Zerkin, recalling the brutal string of murders and assaults in the Richmond area that Briley and his brother, Linwood, committed. "He was also perhaps the most courteous client of all the people I've ever represented. He was pleasant to talk to, he thanked you for what you did." Over the years, Zerkin encountered similar swings among others on death row. He reconciled the extremes, he said, by remembering that "we're not simply the worst thing we ever did . . . nor the best. None of us is."[14]

Intrigued by the intellectual challenge of death penalty litigation, Zerkin quickly recognized its limitation. "The punch line is terrible," he said, recalling a surreal scene at James Briley's 1984 execution at the Spring Street penitentiary: "It was horrible. I didn't go downstairs (where the electric chair was located). Marie and I were upstairs. They would come around, and I wasn't prepared for this. Marie and I were upstairs in this room on the first floor in the warden's office or something, and they come in and they say, 'We're going to read the execution order to him. Do you want to be there?' This is just one of these things in these ceremonies that you say, 'You've got to be kidding. You're about to kill him. This is so ridiculous.' I just sort of looked at Marie and I said, 'Do I have to do this?' and she said, 'No.' I just looked at the guy and I said, 'Put me down as, seen and objected to.' I was devastated by it, and I wasn't going to do it again."

That resolve changed, however, after Zerkin agreed to let his office be used by an out-of-town legal team that was mounting a postconviction defense for Alton Waye, who was executed in 1989. During the three-week period, "I just sort of marveled at what they did. It was brilliant litigation, incredibly invigorating. Then I was hooked," he said.

Even so, "the time came when I went out of my way to avoid being at the death house for an execution," he said. "I only witnessed one and after that, if I could figure out some reason I had to be elsewhere at the last minute, that's where I was."

When the evidentiary hearing opened in Alexandria, Virginia, on April 6, 1992, Jerry Zerkin and Bob Hall were on hand, as was assistant attorney general Wells for the state. Since habeas petitions are civil matters, Earl Washington's presence was not required. Zerkin's role was to introduce the case to Judge Claude Hilton and to question the first two witnesses, John W. Scott Jr. and Gary Hicks, Washington's former defense team. Then Hall would take over.

Zerkin began in a crisp voice. The issues in the hearing were narrow, he said. First, was there a strategic explanation for Scott's failure to investigate and introduce certain forensic evidence? And second, what was the meaning of that evidence? The critical point was not whether the evidence conclusively proved Washington innocent, but whether "it could have created a reasonable doubt in the minds of the jury" about his guilt. Beyond that, might it have created sufficient "residual doubt" to reduce the death sentence?

Zerkin's initial questioning was brief. Scott, now a state district court judge, acknowledged that he detected nothing exculpatory in the forensic reports. Hicks, who obtained the lab reports, also noticed nothing important.[15]

On cross-examination, Linwood Wells laid out the state's new theory: true (and contrary to what the state had argued in some of its appellate briefs), the semen on the blanket probably was not Earl Washington's, but that was of no moment, because it belonged to Clifford Williams. Semen stains on a blanket on the bed of a sexually active, married couple were to be expected and knowledge of them would not have swayed Washington's jury. Wells did not at that point say how he intended to explain the inconsistency between the Type A antigens in the stain and Clifford's Type O blood.

For now, Wells wanted to know how Scott would have dealt with the stains, had he received expert advice that they were Clifford's. What followed was one of the memorable moments of the evidentiary hearing.

Wells: "Let's assume that the seminal, that the stains on the blanket, excluding the blood stains, could have been excluded by you scientifically by the use of someone on the stand or otherwise, could have excluded Earl Washington as the cause for those stains. But at the same time assume that the stains, according to experts, would probably have been caused by the husband of the victim. What, if anything would you have done in that event?"

Scott: "Let me make sure I understand your question. You are saying that the stains were not those of Earl Washington?"

Wells: "I am saying if you assume that the experts would have said that those stains were not caused by Earl Washington, yes."

Scott: "But that the stains—"

Wells: "Were in all likelihood caused by the husband."

Scott: "In that case—"

Zerkin interrupted. "Your Honor, I object to that question. I don't know that 'in all likelihood' is a legal standard applicable to anything, and I would object to the form of the question therefore."[16]

Zerkin's objection was greeted with silence. There was a long pause, and it occurred to the defense team that the judge had been caught dozing. A clerk rose, quietly approached Hilton and whispered something in the judge's ear. "Objection overruled," the judge responded. Later, the lapse would figure in Hilton's ruling.

Continuing, Scott replied that he would not have called Clifford Williams to testify if he had received expert advice that the stains were consistent with the husband's blood work. "The last thing I would have wanted to present to a jury would have been a family member testifying," he said. Seconds later, under cross-examination, Scott clarified that his response was based purely on Wells's hypothetical scenario.[17] In fact, no such "expert advice" linking Williams to the stains had been given.

For almost seven years since he first analyzed the state forensic reports, Bob Hall had been trying to find out what discussions had gone on between the Culpeper prosecutor's office and the Virginia Division of Forensic Science. Who had decided not to test Washington's hairs, and why? What had state forensic investigator Deanne Dabbs told prosecutor John Bennett about the origin of the stains on the blue blanket, and had the state's interpretation shifted when Washington replaced some earlier suspects as the prime focus of the investigation? What did the police notes reveal about various conversations? Had he been Washington's trial attorney, Hall might have been able to get at some of that information; as the habeas attorney, he was stuck largely with the earlier trial record and his own speculation. An attempt to subpoena the laboratory notes had been quashed in the courts. Now, he was hoping for some answers.

Henry C. Lee, director of the Connecticut State Police Forensic Science Laboratory, was on hand that morning to analyze the available information from the defense perspective. After reviewing the blood characteristics of Washington and the Williamses for the court (Washington was a Type O secretor, PGM 2–1; Rebecca was a Type A secretor, PGM 1; Clifford was a Type O nonsecretor, PGM 1, and the stains were Type A, PGM 1), Lee reported his conclusions. "If the stains are a seminal stain, I wrote Earl Washington out as a donor of that seminal stain," he said. Pure seminal stains from a person with Type O blood could not show up as Type A. The same was true of Clifford Williams.[18]

Two of the earlier suspects in the case were Type A, PGM 1, the precise typing found in the stains. Moreover, the facial hairs of one of them—James Pendleton, Rebecca Williams's former neighbor—were consistent with the hairs found in the shirt pocket, according to a lab report.

Foreshadowing the state's rebuttal, Hall then asked Lee whether the stains might be a mixture of semen and vaginal fluids, rather than pure semen. In deciding if a stain is a mixture, Lee testified, an analyst would determine whether any vaginal epithelial cells were present. Since none were mentioned in the lab report, which cited only the presence of "spermatozoa and/or spermatozoa heads," he concluded that there were not.

Lee's point highlighted the disadvantage to the defense team in not having access to either the laboratory notes or the blue blanket itself. In some states, such material might have been available to Washington; in Virginia, it was not. Testifying later, Dabbs contradicted Lee. Even though her report did not say so, the visual appearance of the stains led her to believe that they contained a mixture of sperm and other fluids, she said. Dabbs acknowledged that her conclusion was not based on any scientific test.[19]

"Masking" was the key word in the state's theory about the seminal stains. If the stains were not pure semen, but a mixture of semen and fluids from Rebecca Williams, then perhaps the forensic results were not as straightforward as they seemed, Wells argued. Perhaps Rebecca Williams's genetic material was "masking" that of the semen donor. By this theory, Earl Washington might have contributed the semen, but a large concentration of vaginal or other fluid in the stain from Rebecca—who had the same blood typing as the stain—was "masking" Washington's blood characteristics. A second theoretical possibility—the one preferred by the state—was that semen from Clifford Williams was being masked.

The defense team thought that both those possibilities were about as likely as that the courtroom bailiff had been the donor. In fact, by the state's theory, the seminal stains could have come from virtually anyone. Still, disbelief was not going to convince a judge. It would take scientific evidence and argument.

Discrediting the notion that Washington might be the contributor was the easier of the tasks. The key was the PGMs. It was extremely unlikely, Lee testified, given the method by which those enzymes are detected, that Washington's PGM 2–1 could have been masked by Rebecca's PGM 1. Deanne Dabbs, who had conducted the original tests for the state, agreed.

Hall: "And it would be your testimony today that of (the four stains in which PGM typing was possible) they are inconsistent with Earl Washington being the depositor of the seminal fluid on that blanket?"

Dabbs: "It would be my testimony that the typings that I detected are most likely—Earl Washington's seminal fluid is most likely not admixed in those results there."[20]

Eliminating Clifford Williams as the donor proved more difficult. For one thing, he could not be eliminated on PGMs alone. Clifford was a PGM 1, the same typing in the stain. Moreover, since he was a nonsecretor, whose blood antigens do not show up in bodily fluids such as semen, it was easier to explain the absence of his Type O.

The state's theory was bolstered by the testimony of John Bennett, who had prosecuted the Washington case. During his discussions with the state laboratory, Bennett said, Dabbs informed him that the blue blanket stains were inconsistent with Washington, but "they were consistent (with), or you could not rule out" Clifford.[21] Had Scott brought up the stains, he intended to put Clifford on the stand in rebuttal, Bennett said.

Bob Hall stressed the flimsiness of any link in the stains to Clifford. In the first place, it was not established that the stains were a mixture. Second, even if there was some sort of masking, there was nothing to prove that the semen being masked belonged to Clifford Williams.

Hall: "You don't have any evidence for or against the seminal fluid stains on this blanket being mixed with vaginal secretions or not?"

Dabbs: "Again, my testimony would be that I have no evidence to the contrary. . . . That is the most conservative approach, is to assume that they are admixed stains."[22]

The attorney pressed the matter with Dr. Lee.

Hall: "Dr. Lee, you have heard the testimony of Ms. Dabbs from the state lab about the possibility that the seminal fluid was that of Clifford Williams, the husband. In the absence of contamination, is that possible?"

Lee: "It's possible."

Hall: "Given your chart and the forensics that were developed by the state lab at this time, looking at all of the parameters that are set forth on your chart, do you have an opinion with a reasonable degree of forensic certainty which of those people tested is the most likely, the most probable depositor of the seminal fluid on the royal blue blanket?"

Lee: "Yes."

Hall: "Who is that? What is your opinion?"

Lee: "James Pendleton."[23]

Why Pendleton? Hall asked. Because his ABO and PGM typings match those found in the stains, and because his hairs were consistent with hairs found in the shirt pocket, Lee replied. And why *not* Clifford? Hall continued. Because, Lee said, if the stain was not a mixture, it definitely did not belong to Clifford. And if it was a mixture, even with Clifford's nonsecretor status, there were still ways that his O typing might have been detected. Nothing scientific linked Clifford to the stains.

On his final cross-examination, Wells honed in on the mixture. From the state's perspective, it was not essential to show scientifically that Clifford Williams was the most likely contributor of the semen, only that he was a possible contributor. A jury could then make its own deduction about who was the likely donor of semen on the bed of a married couple.

Wells: "If you assume it's a mixture, then isn't it true that the husband could just as well have been a contributor to that stain as James Pendleton?"

Lee: "Yes, as a matter of fact, you're correct, and William White (another early suspect) could be the contributor, Clifford Lacey could be a contributor, maybe I'm a contributor, you're a contributor. It could be everybody included."[24]

In other words, by the state's theory, the male ejaculate could have belonged to anyone.

It was the best that the defense could do. They could show with near certainty that the stain did not belong to Washington. They could produce an expert witness, a respected serologist from another state, to say that the stain most likely belonged to another suspect in the case. They could argue that such evidence, had it been introduced at the 1984 trial, would have been a critical warning flag to a jury. But they could not prove with 100 percent certainty that the semen in the stains did not belong to Clifford Williams.

It was up to Judge Hilton, himself a former criminal defense attorney, to judge how such information might have impacted the Culpeper jury that heard Washington's case.

Three and a half months later, in July 1992, Hilton ruled. Once again, Earl Washington was the loser in a court of law.

Astonishingly, the judge opined that Scott's decision not to pursue the forensic evidence was a strategic choice. "The decision was based on Scott's desire to keep the victim's husband from testifying any more than necessary and, thereby, minimizing the jury's sympathy toward the victim's family," the judge asserted, even though Scott had testified that he simply failed to recognize anything significant in the lab report.[25]

Scott himself had as much as said that his decision to move on was not a matter of strategy; it was a matter of omission. To what extent was that clearly erroneous interpretation of Scott's testimony influenced by Hilton's lapse in attention? No one knew.

It was less easy to dismiss Hilton's conclusion that "the forensic evidence in this case is inconclusive as to who was the cause of the seminal stains on the blanket."[26] In truth, the evidence *was* inconclusive. There were several ways of looking at the results. Hilton chose the one least favorable to Earl Washington. The judge could have elected to stress the likelihood that Washington had not been the contributor or the fact that no more evidence pointed to Clifford as the contributor than to thousands of other males. Instead, he preferred the state's theory. "If anything, the evidence leads to the conclusion that the stains were on the blanket prior to the murder and, in all probability, were produced by the victim and her husband," the judge wrote.[27] Hilton concluded that ineffective assistance of counsel had not been proved. Claims to the contrary should be dismissed.

The 4th Circuit appeals court had overridden the judgment of a lower court once in the Washington case; it was defying all odds to hope that the three-judge panel would do so again. A year later, at a June 9, 1993 hearing on the matter, the questions of Phillips, Butzner, and Wilkinson were pointed.

The trio questioned Hilton's conclusion that Scott had followed a deliberate strategy in not presenting the blue blanket forensic evidence, a conclusion the state made no attempt to defend. "That's taking so horrible a risk, not to put on exculpatory evidence, that I would find that hard to accept," Judge Phillips told assistant attorney general John McLees, who was arguing for the state.

On the other hand, Wilkinson sounded increasingly impatient with the defense. "How could an innocent man have supplied the details of the crime?" he asked.[28]

Leaving the courtroom, Eric Freedman—who by then had secured tenure at Hofstra and was back on the case—once again felt mildly optimistic. Jerry Zerkin, walking at his side, put a damper on hope. Zerkin's assessment was matter-of-fact, grounded in years of experience with the 4th Circuit. "You're going to lose this," he said.[29]

Experience trumped. On September 17, 1993, three years and three months after the Washington case first appeared on the 4th Circuit's docket, the panel upheld Judge Hilton's conclusion that Washington was not prejudiced—or substantially harmed—by Scott's performance. Phillips and Wilkinson formed the majority in the 2–1 decision. Butzner dissented. Hilton was wrong in concluding that Scott made a strategic decision not to introduce the forensic information, the majority said, but that error did not negate the correctness of his larger ruling. Inconclusive evidence such as the blue blanket seminal stains was unlikely to have swayed a jury. Judge Phillips, who wrote the earlier 4th Circuit opinion sympathetic to Washington, now signed on to a Wilkinson opinion that took an opposite view of the soundness of the evidence against Washington.

Wilkinson concurred with Hilton that the blue blanket stains most likely came from intercourse between Rebecca Williams and her husband, and the judge listed factors pointing to Washington's guilt. His comments paralleled those in Bennett's closing arguments at trial. "Defendant . . . confessed no fewer than three times to the murder, and was convicted on the basis of these confessions and his acknowledgment that he owned a shirt linked to the crime scene," Wilkinson wrote.[30]

He continued: "The strength of the prosecution's case, however, lies beyond the mere voluntariness of the confessions. It rests in the numerous details of the crime that Washington provided to the officers as they talked with him. . . . According to the testimony of the officers present and Washington's own signed statement, it was Washington who volunteered that he 'took (the victim) to the back bedroom' of the apartment to rape and kill her. . . . While officers mentioned only that the victim had been stabbed, Washington brought up his sexual assault of her. . . . When officers later asked whether he had left anything in the apartment, Washington responded that he had left his shirt, explaining that '(I)t had blood on it and I didn't want to wear it back out.' When asked where he had left the shirt, Washington stated that he '(l)aid it on top of the dresser drawer in the bedroom.' Petitioner identified as his a shirt that had been found with blood on it in a dresser drawer from the bedroom. . . . In answers to other questions, Washington volunteered that a radio had been playing in the apartment 'but it wasn't too loud,' and that the victim was about 5'6" or 5'7" and weighed maybe 170 pounds. Police confirmed that when they entered the apartment, a radio was playing; the victim was 5'8" and weighed approximately 180 pounds."[31] In conclusion, Hilton's opinion was affirmed. The various errors and omissions that figured so prominently in Judge Phillips's earlier opinion were not mentioned.

Butzner, the court's old liberal, wrote a scathing dissent. Early in the investigation, when James Pendleton was a prime suspect, there was no talk of fluid mixtures or masking, he wrote. Only when it became necessary to explain how Washington had committed the murder did the state begin to espouse such theories.

"To mend its own report, the Commonwealth now advances the theory that vaginal fluid masked the stains. But this theory is not based upon scientific evidence. It is based upon anecdotal testimony of the technician that she assumed vaginal fluid was present because she usually observed it in other instances," Butzner wrote.[32] "The Commonwealth's laboratory report, together with the Commonwealth's subsequent test of Washington's blood when he was arrested about a year later, exonerated Washington. Because Washington's counsel did not appreciate the significance of the report, he did not present this fact to the jury."[33]

Ultimately, Butzner concluded, deciding whether a defense attorney's unprofessional conduct was sufficient to alter the outcome of a trial is a matter of judgment. In his judgment, Scott's failings rose to that level. "I believe that Washington has shown the prejudice required by *Strickland*. He is entitled to a new trial on the issues of guilt and death. I would grant the writ."[34]

Years later in an interview with the *Washington Post*, Phillips said that, having sent the case back to Hilton for an evidentiary hearing, he felt compelled to uphold the findings of the district court. But he acknowledged his unease: "My intuition was that there was something very, very wrong about the case in the first place."[35]

11

Strategies

IN THE SUMMER leading up to the 4th Circuit's September 1993 opinion, Earl Washington's case moved to the forefront for Marie Deans, Bob Hall, Eric Freedman, Jerry Zerkin, and Barry Weinstein. The five began conferring as a team.

After the June 9 hearing before Judges Butzner, Phillips, and Wilkinson, Washington's supporters expected that the 4th Circuit panel would rule promptly. If the ruling was negative, and there was reason to think it would be, the slow pace of the last eight years would accelerate. The U.S. Supreme Court likely would reject a petition, and Washington might be scheduled for execution sometime early in 1994. A strategy needed to be in place before the 4th Circuit ruled.

"Somewhere in the summer of '93, all of us collectively became 'the team,'" recalled Weinstein, who had moved to Virginia a year earlier to become the first director of the Virginia Capital Representation Resource Center. "The discussions probably ensued with me and Marie asking, what were we going to do, because part of the decision was going to fall on the Resource Center. I had assigned Earl's case to myself."[1]

When Barry Weinstein arrived in Virginia on April 1, 1992, his reputation preceded him. As a public defender in Dade County, Florida, and later as chief of the capital division in the West Palm Beach public defender's office, Weinstein had an almost unbroken record of courtroom success. In his two and a half years at West Palm Beach, no defendant represented by his office was sentenced to death. He hoped for comparable success in Virginia.

The aim of the Virginia Resource Center, and similar ones in eighteen other states, was to provide expert assistance for indigent inmates in state and federal habeas corpus proceedings. Public funding for such offices grew out of awareness in the mid- to late 1980s that prisoners were approaching their executions without a full constitutional defense. The ad hoc system, in which advocates such as Marie Deans desperately sought volunteer lawyers to oversee life-and-death matters, was inadequate. Virginia was one of the last active death penalty states to fund a resource center, but due to the relentless efforts of advocates such as Deans and Zerkin and several prominent attorneys and jurists, the Virginia center was born.

In accepting the directorship, Weinstein aimed to reverse the trend by which thirteen people had been executed in Virginia in the previous decade. Instead, almost as soon as he arrived in the state, he was swept up in a flood of deaths that never abated. Eleven people were executed in the two and a half years that he headed the center. The memories of those multiple countdowns to death haunted even his peaceful days. It was telling that almost a decade later, Weinstein could recite without hesitation the precise dates on which he witnessed four Virginia executions: Eddie Fitzgerald on July 23, 1992; Joe Wise on September 14, 1993; David Pruett on December 16, 1993; and Timothy Spencer on April 27, 1994.

Barry Weinstein grew up in Florida in middle-class comfort, but he developed a sympathy for the downtrodden and an abhorrence of any form of killing in part because of his Jewish heritage. His father, a successful produce wholesaler, wanted his only son to appreciate the family's roots. And so the father frequently left books in the son's room about Jewish history. Many of the volumes were uninteresting to Weinstein; tales of the Holocaust and World War II were the exceptions. "I became obsessed with how a government and the simple folk behind this government could permit all this killing," he recalled. "I began to get this feeling that any state-sanctioned killing is wrong. It just encourages more of the same."[2]

After undergraduate work and antiwar activism at the University of Tennessee in the late 1960s, Weinstein enrolled at Nova Law Center in Ft. Lauderdale, Florida. His personal hero was Clarence Darrow, defender of underdogs and difficult causes, and from the first day of law school Weinstein's dream was to practice civil rights law and criminal law with an emphasis in death penalty litigation. Even as a student, he logged extensive time working on capital cases, and when he graduated in two and a half years, he went straight to work as a public defender. Occasional stints in private practice never satisfied him for long. Within a year or two, he was usually back to his first love, working as a public defender.

While Bob Hall, Eric Freedman, and Jerry Zerkin focused on court actions involving Washington, the human dimension of the client-attorney relationship was left first to Marie Deans and later to Deans and Barry Weinstein. That was in part due to geography. But it was also a dimension of personality that their lives became more entwined with the prisoners they committed to defend. Whatever mechanisms might allow others to distance or protect themselves from the harshness of death row and the devastation of watching a client die, those defenses were not part of the makeup of Marie and Barry. They repeatedly took the punishing step of developing personal relationships with condemned men. It was no accident that both of them, over time, were diagnosed with post-traumatic stress disorder. Where many in society saw monsters, they saw human beings.

Like Jerry Zerkin, Barry Weinstein was a philosophical iconoclast in the conservative, tradition-laden atmosphere of Richmond. But while Zerkin learned to meld into the legal and political culture, Weinstein never did. He remained the outsider, more emotional in his opposition to executions, and unable or unwilling to hide his disgust with Virginia's mannerly, smug confidence in the superiority of its institutions.

"I carry all this emotional stuff that irritates everybody, or it seems to," said Weinstein, recalling an e-mail in which Zerkin once demanded that he "stop raving and ranting." But zeal had its purpose. "There needed to be that person who would drive every other week to see Earl," he said. Someone had to give hope a face. For Washington, that was Marie Deans and Barry Weinstein.

Arriving in Virginia, Weinstein reviewed the cases of every death row inmate. Two stood out for him, those of Joe Giarratano and Earl Washington, both of whom he suspected might be innocent. As a public defender and private practitioner in Florida, Weinstein had represented numerous defendants who were either mentally ill or mentally retarded. He became schooled in the interplay between the criminal justice system and mental disability issues. Informed by that experience, the attorney was horrified when he read the transcript of Washington's trial. "Scott had so much to work with and he was totally out of his league," Weinstein said. "He should never have taken on a capital case. He was not qualified to do this."

Barry Weinstein's first meeting with Earl Washington at Mecklenburg in the early summer left him equally incensed with law enforcement officials in Fauquier and Culpeper counties. The man who sat
across from the attorney was soft-spoken, respectful, and—to Barry—
obviously retarded. Earl was smiling, but Weinstein thought the expression masked nervousness. Any question that required more than a
simple answer elicited a "whoa" or a "whee" and a long pause. How,
Weinstein asked himself, could the police officers not have recognized
Washington's obvious handicaps? "This is why I personally ascribe suspect motives and tactics to them," he said. "They knew what they had,
and they knew what they could get."

In subsequent months, telephone calls and periodic visits with Earl
became routine. The prisoner would place collect calls to the Resource
Center just to chat. Weinstein always took the calls. "Most of it was not
about the case," he said. "We'd talk about his sisters, his mother, his father, ball games, especially basketball, what his day was like. Very
rarely would I talk to him about specifics of the case on the phone."

Two questions loomed as Washington's team coalesced in the summer of 1993. One was whether to press a clemency petition with Governor L. Douglas Wilder immediately if the 4th Circuit ruled against
Washington. The nation's first—and only—elected black governor and
a former criminal defense attorney, Wilder might be Washington's last,
best hope for living. But Wilder was due to leave office in January. There
probably would not be enough time for the U.S. Supreme Court to review a negative ruling from the 4th Circuit before a new governor took
office.

The possibility of DNA testing was the second issue. The question
of testing Washington's DNA had been in the background for a while.
Even as the litigation on the conventional serology results and the ineffectiveness issue was winding its way through the federal courts, Eric
Freedman consulted with civil rights attorney Barry Scheck, cofounder
with Peter Neufeld of the pro bono Innocence Project at Cardozo School
of Law, about the prospects. The Innocence Project is committed to unearthing wrongful convictions through the use of DNA. "I remember
suggesting that we try DNA tests then, but it was decided that first a
shot should be taken for relief in the federal courts," recalled Scheck.[3]

The ability to fingerprint criminals by comparing the deoxyribonu-
cleic acid (DNA) in human tissue or fluids—blood, hair, semen—left at

a crime scene with the genetic makeup of a suspect was just coming into its own. The principle behind DNA testing is that each individual, save an identical twin, has a unique genetic makeup. Genes, which determine everything from eye color to the shape of limbs, are composed of strands of DNA, which is sometimes referred to as the "master molecule of life." The goal is to isolate a distinctive segment of genetic material from an individual and then analyze it in one of several ways for a match.

DNA analysis was developed as an identification tool in the mid-1980s in Great Britain. By the end of the decade criminalists were realizing its potential as well. The first criminal conviction in the United States based on a match between a suspect's DNA and crime-scene evidence occurred in 1988. In the original technique, known as restriction fragment length polymorphism (RFLP), scientists separate a DNA sample into segments that can be manipulated to produce a visual pattern on X-ray film of a so-called DNA fingerprint. The steps are to extract the sample from body tissue or fluids, divide it into segments using enzymes, arrange the segments according to size through electrophoresis, and then tag the segments radioactively to produce the X-ray picture. Varying widely from individual to individual, such pictures gave criminalists the ability, under proper conditions, to connect or exclude a suspect from a crime scene with near certainty. By 2002, eleven individuals nationally had been freed from death row on the basis of DNA testing.[4] The first such release did not occur until nineteen days after the 4th Circuit Court of Appeals held its second hearing in the Washington case. Kirk Bloodsworth, a Maryland waterman twice sentenced to die for the 1984 rape and murder of a Baltimore County third grader, was released from prison on June 28, 1993 after a tiny spot of semen found on the child's underwear turned out not to be Bloodsworth's.[5]

Closer to home, Governor Wilder was confronted that spring with DNA evidence exonerating Walter Snyder, a young black man sentenced to forty-five years in prison for the 1985 rape of an Alexandria woman. Snyder's prospects for release appeared doomed when there was insufficient genetic material from the crime scene to conduct a RFLP-DNA fingerprinting test. But the timely development of a new process known as PCR (polymerase chain reaction)-DNA, in which amounts as minuscule as 2 billionths of a gram can be tested, saved him. PCR testing amplifies available DNA by making multiple copies of it. Then the makeup of a specific gene, the HLA DQa, is analyzed. The advantages over RFLP testing are substantial. The tested material can be older and of poorer quality, less is needed, and the test can be completed in days rather than weeks. However, the first generation of PCR-DNA tests were less discriminating than the RFLP test. PCR at that point was more helpful in ruling out a suspect than in making a positive identification. Tests conducted on October 27, 1992 at a Boston lab by Dr. David Bing, one of the early users of the PCR-DNA process, showed that Snyder was not the contributor of the crime-scene semen. It would be another six months before Snyder walked free, however. With Virginia's Twenty-One-Day Rule, options were closed for introducing the evidence in court. Finally, after the Innocence Project waged a campaign in the press and a second test confirmed the results, Wilder agreed that the scientific evidence could not be ignored. He signed an executive order releasing Snyder on April 23, 1993. "To the end, everyone in power insisted that there was good reason Walter Snyder spent seven of the prime years of his life locked in a cell," wrote Jim Dwyer in a book detailing the story. "The case against him was built on evidence that was, by any reasonable standards, compromised, corrupted, and unsafe. Yet his trial was judged fair by the highest court in Virginia."[6]

The story did not go unnoticed at the Virginia attorney general's office where, far from the public eye, the Earl Washington case was getting an unexpectedly skeptical review. Surprisingly, Washington's initial DNA test was sought first, not by his attorneys, but by an interim attorney general appointed to fill out the term of Mary Sue Terry, a steadfast defender of capital convictions who resigned to run for governor. As a one-year appointee without political ambitions, attorney general Stephen D. Rosenthal had no need to build a tough-on-crime reputation for voters. The possibility of DNA testing came to Rosenthal's attention in part because of another fluke. Gail Sterling Marshall, also serving just one year as the top deputy in the criminal division, read Washington's file and reached a heretical conclusion—he was not guilty.

Marshall was no stranger to long odds or unpopular stands. Her father was a labor organizer for the United Auto Workers in Georgia, hardly a hotbed of union activity. Later, Thomas Starling became a national labor leader, sitting on the UAW's national board with President Walter Reuther. Marshall was one of two women in the Class of 1968 at the University of Virginia law school, and when she joined the prominent Washington, D.C., law firm of Hogan & Hartson, the attraction was the firm's full-time unit focusing on pro bono work. By the time she left in 1986 to become a deputy to Virginia's first female attorney general, Marshall was a litigating partner. Seven years later, when Terry resigned and Rosenthal advanced, Marshall assumed oversight of the criminal division. Part of her job was to review every capital conviction in which a prisoner was approaching execution. Washington was on the list.

Marshall was personally opposed to the death penalty. "Outside some strict self-defense principles, murder is not morally acceptable," she said.[7] Still, as part of her job, she was prepared to sign off on those cases in which she felt that a proper trial and sentencing had been awarded a guilty defendant. Deciding what is or is not proper is often a matter of judgment, however. And no top deputy in the criminal division, before or since, brought so skeptical an eye to the task as Marshall. "In reviewing cases, I came to it with a you-prove-it-to-me attitude, and in Earl Washington's case, they didn't prove it to me," she said.

In the course of her review, Marshall dispatched a paralegal to Culpeper to collect all the newspaper stories written about the Williams case. She wanted to know how many details of the murder had been in the paper prior to Washington's confession. Marshall also spoke with Richard Bonnie, a University of Virginia law school professor and expert on mental retardation and the criminal justice system. "The general information I learned is that there is a demonstrated tendency of the mentally retarded to try to agree with and please the person interrogating them. They become extremely adept at reading body language and intonation. You can ask what appears to you to be a neutral question, and body language, even tone, can inadvertently telegraph to them the answer you want," she said.

Marshall was struck by the inconsistencies in Washington's testimony. She also questioned the police tour of Culpeper, noting that the only apartment complex to which Washington was taken more than once was the one where Williams was murdered. "The investigators found it significant that he pointed to 'exactly the opposite end'" of the row of apartments. "I did not find that confirmatory," she said.

For every objection Marshall raised, the state lawyers who had been handling the case had a rebuttal. If Washington did not mention the two children, it was because he was embarrassed about their presence. If he said he stabbed Williams two or three times, not thirty-eight, it was because he did not want to admit to such a brutal act. If he identified the victim as black, not white, it was because he believed the law would be harder on him if she were white. "They had all sorts of reasons why I was wrong, but the reasons were not convincing to me," she said. "I said, 'This guy in my view is innocent. I cannot certify that we ought to go forward.'"

In the face of that dilemma, the idea of DNA testing surfaced. The state forensic lab confirmed that there was enough material left on the vaginal swabs to conduct a PCR-DNA test, the new procedure requiring minimal DNA. Rosenthal was approached about the prospect, and he immediately agreed.

"This one was pretty simple and straightforward from my perspective," said Rosenthal.[8] He had reviewed the Washington file, Rosenthal said, and saw nothing that struck him as an obvious mistake on the jury's part. Moreover, he had no qualms about carrying out the death penalty when it was deemed appropriate by a properly impaneled and instructed jury. His review of the horrid details of various capital crimes convinced him that the penalty was at times acceptable. But he also believed that acting justly was more important than saving face. If a DNA test could determine Washington's guilt or innocence, then of course it should be done.

Rosenthal extended the offer to Bob Hall in a letter written on June 2, a week before the 4th Circuit's second hearing. If Washington would allow the state police to collect a fresh blood sample, the PCR-DNA comparison test could be performed promptly, Rosenthal wrote. "I think we both acknowledge that the most important goal is that justice be done. . . . In my opinion, this will allay any reasonable concerns about Mr. Washington's conviction."[9] In later years, a consensus arose that only the governor could order such tests if time limits on introduction of new evidence had expired in the courts. But DNA testing was so new in 1993 that the issue of whether Rosenthal was acting within his authority did not even come up. Two weeks later, Hall wrote back, requesting more information about the procedure. On June 29 Rosenthal replied. There was no further correspondence until eleven days after the 4th Circuit September 17 decision upholding Washington's conviction. In a letter dated September 28, Rosenthal expressed veiled annoyance at the defense attorneys' delay. "I made the offer because it is in the best interests of everyone involved, and particularly, I believe, your client," he wrote.[10] This time, with the 4th Circuit's decision announced, the offer was promptly accepted. Writing for Hall, who was out of the country, Zerkin negotiated the details of the testing arrangement. In an October 13 letter, he outlined a six-step agreement in which Washington would submit two vials of blood, one for a comparison test conducted by the Virginia state lab, the second for a similar test to be conducted by a scientist of the defense team's choosing, Dr. David Bing.[11]

The team had stalled on the tests for four months for two reasons. First, the members were not entirely sure that they trusted the state's intentions. Second, much as the team believed in Washington's innocence, they could not be positive. In their view, it would be bad lawyering if the 4th Circuit ruled in Washington's favor only to have DNA results prove the panel wrong. "You can convince yourself of a client's innocence, which I had done in Earl's case, but there's still this gnawing thing. . . . You weren't there," said Zerkin.[12]

Once the 4th Circuit rejection was in, there was no dispute about going forward. The day after Zerkin and Rosenthal signed off on the DNA test agreement, state police delivered a sample of Washington's blood to the state laboratory. The countdown began. It ended twelve days later with a flurry of charges and countercharges about Washington's innocence and about who had said what, when, and to whom regarding the test results.

According to Zerkin, John McLees, an assistant attorney general and former Richmond public defender assigned to the Washington case, called him on a Tuesday—five days after the blood sample was delivered to the state—with a stunning report. "He stated that he had 'monumental news' for me, that their DNA test had resulted in an exclusion of Mr. Washington," Zerkin said in an October 26 letter to Walter A. McFarlane, Wilder's chief legal adviser. "His only caveat was that the test might not exclude Washington if there were more than one perpetrator, but, of course, there was no evidence of that. At my suggestion, we agreed to limit that information to the defense team and his superiors."[13] Not even Earl Washington was to be told until the following Monday, the day the formal state lab report would be available.

For twenty-four hours, elation reigned among the Washington defense team. The next day, Wednesday, Jerry Zerkin telephoned attorney general Rosenthal and suggested that they meet to discuss the findings and their public release. Present at the afternoon gathering, according to Zerkin's letter to McFarlane, were Zerkin, Bob Hall, Rosenthal, and deputy attorney general Deborah Love-Bryant. "At that meeting, General Rosenthal implicitly confirmed the information I received from Mr. McLees," Zerkin wrote. Both Zerkin and Hall recall that the meeting, which began congenially, was interrupted with a message to Rosenthal from someone within the criminal division. After receiving it, Rosenthal turned grim. Zerkin recalls him saying something on the order of, "This is what I was afraid of."

"It was all going along hunky-dory. Then this note comes in which says the results may not be as conclusive as we thought," Zerkin said.[14] Washington's lawyers were furious. Now the state was suggesting that Washington might not have acted alone. If so, he could still be connected to the crime.

"We argued that the victim [Rebecca Williams] said it was one individual," added Hall, "but the die was cast."[15]

A decade later, Rosenthal recalled nothing of the meeting, but agreed that the joint memories of the two lawyers indicated that one had occurred. Even so, Rosenthal insisted he never concluded personally that the first DNA test results excluded Washington. "Whatever discussion John McLees had with Jerry Zerkin was before I saw the results of the DNA test," he said. "He [McLees] either saw the results first or he'd gotten a call first." In any event, if Zerkin and Hall believed they were in his office to decide how best to inform the public that Earl Washington had been found innocent, they were mistaken, he said. His only intention, ever, was to pass the test results along to Governor Wilder without recommendation.[16] Precisely why he met with Hall and Zerkin eluded Rosenthal, since he did not remember the meeting.

The following Monday, October 25, 1993, Rosenthal appeared at a press conference, flanked by Dr. Paul B. Ferrara, head of the state's division of forensic science, to announce the results of the PCR-DNA test. The test works by determining the pattern of alleles, or genetic markers, in the HLA DQa gene. Each individual has two of six possible versions of the gene. Both Rebecca and Clifford Williams had a 4, 4 allele pattern. Washington had a 1.2, 4. What the state lab discovered in the sperm fraction of the vaginal swabs taken from Rebecca Williams was the presence of three alleles: a 1.1, a 1.2, and a 4.

Jeffrey Ban, the forensic scientist who conducted the test, provided an explanation: "Neither Earl Washington, Jr., Rebecca Williams, nor Clifford Williams, individually or in combination, can be the contributor(s) of the 1.1 allele previously detected on the vaginal swab." However, he continued, "none of these individuals can be eliminated as contributing to the mixture if another individual possessing a 1.1 allele is also present."[17]

Asked how he interpreted the results, Rosenthal replied: "It's too early to judge the precise meaning. . . . He could be innocent. He could be guilty. . . . It's up to the governor and the governor will draw his own conclusions from the test." Ferrara's reading was more positive for Washington. While the PCR-DNA test did not conclusively prove Washington's innocence, the forensic scientist said, it "cast 'substantial doubt' on his guilt."[18]

Outside the press conference, Zerkin erupted in anger. "I'm morally outraged by Mr. Rosenthal's comments today. . . . [T]he proposition [that the tests are inconclusive] is absurd," he said.[19] As far as Washington's supporters were concerned, the obvious interpretation of the results was that Rebecca Williams had contributed the 4, and the rapist had donated the 1.1 and 1.2 alleles. That meant the rapist was not Earl Washington. For the results not to exclude Washington, as Rosenthal suggested, there could be only two explanations: either Rebecca Williams had consensual sex with someone other than her husband shortly prior to the murder, in which case there was no evidence that a rape had occurred, or the murder had been committed by Washington and another individual, who raped Williams.

Over the course of ten years and three months, through endless courtrooms and countless legal briefs, the Culpeper prosecutor and lawyers for the state had never once suggested that Rebecca Williams's murder had been conducted by two people or that the victim had been promiscuous. The victim herself had told three individuals that she was assaulted by a single black male. But in an instant, the state's position had changed. While Rosenthal defended his neutrality as the proper position for an attorney general passing on information to a governor, with whom any decision rested, the implication of his comment was unavoidable. The only way in which Earl Washington could still be guilty was for the whole theory of the case, as it had been argued for years, to change. If two people had committed the murder, then the state was acknowledging that the confession which carried so much weight in convicting Washington was a lie. Save two footprints on a plastic runner, one of which could easily have come from a law enforcement officer, there was not a single piece of evidence pointing to *two* perpetrators. As for the second alternative, that the 1.1 allele had come from a lover, testimony at trial said that the semen was no more than twelve hours old when Williams died at 2:05 P.M. Clifford was due home from work at 7 A.M. There would have been a narrow window of opportunity for an affair.

The state's case had been exposed as false. Rather than own up, the powers that be were trotting out an unsubstantiated theory at odds with anything that had been argued in a courtroom. Defense attorneys had a term for the mystery accomplice who often cropped up in the prosecution's revised theory of a case after DNA pointed to a defendant's innocence. They called the figure "the unindicted coejaculator." Now Earl Washington had one.

Jerry Zerkin was not the only one upset about the day's events. The next morning's paper reported that Barry Weinstein had credited the defense team, not Rosenthal, with initiating the idea of DNA testing. "Let me make this very clear. I was the one who asked for this DNA test, for a variety of reasons that I'm not going to get into here," snapped the attorney general in reply.[20] Rosenthal angrily telephoned Hall and Weinstein demanding an apology. Weinstein acknowledged that he had erred.

Years later, Washington's defense team complimented Rosenthal for fairness in ordering the DNA test. Indeed, without Gail Marshall's skepticism about Washington's guilt, without the subsequent proposal for DNA testing, and without Rosenthal's ready acceptance of the idea, events might have taken a disastrous turn. Over the next few days Governor Wilder showed a marked reluctance to involve himself in the case. Had the DNA results not been pressed into his hands, he could have easily left the Washington case to his successor, crime fighter George F. Allen. But during a week in which it took only a tiny leap of faith to understand that Earl Washington had been exonerated, it was hard for his defense team to recognize that thin silver lining.

Far from the fray on the day of Rosenthal's press conference, Earl Washington knew only that a DNA test had been conducted and that the results were favorable. He was unaware of the tense debate over the meaning of the findings. Contacted at Mecklenburg by a reporter for the *Washington Post*, the prisoner termed the DNA report "the best news I ever got."[21] To a Richmond-based reporter, he added: "I feel good right now."[22] The same could not be said for the defense team.

Their continued public optimism about Washington's prospects did not erase the chill of Wilder's reaction. Wilder was widely reputed to be at least skeptical, and perhaps privately hostile to capital punishment. But the governor was not one to follow a predictable political path or to be subject to manipulation, even—and perhaps especially—by those whose philosophical sentiments he shared. Speaking to reporters during a trip to Roanoke hours after Rosenthal's press conference, Wilder said he had no intention of considering Washington's case while it was still pending in the courts. "I don't involve myself in any of those cases as long as they are pending," he said. "I don't propose that I will intervene as long as that is the situation. . . . I have never intervened in any case that is pending in court."[23] The governor released a three-paragraph press release saying much the same thing.[24]

Given Wilder's reaction, the radical option that the team had discussed during the long summer wait resurfaced. The defense team was considering dropping Washington's appeal of the 4th Circuit decision to the U.S. Supreme Court, Zerkin told a reporter. "What we would do is simply advise the governor we will not pursue (litigation) any further," he said.[25] That appeared to be the only way to get the case before Wilder before his term expired.

Earlier in the summer, the team had confronted the question of what action to take if the 4th Circuit agreed with Judge Hilton in rejecting the ineffectiveness of counsel claim. If that happened, two steps remained to Washington in the courts. The team could request that the full 4th Circuit Court of Appeals reconsider the three-judge panel's rejection. But if a panel including Phillips and Butzner turned down the appeal, there was no practical hope that the full panel would act otherwise. Alternatively, a petition for certiorari could be filed with the U.S. Supreme Court, but there was no reason to think that the high court would be any more accepting of the issues rejected by the lower courts. Gradually, the team came to feel that Washington's best—and probably only—hope of avoiding execution was to get a clemency petition into Wilder's hands. Neither of the candidates competing to replace him, Democrat Terry or Republican Allen, had shown any sympathy for those convicted of capital crimes.

The decision was not taken lightly. The lawyers were cognizant throughout that their client was a mentally retarded man and that they were making life and death decisions on his behalf. Years later, Douglas Wilder was highly critical of the action. "Earl Washington's lawyers dropped his appeals. I think it's unforgivable. . . . It was a stupid thing for them to have done, almost unprofessional," he said.[26]

The attorneys thought otherwise. In a December 2 letter to Governor Wilder, Hall explained their viewpoint. "While technically a Petition for a Writ of Certiorari could be filed with the U.S. Supreme Court, there is no likelihood that it would be granted," he wrote. Moreover, the DNA test results would not be considered because they were not part of the record before the 4th Circuit. "Asking the Supreme Court to adjudicate the merits of this case on a record which did not reflect the single most important fact of Earl's innocence, the DNA findings, would be meaningless exercise and a breach of faith to the Court, to the law and to Earl," Hall wrote.[27]

Bob Hall informed the governor that "there is no court before which Earl's fate is now pending, and, in my judgment, there is no court to which he may now turn for relief. No judicial process will be derailed or otherwise interfered with" if Wilder agreed to review the case. Hall urged the governor to do so.

With Rosenthal's release of the DNA results and the decision to forgo further appeals, the team zeroed in on clemency. At the time of Rosenthal's press conference, Wilder had eighty-one days—less than three months—left in office. It was not nearly enough time to mount an effective political campaign, which a clemency appeal essentially is. Supporters of Joe Giarratano had spent almost three years building the momentum that resulted in Wilder's decision in February 1991 to commute the prisoner's sentence to life in prison. It would be impossible to orchestrate a similar effort on Washington's behalf. Nonetheless, there was no choice but to try.

Meanwhile, there was some bad news on the DNA front. After a month's wait, Dr. David Bing reported that the slides of the vaginal swabs sent by the state lab for his analysis had insufficient DNA for a test. "No conclusion can be reached as to the contributor of the DNA typed," he wrote on December 8.[28] Team members were back on the telephone with Barry Scheck, their informal DNA consultant, to determine the prospects for further action.

The clemency drive proceeded on two fronts. First, it was critical to rally as much public support as possible. That meant soliciting letters or telephone calls from congressmen, legislators, and community leaders. Each of the team members tapped contacts in high places. Letters went out to an assortment of members of the General Assembly. A private investigator who had assisted on the Washington case and who worked previously on the House Select Committee on Assassinations, investigating the death of Martin Luther King Jr., among others, urged key members of the committee to contact Wilder. The executive director of the Arc (formerly the Association of Retarded Citizens of the United States) wrote on behalf of its 120,000 members, noting that Washington's mental retardation "produced many opportunities for miscommunication, misinformation and the general failure to consider these and other mitigating factors."[29] *Washington Post* columnist William Raspberry contributed a column, urging Wilder not only to spare Washington's life but to pardon him altogether. "It may not turn out to be the most politic act of Doug Wilder's career, but it's the right thing to do," Raspberry wrote.[30]

One of those who did not respond to a request for support was James Weeks III, the son of Hazel Weeks. Jimmy Weeks did not want to see an innocent man executed, but he felt little sympathy for the man who had assaulted his mother. "I'm not the judge and the jury. You want to know if I feel any remorse for him, no," Weeks said, explaining his decision years later.[31]

Before the campaign ended, Wilder had received some two hundred sixty letters, including communications from public officials, advocacy groups, and the British House of Commons.[32] Even so, that was far less support than in some other high-profile cases. "I was not happy during that campaign," Deans recalled. "We made the decision too late in my opinion. . . . Everything was one shot" as compared to the Giarratano campaign where, for instance, conservative columnist James J. Kilpatrick wrote columns and made public appearances over a lengthy period. She was frustrated, Deans said, that no one of similar prominence agreed to become the public face for the opposition in Washington's case. Her suspicion was that race and retardation made him a less sympathetic figure.[33]

The second, more critical task during the autumn of 1993 was to persuade Wilder even to entertain the clemency petition. There was no guarantee that he would grant Washington's attorneys a hearing, given his obvious displeasure with the course of events. Bob Hall, who was esteemed with the trial bar, had a reputation for civility, and—unlike others—had not dealt with the governor on prior clemency petitions, became the designated spokesman. In the December 2 letter, he pleaded the case. Noting that a request for a meeting with Wilder's legal counsel, Walter McFarlane, had been rejected, Hall urged reconsideration.

He outlined, once again, the many inconsistencies in the Washington confession, the ambivalence in the 4th Circuit's decision, and the impossibility of squaring the DNA results and Rebecca Williams's dying words with Washington's guilt. "Your great office has always been the safety net through which innocent people were not allowed to fall, and, I've always assumed, perhaps in error, that in a case of clear innocence there was no fixed timetable in which a petition for a pardon must be presented," he pleaded.[34] Hall asked leave to submit a clemency petition and to meet with McFarlane.

Two weeks later, the request was granted without explanation, prompting cautious celebration on the defense team. Behind the scenes, Wilder had been persuaded by the argument that Washington would not be able to present the new DNA evidence to a court of law. He instructed McFarlane to begin reviewing the case. On December 20, with twenty-five days remaining in Wilder's term, a formal clemency petition filled with transcripts, lab reports, affidavits, police notes, and a ream of other materials was delivered to Wilder's door. At a press conference three days before Christmas, the team confirmed that they were not going to take the case to the U.S. Supreme Court. The deadline for filing a certiorari request would pass unmet on January 7. Meanwhile, national and local branches of the NAACP added their voices to those calling for Washington's pardon.

The push came at an inopportune time for the governor. Winding up a sometimes tumultuous four years, Wilder was involved in a host of farewell transitional activities, including a trip to Africa slated to begin on New Year's Day. Engaging in the sort of political imbroglio at which he excelled, the governor was cagily taking advantage of a misstep by his successor, George Allen, who had asked 643 state government employees to submit their resignations by December 20, almost a month before he was due to take office. After several days of sparring, Wilder with typical bravado issued an executive order directing the fired employees to disregard Allen's directive.[35] And the governor was deciding whether to grant clemency to future NBA superstar Allen Iverson. Considered the nation's top high school basketball recruit, the Hampton teen had been sentenced the previous September to fifteen years, ten suspended, for his participation in a bowling alley brawl that injured several people. When Washington's team heard that Wilder had met with Iverson's attorney and that the player was getting a "furlough" from prison, while their own case remained in limbo, they traded cynical quips. "What position do you think we need to get Earl to play?" one asked.

From the governor's standpoint, there was ample reason for irritation with Washington's lawyers. Not only were they hitting him and McFarlane with a tremendous amount of new work at a frenzied time, but the governor had more than paid his dues to the antideath penalty movement. Given the conservatism of Virginia voters, the pluses of showing leniency in a capital case were few. "Wilder was angry at us," Deans recalled. "It wasn't on his watch, and we had to make it on his watch."

Already, Wilder had commuted two death sentences—those of Joe Giarratano and Herbert Bassette—to life in prison. And he had gone the extra mile to provide DNA testing and a last-minute lie detector test to a third, Roger Keith Coleman.[36] The cases of Giarratano and Coleman had drawn international attention, flooding the governor's office with thousands of letters and telephone calls pleading for clemency. Commentators factored Wilder's various political ambitions into his actions in both cases. The 1991 decision to spare Giarratano's life, but leave him on death row, "pleased every side on the issue and covered his own political future," observed Virginia Commonwealth University political scientist Robert Holsworth.[37] At the time, the governor was just a month away from announcing the formation of a fund-raising committee on behalf of his possible bid for the Democratic presidential nomination. The following year, Wilder considered granting clemency to Coleman, who was featured on the cover of *Time* magazine as a death row inmate whose appeals were cut short due to a filing mistake. Wilder agreed to DNA testing in the case. When the results of the PCR-DNA test showed that Coleman was within the 2 percent of the population that could have committed the crime and he also failed a lie detector test just before his scheduled execution, the governor let the verdict stand.[38]

As the Washington team prepared for a January 5 meeting scheduled with McFarlane, it was clear that they were not the only ones knocking at Wilder's door. Culpeper law enforcement officials and the local prosecutor were not sitting idly by. Any illusions that the meeting with McFarlane might go smoothly were erased when he issued a media advisory a week in advance. The governor wanted the public to know that "the matter is not as simple as has been projected by the media," McFarlane said. It listed fourteen steps to be taken by Wilder

and McFarlane, including the need to "review all other prior indictments and convictions and their bearing on his propensity for violence
and/or rape." In Fauquier County, Washington was convicted only of
the assault and break-in at the home of Hazel Weeks, but now the discredited confessions involving Eugina Hecker, Lynn Rawlings, and the
rest were back in the mix. Focusing on the new theories of the Williams
case, the governor had to assess whether there might have been more
than one perpetrator and whether the unidentified allele might have
come from someone other than Clifford Williams or the perpetrator, the
statement said. That subtle phrasing masked the unspoken question of
whether Rebecca Williams was having an affair. Then, Wilder needed to
know if other DNA tests could be performed, and he had to review the
voluminous record. Underscoring the governor's irritation once more,
the advisory asked: "Why did the defense counsel abort the criminal
appeals process which they had so vigorously pursued? Was this action
appropriate or does it reflect an attempt to replace the decisions of the
Judicial Branch with that of the Executive?"[39]

Answering all those questions to Wilder's satisfaction in a two-
week period appeared difficult, if not impossible. The range of concerns
underscored the difference between a judicial proceeding and a
clemency petition. More was at issue than Washington's guilt or innocence in the murder of Rebecca Williams. Of course, Wilder needed to
be clear about the legal facts, but as a politician he also wanted a guarantee that releasing Washington would not come back to haunt him. It
was as important to evaluate Washington's propensity for violence as to
weigh the specifics of the case. That fact was underscored by a private
conversation between Hall and a close friend and confidante of the governor. First, the confidante advised, Wilder intended to give the petition
personal attention, but if he pardoned Washington, it would be from the
capital charge only. Because of the Hazel Weeks assault, the governor
did not want to be seen as speeding Washington's return to the community. Action on that matter would have to come from the parole
board. Wilder did not want blood on his hands if Washington turned
violent again. Second, one of the major bars to an outright release was
the defense team's failure to have in place a specific plan for where
Washington would live and work if he returned to the community.
Sending a man who had been violent—even if only once—back to the
same dysfunctional setting from which he emerged was a risky idea.
Third, the more elected representatives stood behind Wilder in support

of clemency, the better. Since Wilder was a Democrat, Republican backing was especially helpful. Politically, it was more critical for Wilder to have elected representatives of the people calling for clemency than interest groups such as the NAACP or Arc. Fourth, an expert should bolster the team's claim that the judicial options had run out. And fifth, public calls for Washington's release, as well as criticism of the governor or attorney general, would be counterproductive.

The team set about addressing these concerns as best it could. Wilder was in Africa, but action could not wait for his scheduled return on January 8. The Arc held a press conference to offer assistance in ensuring Washington's safe placement if he were released. The group used the moment to reiterate the problems that can occur when the mentally retarded confront the criminal justice system. When a retarded person is a suspect, "you give them a list [of crimes] and they will admit to it simply because they think they are being friends and they're helping out the police," said Elizabeth Campbell, executive director of the state organization.[40]

Jonathan Lynn, who was Washington's lawyer on the Fauquier County charges and had since been elected Commonwealth's attorney, submitted an affidavit. From his first meeting with Washington in 1983, it was apparent that the prisoner had a "fairly low level of intelligence," suffered from both long- and short-term memory loss, and had limited capacity to understand basic legal principles, Lynn said. Concerned about his client's ability to have waived his Miranda rights, Lynn secured a psychological evaluation. "My impression of the results of the evaluation was that there was a serious question as to whether Mr. Washington could have knowingly waived his constitutional rights," Lynn said.[41] Because of the plea agreement, that information was never presented in court. Lynn had passed the information on to the Scott-Hicks defense team, but he did not know if the pair had contacted the psychologists during the Williams trial. They did not.

Earl Washington never wavered in admitting the Weeks break-in and assault, but he consistently denied having committed the other crimes to which he confessed, Lynn continued. Lynn then reiterated why he believed Washington had not committed the attack on Lynn Rawlings, the most serious of the charges that were dropped. And he pointed out that Mrs. Weeks's testimony at the preliminary hearing discredited Washington's "confession" of an attempted rape.

On behalf of the team, Hall also submitted a long letter to McFarlane, attempting to answer as many questions as possible before their formal meeting.

On January 5, ten days before Wilder was to leave office, Weinstein, Hall, and Deans journeyed to McFarlane's office on the third floor of the Virginia Capitol for the long-sought meeting. It was a trek Deans had made several times before, and she reassured her colleagues that they were meeting with a man who was straightforward and honest. They might or might not like his conclusions, but they would get a fair hearing, Deans promised. From the start of the conversation, it was apparent that the obstacles were great, probably too great to overcome. The governor had deep concern about the implications of the Hazel Weeks assault. That was expected. But Deans thought McFarlane also seemed to misunderstand the DNA results. Barry Scheck, whose expertise in such matters was great, kept reassuring the team that the intensity of the 1.1 allele meant Washington was excluded as the donor. That message was not getting through.

Leaving the Capitol, there was a grim silence among the three advocates.

"I felt awful. . . . I felt Earl wasn't going to be pardoned," recalled Weinstein. "We felt we had the strongest clemency petition of any in the last couple of years, but when we had to spend so much time with McFarlane" it was an ominous sign.

"We went from this point in October when were we all high (after the McLees telephone call to Zerkin), and then walking out, we were wondering if Wilder's even going to commute" to life in prison, said Hall.

Deans also remembered an overwhelming sense of loss. "Part of me was just sad because I knew Earl was going to be spending the rest of his life in prison," she said.

Despair was an unaffordable commodity. With a week remaining, the team had to do what it could to turn the tide. Somehow, Wilder had to be convinced that the DNA results excluded Washington. There was a flurry of telephone calls to Scheck, who was helping put on an annual trial practice program at Cardozo Law School. More than a hundred lawyers and judges from across the nation were gathered for the two-week course in trial advocacy. "I remember spending most of my time on the phone dealing with Earl calls instead of the course, to the consternation of my faculty, who saw me freaking out at each bizarre turn of events," Scheck recalled.[42]

Action came in the form of a decision to send negatives of photographs of the state's PCR-DNA tests to Dr. Henry A. Erlich, a developer of the PCR process, for an interpretation. The negatives reached Erlich's office at Roche Molecular Systems Inc. in Alameda, California, where he was director of human genetics, on the night of January 12, with less than three full days remaining in Wilder's term. The next day Erlich faxed his conclusions. The presence of three alleles in the vaginal DNA made it impossible to unambiguously determine the specific combination of genotypes or pairs, he said. Even so, based on the relative dot intensities of the three alleles, "it is my view, and that of my colleagues, that the most likely interpretation of the test results . . . is that the sperm donor was a 1.1, 1.2 genotype." The "4" allele was most likely the result of contamination of the sperm fraction with vaginal epithelial cells from Rebecca Williams, who was a 4, 4. Such contamination "is a fairly common occurrence in the analysis of vaginal swabs and semen stains," Erlich wrote.

He concluded: "However one wished to interpret these test results, the directly determined presence of a 1.1 allele is significant since it cannot have been contributed by the victim, the victim's husband, or by Mr. Washington. In summary, it is my view that these test results cast very significant doubt about Mr. Washington's contribution to the sample."[43]

Dr. Paul Ferrara, head of Virginia's forensic science division, had said much the same thing at Rosenthal's press conference two months earlier.

Washington's defense team was not the only party hoping that DNA might magically resolve the quandary. A January 13 article in the *Richmond Times-Dispatch* reported that Wilder had ordered a separate, last-minute DNA test on the seminal stains found on the blue blanket. A sealed package with the results was to be delivered to his desk at 10 A.M. on January 14, the last full day of his administration. Meanwhile Wilder was urging lawmakers convening for the 1994 General Assembly to approve legislation allowing newly discovered evidence to be introduced in court in capital cases. Had such a law been in effect, Washington's DNA test results could have been placed in the hands of the judiciary, sparing the executive branch.

At Mecklenburg, Washington was led from death row to the administration building for an interview with Frank Green of the *Rich-*

mond Times-Dispatch. His hands were cuffed and his head was uncovered, but according to the reporter, "there was a smile a yard wide" on his face. All the attention was making him uneasy, but also hopeful, the prisoner said. He had been thinking about what he would like to do if Wilder should free him.

After a decade on death row, Washington figured he would like to travel far, far away. "I think I would like to go to Australia," he said.

Why Australia?

"Who-o-o-a," he laughed, using his standard verbal device for buying time when answering a difficult question. "It's a nice place." Beyond that, Australia was someplace else. "I think I would like to leave Virginia," he said.[44]

12

An Ending

BARRY WEINSTEIN had not slept well for three days. He'd spent the last week capping the clemency campaign. Calls zipped back and forth to the governor's office. Letters were written, contacts made. Henry Erlich's analysis of the vaginal swabs taken from Rebecca Williams had been rushed to the Capitol. Now, it was the last full day of Governor Wilder's administration, and there was nothing to do but wait.

Team members in Northern Virginia, New York, and Richmond were staying close to their telephones. Weinstein was trying to perform a normal day's work in his office at the Resource Center, but his eyes kept darting to the clock. "All I know is, at 11:59 A.M. the next day, Wilder's out," Weinstein recalled.[1]

The call came a little after 3 P.M. Weinstein motioned Deans, who was sharing the vigil, into his office. McFarlane told them the governor was prepared to grant Washington a conditional pardon only. Wilder would commute the death sentence to life in prison, and he would allow eligibility for parole in the Weeks case at a future date. Washington's lawyers figured that meant their client would get his first chance at a parole hearing in about twenty-two years, but there was no reason to expect he would ever be freed. In a five-page order, Wilder provided his rationale. After reviewing the history of the case, including the recent discovery of the unidentified allele in the vaginal swabs, Wilder said he believed a jury apprised of the new information might have reached a different conclusion about Washington's guilt. But he added that the depth of Washington's apparent knowledge about the particulars of the Williams murder remained troubling. To bolster his position, he quoted from the final 4th Circuit opinion, written by Judge Wilkinson: "[Washington] knew so much about this crime that a jury could afford his confessions substantial probative weight." Wilder also observed that, while he had heard from many "sincere and well-meaning people" about the case, "it is clear that the large majority do not enjoy a grasp of the specific facts in the case."[2]

There was no mention of the DNA test results on the blue blanket that were due at his office that morning. Moreover, Wilder was giving Washington until 5 P.M.—less than two hours—to sign or reject the offer.

Quickly, Weinstein arranged a conference call among the entire team, including Barry Scheck. The offer was no less than what Hall, Deans, and Weinstein had expected when they had walked out of Mc-Farlane's office nine days earlier. In fact, it was better than their worst fears. But the loss of their remaining hope, however slight, that Wilder might grant Washington a full and unconditional pardon in the Williams murder was bitter. Team members fumed, their anger exacerbated by the difficulty of making a life and death decision in less than two hours. "We were all upset and attracted by the 'tell Wilder to take his pardon and shove it' option," Freedman recalled, "but nonetheless we applied professional judgment to reach the conclusion to do the rational thing."[3] A twofold strategy emerged. Deans and Weinstein would drive to Mecklenburg to talk with Washington. This was one decision no one wanted to make for the client. The options must be laid out as simply and completely as possible, and Washington must choose his own fate. Second, Hall—who knew Ferrara well—would do his best to unearth the results of the blue blanket test from the forensic scientist, and Hall would communicate to McFarlane that two hours was simply not enough time. As for a recommendation to Earl, everyone was of two minds. No one wanted Washington to give up the fight for his freedom. No one wanted him to die either.

Deans and Weinstein rushed to pick up Weinstein's car and then maneuvered their way through late Friday afternoon traffic onto Interstate 95, heading south. Already it was after 4 P.M. At Petersburg, Weinstein steered his blue, four-wheel-drive Blazer with its "NOMADS" license plate onto Interstate 85 toward North Carolina. The pair headed into a gray expanse of lonely forests and farmland that matched their mood. "We both were commiserating about what Wilder didn't do, heavy commiserating," said Weinstein. "We both felt like 'life with parole' was forever. I personally had put a lot of faith in Wilder. I hoped he would do what nobody else would have done. Even though this was what was expected, I just felt if he'd truly stepped back, there was more than enough to grant Earl a full pardon."

As the miles slipped by, the pair talked about how best to approach Washington. Weinstein would lay out all the options; Deans would provide emotional support and try to divine whether Earl understood what was being said. In fact, there was not much to explain. Earl could take the conditional pardon, and in a couple of decades he could make his case to a parole board. Most likely, he would never be freed. Or he could reject the pardon and follow one of two courses. The team could try again on clemency with incoming Governor George Allen, but Allen had been elected on a tough-on-crime, no-parole platform. There was no reason to think Allen would be more generous than Wilder. Or the team could try to bring another habeas petition in federal district court based on "actual innocence." That route was even more perilous. In the first place, it was not entirely clear that federal case law allowed such a claim in Washington's case, but if it did, it was probably essential that the prisoner be on death row. If Washington accepted the commutation to life in prison, an "actual innocence" claim appeared to be precluded. In other words, if he turned down Wilder's offer, Washington still had options, just none that had any likelihood of working.

Seething, Weinstein kept the speedometer at about 50 MPH. He was in no hurry to perform one of the most difficult tasks of his life. A health-conscious vegan, Weinstein shunned tobacco, but when Deans wanted to light a cigarette, he did not object. Approaching the exit to South Hill, a small manufacturing town near the North Carolina border, Weinstein announced: "We're going to run out of gas."

"When?" Deans asked.

"Now," Weinstein said as the car coasted to a halt on the side of the road.

Switching off the ignition, he strode into the middle of the lane closest to the shoulder and began waving his arms up and down at the few approaching cars. "Damned if somebody doesn't stop," recalled Deans.[4] Two men in an aging Buick pushed Weinstein's vehicle down the exit ramp and to a nearby gas station. After filling up, the pair were back on their way through the countryside toward Mecklenburg.

When they pulled into the parking lot, it was nearing 7 P.M. A guard rushed to meet them at the entrance.

"Where have you been?" he demanded. "We've got state troopers out looking for you."

"I remember thinking, 'Well, they're really ineffective,'" said Deans. "I was kind of in a blur."

Before joining Washington, the pair placed one last conference call to the team. Hall had had no luck in getting the blue blanket test results. There would be no relief on that score. Wilder was a governor, not a judge, and he had no legal obligation to reveal information that had influenced his decision. All the team could be sure of was that the results did not implicate Washington. Otherwise, Wilder would not have reduced the sentence. McFarlane did agree to an extension on the deadline, but even that time had passed. Deans and Weinstein should simply proceed. Fate would determine the outcome.

Surrounded by guards, the clang of closing metal gates echoing in their ears, the pair arrived at a small, glass-enclosed cage adjacent to the prison library. Earl was waiting for them. When he stood, drawing in a deep breath and eyeing them with an anxious half-smile, Marie struggled to keep her composure. Somehow, Earl already knew that the news was not good. For close to an hour, they talked, Barry outlining all the points that had been discussed en route to the prison, Earl listening intently, Marie breaking in to repeat one point or elaborate on another.

"Barry, he explained it to me," Washington said years later. "He said, I ain't going to tell you which one to choose. I was mad at first. It didn't come out the way I thought about it. I was thinking when Doug Wilder did the DNA tests, I'd be a free man. We talked a little longer. I had to think about it. But if I didn't take it then, by March, they would be setting a date for execution."

Weinstein summed up the situation one last time. If he took the deal, Earl would most likely spend the rest of his life in prison. If he did not, the team would go on, but Earl might well be executed, and soon.

"So if I take this, I won't die?" Earl asked.

Barry and Marie nodded.

"Then I'll take it," he said.

Marie started to weep, but Earl took hold of her hand. "I'll be all right," he said.

"He signs, and I was just devastated," Marie recalled. "There was a huge part of me saying, 'Don't sign. Don't sign. Keep fighting. Maybe we can win.' But this other part of me was going, 'Yeah, but they'll kill him.'"

With the copies of the signed order in hand, Weinstein went in search of a telephone. Reaching Bob Hall in Fairfax, the attorney said simply: "He took it."

Hall immediately telephoned McFarlane's number in Richmond, but there was no answer. The office was closed. Inaugural balls and private parties soon would be getting under way. Wilder had appearances to make. An operator switched Hall to a Capitol guard.

"Can you get a message to Mr. McFarlane?" he asked.[5]

"I don't know if I can find him," the man replied.

"If I told you it involved whether an innocent man might be executed, could you?" he pressed.

"Yes, sir. I'll try," the officer said.

A short time later, the telephone rang. McFarlane, who had been working in his office, was on the other end.

"You've got a deal," Hall told him.

"Your time came and went," McFarlane said.

"You could have called us earlier," Hall replied, his voice starting to frost.

Bob Hall was not one to show his anger, but there was no mistaking his outrage now. "You advise the governor that once we determine what ball he's attending tonight, we'll be having a press conference outside, and I have reason to believe it will be well attended by the press," he snapped.

Within half an hour, McFarlane called back. Washington's acceptance had been approved. The story was about to go out over the newspaper wires.

Years later, McFarlane said he had no memory of such a contentious exchange. What he recalled was "the ungodly mess" of boxing papers and sorting files while simultaneously dealing with a person's life during his last night in the governor's office. No one wanted to force Washington into a two-hour decision, but time was simply running out, he said. It was, after all, Washington's attorneys who had opted to bring the petition to Wilder at the eleventh hour.[6]

"We in the most hectic period of trying to close our office were willing to look at this issue and work our butts off on this thing," said McFarlane. The DNA tests were not 100 percent conclusive. The former prosecutor and investigators were insistent that Washington had not been fed details of his confession. "We'd have almost had to say they were liars," he said. "I think we made the right decision based on the information we had. What the governor did was save his life."

And so, the struggle was over, the weeks, months, and years of effort to free Earl Washington jolted to a halt. It was almost a decade since

Marie Deans had first encountered the tall, skinny prisoner at Mecklenburg and asked, "Do your parents live on a particular road?" It was over eight years since Eric Freedman and Marty Geer had catnapped on office couches in Manhattan and pushed themselves through an exhausting week to file the first habeas petition and since Bob Hall had recognized that the seminal stains on Rebecca Williams's blanket were not Earl's. Nearly three months had passed since Jerry Zerkin had received a telephone call reporting the "monumental news" that the first round of DNA testing had excluded Washington. Since then, Barry Weinstein and the rest had spent long days and nights struggling to convert a reluctant governor.

Now the work was done, and it was hard to say what had been gained. Washington was not going to die, but a life in prison was scant victory for an innocent man. Based on the DNA results, officials could argue that it was conceivable that Washington had been at the crime scene, but only if the authorities ignored Rebecca Williams's dying words and only if the entire theory of the case changed. A series of tests had been done, each more sophisticated than the last, and none of the results dislodged the essential truth: not a single piece of forensic evidence and not a single witness linked Washington to the Williams murder. A retarded man was going to spend his life behind bars based solely on his own error-filled confession.

"I felt terrible," recalled Hall. "Earl hadn't gotten what he deserved."

Driving back to Richmond that night, Weinstein and Deans were quiet. Each was physically and emotionally spent. The silent, shadowy fields mirrored their gloom.

"I was almost hoping Earl would have turned it down," Weinstein said.

Deans could not remember a lower moment in her years of death work. She had suffered with other prisoners, but Washington's case was different. "I felt like a puppet on a political string, hopeless, devastated," she said.

Returning to death row, Washington was greeted by fellow prisoners curious about his fate. He would be leaving them, Washington replied, but he would not be going to Australia or even home. He would be transferred to a different prison, somewhere else. At least, unlike most of them, he would not be going to the electric chair. "I was upset," Washington acknowledged. He spent a restless night, but by the morning his emotions were in check. "I just made up my mind, ain't no use getting mad and upset about nothin'," he said.[7] Being "mad" was what had landed him in prison in the first place. Anger was an unaffordable emotion.

Earl Washington was thirty-three years old, and that was one lesson he had had plenty of time to learn.

Coming to terms with the loss would take longer for Deans. Her grief reflected not only Washington's continued imprisonment but the demise of the Virginia Coalition on Jails and Prisons. Out of money, Marie had closed operations in September. Officially, she was still seeking benefactors, but the prospects for reopening were dim. "I had no clue where my next meal was coming from. You didn't even know if you had fought the good fight at that point. None of it was working out; at the very least all you could do was get a sniff of justice," she said.

The announcement that the Virginia Coalition was ceasing operation was startling for the many who had come to equate death penalty opposition in Virginia with Deans. A reporter who had followed her during the hours leading up to an execution in 1992 captured the essence of her role through the words of the condemned man. "Without Marie Deans, there'd be no me, right?" said Willie Leroy Jones in the hours before his death. "They been trying to execute me for the last eight years, right? She's the reason I hung on. She's been a friend to me. She's been the person I could call and talk to any time of day. I could always pick up the phone and call Marie, no matter how big or small the problem was."[8] The night before his execution, Deans spent five hours with Jones, who had committed a double murder, talking about life and death.

Since her arrival in Virginia in 1983, there had been dozens of Willie Leroy Joneses and only one Marie Deans. From the start, the operation had been touch and go financially, but the last year was the worst. Deans had received none of the $23,000 salary allotted her in the organization's budget.[9] In fact, in all her years in Virginia, she had never made anything approaching that amount. At its peak, the Virginia Coalition had an annual budget of between $50,000 and $60,000, funded with foundation and public interest law grants. Over the decade, the most she had received in salary in a single year was about $18,000.

The Coalition's undoing stemmed from the 1992 execution of Roger Coleman. Convinced of Coleman's innocence, several supporters went so far as to identify in national publications the people they believed were responsible for the murder. Because the names of Deans and the Coalition appeared on various papers associated with Coleman's defense, they were listed as defendants when the accused sued for libel. Eventually, Deans was dropped from the proceedings, but for almost a year while the claims were pending, foundation grant money dried up.

Years later, Deans could speak with some satisfaction of the successes of the Virginia Coalition. During her watch, she found attorneys for dozens of death row inmates. No one died without a lawyer. She assisted in over 220 capital trials and only two of the defendants were sent to death row. Moreover, although Deans did not say so, the emotional bridge she extended to condemned men was invaluable. But in the winter of 1994 Deans saw her efforts as failed. A couple of weeks after Washington's sentence was commuted, she visited him at the Powhatan Reception Center where he was awaiting a transfer. He was out of his cell, playing cards, seemingly happy at the changes in his life. "I got a little weepy," Deans said. "I wished I could have enjoyed his being happy, but I was afraid for him. I didn't think Earl was prepared to live in prison without getting hurt."

It was the last time Marie Deans saw Washington face-to-face for eight years. She sent cards and greetings through Weinstein, but the geographic distance as Washington rotated among various prisons and her growing psychological resistance to being within confined spaces dictated against face-to-face meetings. "I had all the background for post-traumatic stress disorder," said Deans, citing her mother's illness, her mother-in-law's murder, and a traumatic train wreck in 1981 in which she was a passenger. "Then I would go into the death house, and I would get emotionally confused. I would feel like I was back in front of Penny's house with the police cars and the blue lights."

By 1994, "I was just so burned out from going into prison. Every time, I'd go into a prison, I'd start shaking," she said.

For Barry Weinstein too, the day-in, day-out involvement became too much. He arrived in Virginia full of vim, but his dream of revolutionizing Virginia attitudes and procedures surrounding capital punishment was not shared by the Resource Center's board of directors. The board's aim was to see that death row inmates received solid representation throughout the appeals process, nothing more. The passion of Weinstein and the contrasting decorum of the board probably set the two on a collision course from the outset. Toward the end of 1994, the year of Washington's commutation, Weinstein was quietly asked to leave. It was a bitter blow that compounded the depression he felt at the escalating pace of Virginia executions, and it propelled him to seek solitude on family property in the Blue Ridge mountains of north Georgia. He lived in a one-bedroom cabin on a dirt road, engaging his interests in reading and hiking, maintaining a small criminal practice that included consultation on death penalty cases in Florida and elsewhere, but spending much of his time in isolation and contemplation. "I was beaten down by Virginia," he said. "I used to be a happy-go-lucky, high-spirited person. I was very, very high on life. I had every reason to be. I loved the law and I found a passion in the abolitionist movement. Then I hit Virginia and it broke me because I couldn't control what was going on. I was just a cog that made the executions work."[10]

Despite his differences at times with the defenders of death row inmates, McFarlane recognized and respected their contribution. "Thank God there are people out there who will do this," he said. "They're very dedicated, and thank God they are, because they stand between life and death sometimes."

But for those doing the work, the toll could be great. Jerry Zerkin also gave up postconviction death work within a few years to concentrate on trial representation in capital cases. "They could have been appointing priests for all the good that we were doing," he said. "It's not just losing. It's feeling like you don't have a chance, that the deck is stacked against you." On that score, Virginia might be worse than many other places, he said, but it was hardly unique.

Whatever the personal cost, none of the members of Washington's team considered walking away from the prisoner. They figured life was worse for him. As Weinstein's own fortunes became more precarious, he seemed only to redouble his commitment to provide an emotional anchor for Washington. On the night when Deans and Weinstein sat with the prisoner at Mecklenburg and heard his decision to accept Wilder's conditional pardon, Weinstein looked Washington in the eye. "We will not stop," he said. "I will not forget you." It was a promise kept.

In granting the conditional pardon, Wilder indicated that he did not think the action should be the end of the road for Washington. Pointedly, the governor repeated an earlier message to the General Assembly, which had just begun its annual session. He urged the lawmakers to adopt legislation that would bypass Virginia's Twenty-One-Day Rule and allow death row inmates to have new evidence of innocence reviewed by a court. "Nothing contained herein," he wrote in the clemency order, "is to be deemed to preclude Earl Washington Jr. from taking advantage of the opportunity to present the aforementioned new evidence and have his case retried from the inception under new provisions for newly discovered evidence which I encourage the General Assembly to adopt at its 1994 session."[11]

Wilder's intentions did not govern Virginia's conservative legislature, however. In the first place, there was a significant quirk in the proposed legislation as it related to Washington. The bill applied only to those on death row. Now that Washington's sentence had been commuted to life in prison, he was no longer eligible. Segueing from the clemency campaign to a push for amendment and adoption of the proposed legislation, Washington's team and other advocates of a less restrictive law ran smack into the immovable opposition of the attorney general's office and a tough, anticrime public mood. Virginia's law was operating well, asserted spokesmen for James Gilmore, the new attorney general. Any change would be yet another loophole allowing death row inmates to delay justice. "Lawmakers were in no mood to be thought of as soft on crime," reported the *Richmond Times-Dispatch*, summing up the action of the 1994 session.[12] The proposed change died.

If the legislators wondered why no one knew what the final DNA tests ordered by Wilder showed, there was no indication. A letter written by Bob Hall almost a year later outlined the repeated rejections experienced by the team in attempting to get the blue blanket results. "On several occasions I have asked the state laboratory for copies of the test results on our client, but have been advised that they first needed to receive your permission to send us the results of the laboratory's analysis. I am further advised that you did not respond to the laboratory's inquiries," Hall wrote in a November 28, 1994 letter to Walter McFarlane, who had become the head of Virginia's department of correctional education after leaving the Wilder administration.

"We are given to believe that the testing of the seminal fluid stains on the royal blue blanket further exonerated Earl from any responsibility in this crime and disclosed some of the DNA genetic information identifying the actual killer or, at a minimum, it genetically identified persons other than her husband with whom she may have had sexual relations." Given the critical nature of such information in possibly exonerating Washington, Hall urged McFarlane to contact Dr. Paul Ferrara at the state laboratory and approve release of the results.

McFarlane did not reply. No approval was given, nor was any required under the Virginia system.

Thus began a six-year period, from 1994 to late 1999, in which any remaining hope that Washington might eventually be freed slowly ebbed.

The prisoner himself felt an initial exhilaration from the attention associated with clemency and his departure from death row. Transfer into the general prison population meant that education and vocational training were available, at least minimally. But the extent of the opportunities varied from prison to prison, and after his departure from death row Washington moved six times. Sometimes months would go by after a transfer before he was assigned regular employment. In a January 1999 letter to Weinstein, Washington noted that he had been at the Sussex I prison for almost four months and was still not working. "I don't know why I am here. I did have a job at Greensville. I have been trying to get a job here," he wrote. In the spring of 2000, several months after being transferred to the Keen Mountain Correctional Center in remote western Virginia, Washington voiced a similar complaint.

A dull monotony soon replaced the initial thrill of leaving death row. On the row, prisoners were by and large left to themselves. In the general population, guards seemed to change more frequently and the interaction with fellow prisoners was less predictable. "A life sentence is just like a death sentence, only you get treated worse," Washington said. One knee tapped nervously as he strained to explain the realities of prison life. "You get treated a little bad on death row, but with a life sentence in prison, it's harder."

Hardest of all was the disappearance of almost all family contact. Washington was at the Buckingham Correctional Center on September 9, 1995 when his sister Alfreda telephoned with the news of their father's death. Having served as a private in the U.S. Army in World War II, the senior Washington was eligible for burial in the national cemetery in Culpeper. When he was laid to rest there on a gently rolling hillside among rows of white stone markers, his eldest son was not allowed to attend. Earl Jr.'s grief was even stronger three months later when Marie Washington, then only fifty-seven years old, joined her husband. Aside from Alfreda, his mother was the person to whom Earl Jr. was the most attached emotionally. The inability to see her before she died or to attend her funeral was the greatest regret of his years in prison, causing him temporarily to break his self-imposed embargo on anger. "I was mad 'cause they passed away, mad 'cause they wouldn't let me go to the funeral. It took me a while to get over it," Earl said. In a letter to Alfreda in March 2000, he referred to the loss: "I wish that mommy, daddy was still liveing [sic] too, and then I could hear from someone in the family too." The letter alternated between bitterness and sadness as he complained in faulty language that the only family member who ever wrote was a niece, Rosemary. "How are you doing?? Fine I hope. I am not doing fine at all okay," he wrote. "But it is something wrong with you and the family to, because you all write me at all to. But the last letter I got from you was in October 19, 1998 to. But it is not like I am asking you to send me any money at all okay. But the way you, Linda, Shirley, Bobby and Duck is doing me now, but if they let me come home this year do me the same way okay . . . I don't BEG no one in life to write me at all okay . . . I am going to close for now. Earl Washington."

At the time, Washington was living at Keen Mountain Correctional Center in the remote wilds of southwest Virginia, a seven-or-so-hour drive from Culpeper. No member of his immediate family, except perhaps his half-sister, had the transportation or the wherewithal to make so long a trip into unknown territory. For years, his only visitors were Barry Weinstein or an occasional reporter checking on his case.

After moving to Georgia, Weinstein made sure that the telephone calls continued, as did occasional though less frequent visits. Their conversations were not long or deep, but each recounting of the humdrum events of prison life or the latest sports contest watched on television was a reminder for Washington that someone outside prison remembered and cared. Weinstein regularly deposited small amounts of money in Earl's prison account so that he could purchase toiletries, and the attorney rarely let an opportunity go by to stress the importance of education and work. "I wanted Earl to take advantage of the prison programs so he could improve his reading, writing, math, and develop a skill or trade and keep busy. I did not want him to languish like most 'lifers' seem to do," he said.

After leaving death row, Washington was assigned to the Literary Incentive Program (LIP), the lowest of three levels in the prison educational classification system. Highest ranked were those prisoners working on a high school equivalency degree. Second were those designated as "literate." And third were prisoners who were either exempt or, like Washington, had minimal educational skills. Six years later, he was still in the LIP program, but his ability to read and write had improved. The advancement was reflected in letters which contained numerous grammatical errors and unclear sentences, but had moved beyond the brief communiqués of earlier years.

Weinstein believed that the improvement was due in part to prison guards and counselors who took an active interest, both because of Washington's disabilities and his seemingly guileless good humor. He was never abused or assaulted in prison, Washington said. When the author asked if that made him feel lucky, he responded with rare wit.

"Lucky," he said, pondering the word for a moment. "I don't think that's a word I'd use."

Did he consider himself unlucky then?

Washington tilted back his chair. His eyes widened and he inhaled as he often did before tackling a difficult question. "I think I'm a good-hearted person . . . at times," he replied finally. "I give people respect. Just like here. . . . Old man I met told me, if you give respect, you'll get respect."

Did that prove to be true?

"No-o-o-pe," he said, characteristically dragging out the first two letters of the word and chopping off the rest. "With some people, yep. With some people, not." Some of the guards treat people well, he said. "Some of them treat you like animals," but none ever hit or abused him. "I ain't given them a reason for that yet." Indeed, prison evaluation sheets show that Washington's behavior was nearly exemplary. Between 1994 and mid-2000, he received 66 out of a possible 70 points for "personal conduct" and 135 out of 140 for (lack of) "infractions" on annual evaluations.

As the years passed, however, Weinstein began to detect a quiet despair. "Our conversations were not as lively. He was upset with his family for they seldom wrote, and he was without money to purchase the basic necessities for prison living," he said.

In a letter to Weinstein dated September 27, 1999, less than two months after his transfer to Keen Mountain, Washington's frustration spilled over. "I have not have a visitor in 3 years to," the prisoner wrote. "What is going on with my family, I have not hear from my family in some times now. But by my book my family is die now to me."

Even as hope waned, Weinstein said, Washington retained an inner faith that seemed to keep him going. "I think God watches out for everyone. God has plans for everyone," Washington replied when asked on the eve of his release to explain the faith to which Weinstein referred.

Did he perceive his years in prison as God's plan for him?

"Nope," he said. "God is a good person. He loves. He don't hate no one. He believes in his work. God is what I call creator, because there wouldn't be nothin' on this earth if it wasn't for God. . . . Someone said, 'Who do you thank most, your lawyer or God?' I said, 'God. Wasn't for God, there wouldn't be no lawyer.'"

But at Keen Mountain in the autumn of 1999, in a land of deep fogs and lonely hollows as distant from the Virginia Piedmont as cliffs from meadows, neither lawyers nor divine intervention seemed likely to unshackle Earl Washington anytime soon.

13

Revival

OFRA BIKEL FEIGNED nonchalance as she asked Dr. Paul Ferrara for copies of the state's DNA tests involving Earl Washington, including—she casually noted—the most recent.

"I'll get them for you," replied Dr. Ferrara, the nationally prominent director of the Virginia Division of Forensic Science.

As Ferrara left the room on this day in the spring of 1999, Bikel and her research assistant exchanged a meaningful glance, then resumed their uninterested pose.

Moments later, the documentary filmmaker held in her hands the January 14, 1994 report that had been denied Bob Hall and the other members of Washington's team five and a half years earlier. Startled by the unexpected good fortune, she scanned the analysis for findings involving the four testable seminal stains found on the blue blanket where Rebecca Williams was believed to have been slain. Bikel's glance fell on the word "eliminated."

"Earl Washington Jr.," she read, "is eliminated as the donor of the HLA DQa types obtained from the blue blanket, Stains A, B and C." Her pulse quickened, but she was careful not to betray her excitement.[1]

Bikel's best-known earlier work was a trilogy, *Innocence Lost*, that painstakingly detailed the charges of sexual abuse against workers at a day care center in Edenton, North Carolina, and the resulting trials. The films, which earned critical acclaim and a slew of prizes, were regarded as a force in freeing all seven defendants. Her credits also included more than two dozen documentaries on political, economic, and cultural subjects in her native Israel and a growing number of pieces for the PBS series *Frontline*. In this latest venture, Bikel was concentrating on men who were still in prison even though their innocence had been corroborated by DNA testing. She was less interested in the science of DNA than in the notion that many judges and prosecutors were unwilling to disavow the results of a trial, even when innocence was established with near certainty.

In the course of her research, Bikel happened across an article about Earl Washington Jr. Bob Hall was quoted in the piece, and she called him up. After their initial interview in the spring of 1999, one curious fact stood out for her—a DNA test had been conducted by the state of Virginia and Washington's lawyers were never able to get the results. Over the years, Bikel had developed a sixth sense about suspicious behavior. The secrecy surrounding the test struck her as a reaction that deserved to be probed. Ferrara's unexpected willingness to hand over the results would allow her to do so with far more ease than expected.

Returning to Virginia on June 7 for filming, Bikel told no one—not even Bob Hall—that she had obtained the January 14 DNA report. She wanted to capture his unplanned response, as well as that of former Governor Wilder and former interim attorney general Steve Rosenthal. A career in film had taught her that few sights are so telling as that of an individual caught unawares and forced to make a spontaneous response about a sensitive matter.

For almost six years, Washington's attorneys had been looking for an opening to reactivate the case. The most hopeful development was an evolution in DNA testing that might answer the questions plaguing Washington's earlier DNA and blood-typing tests. Through a new process, known as "short tandem repeats" (STR), it was now possible to sort out the contributors to a DNA mixture.

The advantage of STR was that it combined the discriminating power of the earlier RFLP (restriction fragment length polymorphism) fingerprinting test with the sensitivity of the PCR (polymerase chain reaction)-DNA test in working with old or extremely small samples of DNA. The STR test analyzed DNA segments at thirteen specific gene sites, identifying up to a dozen different versions of each gene and reducing the chance for misidentification to one in several billion. Most significant for Washington, an STR test ought to be able to say whether Clifford Williams or someone else had deposited the semen on the blue blanket.[2]

Eric Freedman first heard Barry Scheck lecture on the process at one of the annual gatherings of death penalty attorneys and activists at the Airlie Conference Center. Soon afterward, Freedman informed other members of Washington's team about the scientific developments and the group began contemplating how to launch a campaign for updated

DNA testing. The courts were not an option. Gubernatorial dispensation was the only hope. The question was how and when to approach a governor with enough force to command both attention and the right results. Dropping a letter in the mail would not do. Even an organized, behind-the-scenes appeal from prominent Virginians might not be enough unless it was accompanied by public pressure. What the team needed was a way to get Washington's case back in front of a broader audience. When Paul Ferrara handed Ofra Bikel the results of the blue blanket test, a way opened.

As the January 11, 2000 airing of the *Frontline* show approached, Washington's team weighed the strategies for approaching Governor James Gilmore. He would not be an easy sell. A former prosecutor from suburban Richmond who had served four years as attorney general before being elected governor, Gilmore was a by-the-book, no-nonsense administrator who took a tough view of criminals. He was a strong believer in the sanctity of local jury decisions and a defender of the appellate courts serving Virginia. On the other hand, he was a pragmatic, linear thinker who might be persuaded by clear, scientific evidence to order additional tests, so long as there was sufficient political cover to protect his substantial ambitions. Gilmore had campaigned on the notion that gubernatorial clemency was the safety valve that protected citizens from the rare miscarriage of justice in capital cases. With the right mix of evidence and pressure, he might be persuaded to reopen the case.

Washington's team had no way of knowing precisely what the *Frontline* documentary would say. But members knew from Bikel's interview with Bob Hall that the program would challenge the state's treatment of their client. Several million Americans might see the program, but only one—Jim Gilmore—could do anything about Washington's condition. It was essential that the governor, or at least his closest legal advisers, know about the upcoming show. In early January Zerkin stopped by the governor's office to tell Walter Felton, Gilmore's counsel and the man who would review any clemency petition, about the show. "It was a courtesy call, just saying, 'This is coming at you, and it's going to take some time,'" Felton recalled.[3]

"The Case for Innocence," as Bikel's documentary was entitled, began with cases in Texas and Louisiana and concluded with Washington. The final segment was stunning. It imparted the clear impression that the state of Virginia in 1994 had deliberately hidden information exonerating an innocent man.

Bikel led into the segment by returning to January 1994 and Wilder's eleventh-hour clemency offer to Washington of life in prison with parole.

Narrator: It was not the victory the lawyers hoped for. They wanted pardon, and they got clemency. Why? The answer, they felt was in the analysis of the blue blanket, which they were not allowed to see.

Bob Hall: The key issue at the absolute eleventh hour was clemency which means, "Earl, you did it, but you should(n't) die for it," versus pardon—"You didn't do it, and you ought to go free." Why didn't we get the pardon? If the blue blanket testing had anything to do with that decision, let us know what it showed. . . . No answer. No answer to this day.

Ofra Bikel: You don't know.

Bob Hall: I don't know.

Narrator: When *Frontline* asked Dr. Ferrara for the test results of the blanket, to our surprise, he handed them to us. To anyone who followed the case closely, the results of the test were explosive. Earl Washington was definitively excluded.

Dr. Paul Ferrara: The results of our testing on the blanket are much more definitive in being able to eliminate Earl Washington as a possible contributor.

Narrator: But there was more. The test pointed to an unknown individual as the possible rapist, a fact that was never investigated or made public. The results were withheld from the defense lawyers.

Bob Hall: I don't know.

Ofra Bikel: Do you want to know?

Bob Hall: I'd like to know.

Ofra Bikel: We found out.

Bob Hall: Well I hope you'll share it with me.

Ofra Bikel: The blanket excluded him. Earl Washington was excluded. Here.

(On camera, Bikel hands the January 14 test results to Hall, who reads from the document.)

Bob Hall: The power of the press. (*reading*) "The sperm fraction of stain D of the blue blanket is an individual possessing a 1.1/1.2 genotype. Based on that opinion, both Earl Washington Jr., and James Pendleton are eliminated as possible contributors."[4]

From there, the documentary switched to separate interviews with Rosenthal and Wilder, both of whom appeared defensive and confused by the report. "This is the first time I've seen this document," said Rosenthal on camera. "Now, should the governor's office have known? Well, obviously. That's something you need to take up with the governor. I—I—this is the first time I've seen this document."

Wilder, who expected to receive credit for commuting Washington's sentence to life in prison, was clearly taken aback at the interview's unexpected turn. He deflected a series of questions about the document, claiming ignorance of why it had never been released.

Narrator: Former governor Wilder is now a professor and host of a radio talk show. When we met him, we did not have to show him the last test. He knew all about it.

Douglas Wilder: They sent the results of that DNA test, and you're saying that no one knew the results?

Ofra Bikel: No one.

Douglas Wilder: I didn't know that.

Ofra Bikel: No one.

Douglas Wilder: Well, I didn't know it. . . .

Narrator: He couldn't imagine, he said, why the lawyers did not know about it.

Douglas Wilder: I don't have any idea what it is they didn't know. And you'll have to talk to those people.

He regrouped long enough to challenge Bikel's assertion that by reducing Washington's sentence to life in prison, "maybe unwittingly you put him in no-man's-land."

"I think you might look back and even think that maybe wittingly I saved his life," snapped Wilder. "Don't you think that would be more positive?"

Two years later, Wilder was still fuming about the documentary, calling it a "butcherous job." In fact, the written analysis in the January 14, 1994 report was not quite as definitive as "The Case for Innocence" suggested. Washington was clearly eliminated as the donor of the blue blanket seminal stains A, B, and C, but according to the report, stain D was slightly more ambiguous. "Elimination of Earl Washington, Jr. as a donor, however, to Stain D is not as clear," the report said. "No specific combination of alleles can be unambiguously determined from these results. However, based upon the relative dot intensities, it is my opinion that the contributor to the sperm fraction of Stain D of the blue blanket is an individual possessing a 1.1, 1.2 genotype. Based on that opinion, both Earl Washington, Jr. and James Pendleton are eliminated as possible contributors."[5] (The report did not mention Clifford Williams.)

The critical fact about the blue blanket report was not the sliver of uncertainty in stain D, however, but the fact that a second DNA test had turned up a 1.1 allele that could not have come from Washington or Clifford Williams. The results, if paired with Rebecca Williams's dying words, excluded the prisoner. Once again, a complete rewrite of the way the case had been argued in a series of courtrooms was necessary in order to link Washington to the crime. The new scenario in which Washington had a partner in crime could be correct only if the confession that convicted him was a sham. The report put the team in position to argue forcefully that new DNA tests should be conducted, using the STR method.

Why was the blue blanket test result denied to Washington's attorneys, and what difference would it have made if they had known the results when weighing Wilder's clemency offer six years earlier?

Walter McFarlane, the counsel who reviewed the case for Wilder, said that he did not recall a conscious decision to conceal the report. His best guess is that the office was wary of fueling growing speculation about Rebecca Williams's behavior. With the release of the October 25, 1993 DNA report on the vaginal swabs, those who continued to insist on Washington's guilt had a dilemma—how to explain the presence of the mysterious 1.1 allele. The October report stated unequivocally that neither Washington, Clifford Williams, nor Rebecca Williams could be the source of that genetic identifier.

The most rational explanation was that Washington simply was not involved in the crime. The 1.1 allele came from the rapist-murderer. At the same time that Washington's attorneys were arguing the case for innocence, however, some of the law enforcement officials and Culpeper citizens knocking on McFarlane's door were painting a less-than-savory portrait of Rebecca Williams. It was entirely possible, those voices said, that she had voluntary sex with someone other than her husband in the twelve-or-so hours preceding the murder. McFarlane and Wilder did not want to feed that chorus, but they were not prepared to grant Washington a full pardon either, both because the community belief in the validity of his confession remained so strong and because the DNA results did not exclude Washington with 100 percent finality.

Out of that dilemma may have come the decision to retain the DNA results on the blue blanket, McFarlane said. While the test on the seminal stains raised no more questions involving Rebecca Williams than the test on the vaginal swabs, introducing yet a second test that called for an explanation of the 1.1 allele might have intensified the focus on Williams. "We didn't know the woman. She's dead. She cannot protect herself. We avoided any kind of speculation relative to that issue. This man, this family had suffered enough. It was an incredibly awkward situation," McFarlane said.[6]

But what of Washington? What was the impact on him of not knowing two things: that the second test, like the first, came close to eliminating him as the donor of the seminal stains and that it also cited a 1.1 allele that neither he nor Clifford Williams could have produced? Might that knowledge have pointed him and his attorneys to a different conclusion in the frantic hours when they weighed Wilder's clemency offer?

Washington would still have faced the dilemma of choosing between a sure thing, Wilder's offer, and the uncertainty of approaching an incoming governor who might offer something better or something worse. But a more timely release might have had several positive results. It would have caused his attorneys to weigh even more carefully whether grounds existed for a new habeas appeal based on "actual innocence." It would have guaranteed louder condemnation by Washington's advocates of Wilder's failure to grant an absolute pardon, a potential political embarrassment. And the knowledge of two tests, neither pointing to Washington, might have focused more persistent media attention on the case, perhaps leading earlier to additional DNA tests. "Maybe it's sour grapes," Hall said years afterward, "but dammit, we should have known."[7]

Despite the controversy it caused, Ofra Bikel's *Frontline* report was the single most important event in reviving public focus on a man who was now deep into his sixteenth year behind bars.

The next critical step was finding out if there was any genetic material left to test. Recalling Bing's difficulty in analyzing the material from the vaginal swabs six years earlier, the team identified its worst nightmare: Gilmore would be willing to conduct additional tests, but there would be no material worth testing. With trepidation Hall contacted the Northern Virginia medical examiner's office. The word came back that some untested slides of specimens remained from the Rebecca Williams murder, and "our excitement level went up tenfold," Hall said.

As news of the January 11 *Frontline* report spread through Virginia, Washington's advocates realized that the moment of opportunity had arrived. Scheck and Neufeld would no longer be advisers to the team but full-fledged members. Their expertise on DNA was critical. It made no sense to have someone else on the team trying to explain the science that the Innocence Project founders knew so well. Moreover, Scheck and Neufeld had strong ties to the national news media, built through their successes in previous cases. Those links could now be tapped on Washington's behalf even as other members of the team were cultivating the Virginia media. This would probably be Washington's last chance for freedom, and the momentum created by *Frontline* could not be allowed to die.

Confirmation that the audience was growing came nine days after the showing of "The Case for Innocence." In an editorial headlined "Set Him Free," the *Virginian-Pilot* newspaper in Norfolk argued: "Justice, if it means anything, demands that Gov. Jim Gilmore reopen the case of Earl Washington Jr. . . . Nothing, save fear of embarrassment for the state, could prevent the governor from reviewing the paltry evidence against Washington."[8] A week later Zerkin and Hall submitted the formal request for new testing. "While we remain convinced that the original tests excluded Earl Washington as the perpetrator of the offense, we are now requesting that the Governor direct that new DNA tests be performed using this technology," the team wrote over Zerkin's signature.[9]

Felton's polite acknowledgment of the letter was followed by silence. As the winter progressed, the team searched for ways to prod the governor without irritating him. Pressing their case too forcefully in the media might backfire. On February 25 Hall sent Gilmore a seven-page letter detailing the background of the case and the results of the prior DNA tests. Four days later, Zerkin dropped a note to inform Gilmore's counsel that a Culpeper newspaper was planning a major series on the case. In strategy sessions the group bristled at the delays but recognized that Gilmore and his staff were preoccupied by the General Assembly session. As spring approached, and still there was no movement, restlessness turned to impatience. Quietly, the advocates began to make sure that their contacts in the media knew that a request for retesting was pending. Across the state, newspaper stories appeared questioning the lengthening delay.

At Keen Mountain Washington continued the routine of prison life, performing janitorial tasks, working out to stay fit, attending occasional classes, spending long stretches alone in his cell. In mid-April, with Weinstein watching protectively, the inmate described for the author his understanding of what Gilmore was being asked to do.

"Tell me what we are doing with the governor," requested Weinstein.

"Oh boy. Whoa," replied Washington who had been briefed the previous day on the push for additional DNA testing. "I didn't think no more about that."

He paused, breathed deeply, and smiled. "My understanding, you all are trying to get Gov. Gilmore, well, Mr. Gov. Gilmore, to do the other DNA test, which I hope he do."

And what would Washington tell the governor if they could meet, face to face? Silence, another smile. "I don't know what I'd say. That would be something hard for me."

Later in the interview, Washington was asked again. What would he tell the governor about why he should not be in prison? This time, he had an answer. "Because I didn't do the crime," he said.[10]

By the beginning of May, the team felt it had waited long enough. Zerkin wrote to Felton on May 1, pressing for a meeting as soon as possible. He enclosed a copy of the U.S. Justice Department's new report entitled "Post-Conviction DNA Testing: Recommendations for Handling Requests." Prepared by a prestigious group that included Virginia's Paul Ferrara, the report suggested dividing DNA requests into five categories, with the highest priority going to those for which biological evidence existed that might exonerate the prisoner. "Mr. Washington's case is the strongest Category 1 case imaginable," Zerkin wrote. He noted that the 1993 test on the vaginal swabs from Rebecca Williams tracked a single genetic marker, whereas the STR test would compare thirteen such markers. "Even a 'law and order' public does not fathom why responsible officials would not allow DNA testing when there exist substantial questions about whether the right person has been convicted. Earl Washington's case provides a perfect opportunity for the Governor to get out front on this issue," he wrote.[11]

A few days later the conservative editorial page of the *Richmond Times-Dispatch* called for tests. "A refusal by the Governor to order a new test would amount to a horrible admission: that the state prefers to accept the possibility of having stolen a man's life over admitting it made a mistake," the editorialist wrote.[12]

Finally, on May 23 Neufeld, Zerkin, and Hall filed into the governor's conference room on the third floor of the Capitol. The meeting with Felton and policy adviser Lee Goodman was cordial. Both the governor's representatives were less overtly political than others on Gilmore's staff. Neufeld suppressed a grin when he noted that the meeting was being presided over by a huge portrait of Thomas Jefferson, another Virginian much in the news because of DNA testing. Eighteen months earlier, DNA tests had established the likelihood that Jefferson had fathered at least one child with his longtime slave Sally Hemmings. Neufeld could not resist nudging Zerkin under the table and raising an eyebrow in Jefferson's direction.[13]

Under an advance agreement, Neufeld acted as the defense team spokesman. Drawing sketches on a legal pad and reducing complex science to layman's language, the New Yorker led the group through a step-by-step explanation of how STR testing works. The procedure could determine with precision whether one, two, or more individuals contributed to the semen left at the crime scene, he said. The old questions about mixtures and masking could be answered.

Moreover, Neufeld held out an enticing option. If Washington was excluded, as the defense team expected, the DNA profile could be fed into the Commonwealth's extensive offender database, the largest such collection of criminal DNAs in the nation. Gilmore might well gain recognition for himself and the state by identifying the true culprit.

The other part of Neufeld's message was less friendly. The team was convinced of Washington's innocence, he said, and they were not going to fade quietly into the night if Gilmore failed to do the right thing. "If you don't consent to test," he threatened, "Dateline NBC, the *Washington Post* and the *New York Times* are going to be camped on your doorstep, and they are not going to go away."

Gilmore did not take kindly to such ultimatums. On the other hand, it was obvious that more and more attention was being paid to the case, both inside and outside Virginia. It was also increasingly clear that a decision to test would put the governor in company he relished, that of Texas Governor George W. Bush. On the presidential campaign trail, Bush—under fire for the relentless pursuit of the death penalty in his home state—announced that he advocated DNA testing to "erase any doubts" from some death penalty cases. To prove his commitment, on June 1 Bush for the first time used his executive power to delay an execution. Just hours before the scheduled death of Ricky Nolen McGinn, a mechanic convicted of the rape and ax murder of his twelve-year-old stepdaughter, Bush granted a thirty-day reprieve to allow a DNA test.[14]

Jim Gilmore chose the same day to make a parallel announcement. After thorough review, he had concluded that further DNA tests should be performed by the state laboratory in the case of Earl Washington Jr. "Since 1994 DNA science and technology have improved to the point that further testing of the samples taken from the victim might produce more conclusive results than were available to Governor Wilder," he said in a statement. "I am informed that additional forensic evidence taken from the body of the victim in 1982 has been located and may be available for further DNA testing."[15]

Privately, Gilmore told Felton, "I don't care what the results are. Just bring them back to me."

In New York City, an ecstatic Eric Freedman and his wife Melissa Nathanson celebrated by going out to dinner at their favorite seafood restaurant on the Upper West Side. "I knew we were home free," said Freedman, recalling his exhilaration. "The victory was getting them to do the test. I had no doubt it would clear Earl. I knew it was just a matter of time."

How much time was a surprise to almost everyone involved.

When Gilmore ordered the DNA tests Washington's team expected that it would be a few weeks, four to six at the most, before their client's fate was known. The group had played the waiting game before, so they knew they would have to be cautious, although the test itself could be accomplished within a few days. Logistics or the decision-making process might drag things out, but surely by midsummer the matter would be settled. In the meantime, there were steps to take. Chief among them was creating a plan for Washington's care and well-being if he should be freed. The team remembered that Wilder, weighing a pardon, was reluctant to see Earl return to Fauquier County. They shared the concern. Release from prison without proper support was a risky proposition, often doomed to failure, especially for those who had been on death row. They wanted a caring, nurturing environment for Earl that included housing, social, educational, and vocational components. During the spring, the team turned for advice to Ruth Luckasson, the University of New Mexico professor and expert in mental retardation who had evaluated Washington in 1993. When Luckasson, then president-elect of the American Association on Mental Retardation, attended an AAMR meeting in Washington, D.C., in May, she was on the lookout for an appropriate care giver. A chance encounter outside a Dupont Circle hotel introduced her to Kay Mirick.

"I believe in synchrony. Things come together in their own time for a purpose," Mirick said later.[16]

A child of privilege, Mirick grew up in Pittsburgh in the 1950s and early 1960s in a world of private schools, dance cotillions, and weekend slumber parties. Her father was a pathologist, her mother a nurse, and the medical world to which they introduced their only child was caring and humane. Arriving in Tuscaloosa, Alabama, in the late 1960s as a new bride, she enrolled at the University of Alabama to complete a degree in psychology. One requirement was a practicum at the Partlow State School and Hospital for the mentally ill and retarded, which a few years later became the subject of a federal lawsuit that launched a national revolution in mental health care. It was an assignment that would change her life.

Mirick arrived at Partlow looking like a Southern debutante in her skirt and sweater set with matching pumps and handbag. She marched straight into hell. Mirick encountered a fly-filled room, heavy with the smell of urine and feces, and ten severely retarded, scarcely clad women screaming in her ear and peeing on her shoes. "I didn't know how to respond," she recalled. "I walked out. I said, 'I will never do that again.' It took me two weeks to understand what had happened. I did not see those women as people. I saw them as animals, and I suddenly realized, it wasn't them. It was where they were put. It became my civil rights movement."

Mirick went on to pursue studies and training in mental retardation and to position herself as an advocate for the fledgling community services movement. Upgrading institutions alone was not enough. Individuals with mental disabilities must be allowed to remain in their communities when possible. Segregation too often marked them as less than fully human. "Now, we look at individuals where they are, at what strengths and weaknesses they have," she said. "We support the weaknesses and build on the strengths."

Moving to Hampton Roads, Virginia, Mirick carried the philosophy to a variety of community mental health settings before launching her own company in 1994. Support Services of Virginia, Inc. allowed individuals with a range of mental and physical limitations to live in the community. Located in Virginia Beach, it operated under a "participatory management model" involving families, clients, and staff. Its motto reflected its mission, "To boldly go where no one has gone before; and have fun getting there." By 2000 the company was providing day services for about eighty people in three support sites and one work site, in-home services for another two dozen families, and residential housing for about forty-five individuals in both three-and-four-bedroom homes and one-and-two-bedroom apartments.

Her increasingly active role in national mental health circles led Mirick to attend the May leadership conference of the AAMR at the Washington Hyatt Hotel. Stepping outside for a cigarette, she noticed a woman wearing a dress emblazoned with a striking embroidered peacock. The two struck up a conversation.

"Where are you from? What do you do?" the woman asked.

"I'm a provider in Virginia Beach, and I only use positive practices. I will not do anything negative," Mirick replied.

"Have you ever heard of Earl Washington?" the woman answered.

Mirick's new acquaintance was Ruth Luckasson. Returning home to New Mexico, Luckasson conveyed her excitement to Barry Weinstein. Kay Mirick, she said, was exceptional and the program she ran near-perfect for Earl. But before any agreement could be reached, Mirick insisted on interviewing Washington. She needed to make sure that the program was a fit.

On June 25 Weinstein and Mirick met at the Comfort Inn in Grundy, the closest lodging to Keen Mountain Correctional Center. They spent the evening discussing Washington's background and needs and what Support Services Inc. could offer him. "I felt like a parent interviewing for my kid's college placement," Weinstein said. "I needed to be 100 percent sure about this program." Before the conversation was complete, he knew his search had ended. For Mirick there was one more critical step, a meeting with Washington the next day.

Walking into the prison, Mirick was on the alert for one thing: anger. She knew that if Washington harbored vitriol toward his captors or accusers, his rehabilitation to the outside world might be more than she could handle. "If he had this sense of being wrongfully convicted, of wanting to get someone, we were in trouble," she said. What she encountered was a man who seemed more at peace than she would have imagined possible.

From the start, the pair clicked.

"He called me, 'ma'am,'" Mirick recalled. "I said, 'Why did you call me that?'"

"He said, 'My mama taught me to call ladies 'ma'am.'"

Washington told Mirick that he had been angry for his first few years in prison, but that he had put the emotion behind him. He learned to live from day to day, without anger, without hope. Mirick also found Washington more communicative than expected. Responding to her clinical questions, he described a day's routine clearly and was able to tell her without hesitation how he would spend $5 in the prison commissary. He expressed pride in the fact that he had never had a serious infraction or physical confrontation with another inmate in seventeen years in prison and he pointed out that he made the highest possible prison wage ironing clothes. When bothered by another prisoner, Washington said, he had learned to walk away. A counselor confirmed that Washington was polite, quiet, and stayed largely to himself. "He did not appear to be angry or hostile in any way. He has a rock-solid value system. He respects people. He respects his work. I immediately respected him," Mirick said.

Four days later, she submitted a formal letter of admission and a community placement transition plan to Weinstein. She outlined Washington's wishes—to live in an apartment without air conditioning in his bedroom, to learn how to cook and take care of his own place, to work outside mowing lawns and making a minimum wage, to learn to talk like people on the outside, to read or watch sports or westerns on the television in his spare time, and to make more friends. Mirick outlined, as well, the ways in which Support Services Inc. would help him achieve those goals.[17]

Washington would live in a two-bedroom apartment in Virginia Beach, initially by himself. Support staff would assist him in purchasing and preparing food, understanding the machines around him, communicating with neighbors, and developing leisure activities. Oversight would be one-to-one from 6 A.M. to 10 P.M. seven days per week during the assessment period. Overnight supervision would be available as needed. To improve social skills, Washington would join structured activities at the day support centers and take outings such as a trip to a convenience store to buy a soda, to thrift stores to buy personal items, and to a park for recreation. Work on lawn and property maintenance crews would give him the opportunity to earn money. He could improve educational skills through community or on-site learning programs.

"All training," Mirick stressed in her letter, "is based on the philosophy of positive practices offering motivation and rewards to build skills as well as achieve self-worth, self-control, self-esteem and self-confidence regardless of the level of disability."

It was everything of which Weinstein had dreamed.

Action on the DNA front was proceeding less smoothly. By mid-July the team learned from sources within the administration that the initial results looked good for Washington. Common sense told them as much. Clearly, there had been more than enough time to analyze the slides. Had the results implicated Washington, by now the matter would have been dropped. Something was holding up the works.

As it turned out, several forces were at play. First, the slides of the vaginal smears from the medical examiner's offices in which the team had invested so much hope had proved useless. The sperm portion of the material was insufficient to yield results. Only one hope remained. In early June, a state police officer delivered to Richmond what remained of the evidence analyzed years earlier in the Northern Virginia office of the state forensic lab. The material had been under lock and key at the Culpeper sheriff's department. Within the mass assembled at Paul Ferrara's office was a remaining vaginal smear. Item 58, as it was labeled, was critical. Had that smear been destroyed or lost in the intervening years, or had it proved insufficient for testing, Earl Washington would have been doomed.

Behind the scenes, a test on Item 58 was going forward. When the STR process was applied to the smear, a profile of seven genes emerged. The portrait did not match the genetic makeup of either Earl Washington or Clifford Williams. This time there was no doubt, no ambiguity. The pair "are eliminated as possible contributors of genetic material to this mixture," read the certificate of analysis, which was still secret.[18]

When those results reached the governor, he decreed that everything possible should be tested, including the blue blanket stains and the shirt belatedly connected to the crime scene. (The hairs found on the shirt had inexplicably disappeared. No one seemed to know when or where.) The shirt and cuttings from the blanket remained in Culpeper under the possession of the clerk of the court. Unbeknownst to the public or Washington's defense team, Gilmore had to go to court to get them.

The degree of resistance in Culpeper to Washington's release had been apparent since Felton began investigating the case the previous winter. As soon as Washington's advocates went public with their pardon appeal, local law enforcement officials and others believing Washington guilty reacted with an equally passionate outpouring.

Almost from the start, "there were people contacting me out of the blue who would never want to be identified. We were hearing from everybody," Felton said. "Some of it was accurate, some of it not." Working through the state police, Felton tried to check out the avalanche of claims. "We would send people out to try to find the truth, and the report would be somebody's memory based on something erroneous. We were getting a lot of information that was simply not reliable."

No one, it seemed, was more convinced of Washington's guilt than the Culpeper Commonwealth's attorney. A former reporter, Gary Close had covered Washington's trial and he remembered clearly his predecessor's persuasiveness in arguing that Washington knew things "only the killer could have known." The short, stocky prosecutor took pride in his own up-by-the-bootstraps rise from a difficult childhood and his bulldog tenacity. He resented what he saw as the national media's intrusion into the Washington case, and he was convinced that any pardon would have more to do with outside forces than Washington's guilt or innocence.

But even Close did not have all the facts straight. He believed that Washington had confessed to the Williams murder in the field where he was arrested after the assault on Mrs. Hazel Weeks. "He just got finished assaulting that seventy-eight-year-old woman. They chase him down out into a field. He had shot his brother in the foot that night, and as I understand it, he first confessed to the crime out in the field," Close said.[19]

The notion that Washington gave a spontaneous accounting of the Williams murder was wrong. Officer Terry Schrum confirmed that the first mention of Williams was made by the officers at the Fauquier County sheriff's office. But a contrary belief was part of the mind-set that Culpeper's prosecutor brought to the case. "That's my understanding; that's what I've been told," he said. "To what degree or what detail [Washington confessed at his arrest], I don't know." Months later, Close confirmed that he erred on the point.

Ultimately, however, Close's belief in Washington's guilt was not embedded in any detail of the case but in the fact that the confession existed. Despite abundant evidence in law enforcement annals of the phenomenon of false confessions, Close simply did not believe that anyone would admit to so horrendous an act unless he was guilty.

"What I find compelling is that he acknowledged responsibility for a heinous crime like this. Now look, you can say, hey, the police led him, fed him facts, you know, he was mentally retarded and therefore he didn't know what he was doing. Well, you know, my son when he was ten years old, there is no way you could convince him that he raped and murdered somebody. He'd deny it, and I don't buy that at all," he said.

Close was not persuaded that there was a difference between a ten-year-old raised in a supportive family environment and an adult with a ten-year-old's intelligence raised in semichaos on the fringes of the social order. "My gut tells me, no," he said.

So convinced was Close of his position that he took the remarkable step of refusing to turn over the blue blanket cuttings and the shirt held in evidence in the clerk's office. Not until August 16 when a local judge ordered him to do so did he agree to let a state police officer pick up the evidence and deliver it to Richmond. Close was unapologetic for the delay. "If you look at it from my perspective, I know where this train is headed, and that isn't a good thing."

From the defense team's perspective, the train was barely creeping. It was almost the end of summer, and still there was no word from Gilmore on Washington's fate. That was unacceptable. The time for restraint was past. On September 7 the team delivered a formal petition for clemency, including Kay Mirick's transition plan, to Gilmore's office. "Earl Washington is innocent of the crime for which he came within days of being executed. To prolong his incarceration would be inconsistent with justice not only to him but to Rebecca Williams and her family," it read.[20]

Five days later ABC's *Nightline* aired a program citing the Washington case and providing contrasting interviews with Gilmore and Illinois Governor George Ryan, who had recently ordered a moratorium on executions in his state because of a spate of erroneous convictions. Virginia's governor, on the other hand, defended the process that moved inmates from sentencing to execution in Virginia faster than any other state. "People have to be very respectful of trials," he said. "We do the best we can and we do exceedingly well."

It was perhaps no coincidence that on the day the *Nightline* program aired, Gilmore's office provided the first official update in weeks on the Washington case. A press release confirmed that Gilmore had received the results of DNA tests ordered in June and that he had ordered additional forensic tests as well as a state police investigation. "He wants justice to be done," said spokeswoman Lila White.

As September wore on, there were almost daily reports in one media outlet or another across the state and nation about the waiting game involving Earl Washington. Why was it taking so long to announce the results of tests that were long since complete? In contrast, Gilmore had wasted no time releasing DNA findings that seemed to confirm the guilt of Derek Rocco Barnabei, who was executed on September 14.

On September 25 the defense team let loose a pent-up cannonade. At a press conference in Richmond, Peter Neufeld termed the delay "simply unconscionable." It had been almost four months since tests that should take a few days to complete had been ordered. Clearly, the results exonerated Earl Washington. If they had implicated him, there would be no reason to prolong the mystery. While Gilmore fiddled, Earl Washington was wasting away in a prison cell. "There is absolutely no justification for Governor Gilmore not to release the information."[21]

In Washington, Virginia Representative Bobby Scott escalated the pressure a notch by joining in the call for Washington's release. He cited the case in urging passage of the Innocence Protection Act, which would codify the right of prisoners to put new information of innocence before a court. It also would require states to provide competent legal representation in capital cases at every judicial stage.

The governor's spokeswoman was indignant. Allegations were being raised without a full understanding of all the facts facing Gilmore, White said. The DNA test results had raised questions "which the governor is having investigated before he takes any action." She called the matter a top priority and said the governor was proceeding with all due haste.

Behind the scenes, the media barrage was taking its toll, however. Earl Washington was becoming an unwelcome distraction for Gilmore.

14

Freedom Delayed

A ONE-LINE NEWS ALERT from the Associated Press sped over the Virginia wires at 7:26 P.M. on October 2, too late for the evening news. Governor Jim Gilmore was granting Earl Washington Jr. an absolute pardon in the death of Rebecca Williams. It was the first such pardon for an individual sentenced to death in Virginia in the almost quarter-century since the death penalty was reinstated by *Gregg v. Georgia.*

Already, telephones were ringing from Virginia to New York to Georgia. In the late afternoon, after Gilmore cemented his decision, Walter Felton made courtesy calls to several members of Washington's team. In each conversation, one question was paramount. Ecstatic as the advocates were to finally have a pardon in hand, they had believed for weeks that the new DNA tests cleared their client. Now they wanted to know, was Gilmore going to set Washington free?

The answer was no. Washington was still serving time for the Hazel Weeks assault. It would be up to the state parole board to act in its normal course of business on a release.

Jerry Zerkin was out when Felton called. His wife, Julie McConnell, answered the telephone. Gilmore's counsel knew McConnell from her work with the American Civil Liberties Union, and he could hear the letdown in her voice. For others as well, the disappointment was keen. Once again, an excruciating wait had ended with a tarnished victory. Washington was getting his pardon, but there was no apology from Gilmore. And because of the thirty-year sentence in the Hazel Weeks case, the prisoner was not even being released. The way Washington's lawyers figured, under prevailing parole practices, their client would have left prison as much as a decade earlier had it not been for the death sentence. No one, it seemed, could go the extra mile of admitting that a terrible injustice had been done.

Gilmore's ten-paragraph pardon statement began with an account of Washington's "brutally beating" Hazel Weeks and ended with an apology to the family of Rebecca Williams. "I am deeply sympathetic to the pain and anguish already suffered by the family and friends of Rebecca Williams, and I regret any reliving of that pain these events may cause," Gilmore said. As for Washington, DNA tests on both the blue blanket seminal stains and a vaginal smear excluded him. "In my judgment, a jury afforded the benefit of the DNA evidence and analysis available to me today would have reached a different conclusion regarding the guilt of Earl Washington," Gilmore said. Period. There was no message of concern or regret about the seventeen years and four months that Washington had served under sentence of death or life in prison. If anything, the statement took pains to breathe life into any lingering doubts about Washington. "It is important for the public to understand that absence of DNA evidence does not necessarily mean an individual is absent from the crime scene—just that he has not left any DNA markers," Gilmore said. There was no mention of how convoluted, unlikely, or far-fetched the scenarios would have to be for Washington still to be involved. The governor concluded by saying that he was directing the state police to reopen their investigation into Rebecca Williams's murder.[1]

Barry Weinstein was at home in Georgia when Bob Hall telephoned with the news: "Gilmore pardoned Earl."

"How about Weeks?"

"Just as we thought. He passed it on to the parole board."

Weinstein refused to let that setback temper his delight in conveying the long-awaited news to Washington. The attorney telephoned the watch commander at Keen Mountain, then waited for a reply. Some minutes later, the telephone rang. It was Washington.

"I've got good news. I've got bad news," Weinstein told him. "The good news is that you were exonerated. Governor Gilmore granted you a pardon."

From the silence at the other end of the line, Weinstein knew that Washington needed further explanation.

"It means that you didn't do it," he said.

There was another pause as Weinstein imagined Washington digesting the news and his face slowly expanding in a grin. The reply, when it came, was matter-of-fact. "That's what I've been telling everybody all along," he said.

Now came the more sobering part. Weinstein explained that Gilmore would not reconsider the Weeks sentence. The matter would go before the parole board, and Earl would remain in prison at least until their decision. The lawyer promised that the team would move as quickly as possible to get the matter resolved. He urged Washington to stay calm and be patient a while longer. "Hang on," Weinstein said.

"How do you feel?" he added as he prepared to say goodbye.

"I feel great," replied Washington.[2]

For others, the victory remained bittersweet. Gilmore's pardon of Washington was perhaps the most affirming event in all the exhausting days and sleepless nights that Marie Deans had devoted to the death penalty abolitionist cause. But her primary responses were anger and fear. Watching the announcement on the 11 P.M. news in her Charlottesville townhouse, her agitation grew.

"I was so angry I couldn't sleep," she said. "Gilmore never said, 'The man is innocent,' or 'Geez, we're sorry.' Nothing. I was very, very concerned that they were going to find some way to keep him in prison. I felt it very strongly, Barry too."[3]

Eric Freedman echoed the sentiment. "They were so grudging and negative about the whole thing that nobody could breathe easy until he walks out the door. Who knew what setups, problems there could be in prison?"[4]

In the aftermath of the announcement, two matters needed sorting out. One was Washington's parole status. How long would it be before he was eligible for release? The team immediately set about getting clarification. The second was the reopened police investigation into who raped and murdered Rebecca Williams. In the flurry of excitement about the pardon, scant attention was paid to the details of the DNA test results. But from a crime detective's perspective, they were fascinating. The critical fact for Earl Washington was that two DNA samples were extracted—one from the blanket, one from a vaginal swab—and neither was his. But the results threw the crime itself into a puzzling new realm. The surprising fact was that the DNA samples came from not one individual, as had long been supposed, but two. Equally startling, one of the two samples, the DNA on the blue blanket, matched the genetic makeup of a man serving time in a Virginia prison for rape. Citing the renewed police investigation, Gilmore refused to identify the man publicly. The DNA on the vaginal swab did not produce a match when it was compared with the samples of 125,000 felons in the state's DNA data bank.

Logically, semen found on the body of a victim following a rape would be assumed to belong to the rapist; but logically also, if the DNA of a known rapist was found at the scene of a rape, it could be assumed to be the perpetrator's. Which was correct? Were two people, neither of them Earl, involved after all? And how did the new information fit with Rebecca Williams's dying statement that she was attacked by a single man? One of the reasons Gilmore delayed so long in announcing the results was that he was trying to get answers from the state police.

The uncertainty, coupled with Gilmore's equivocation in the pardon announcement, allowed Culpeper officials to intimate that they had the right man all along. By their new theory, there were two guilty parties, one of them Washington, one of them the unidentified blue blanket rapist. The semen found on Williams's body was taken to be the result of consensual sex. It was of no matter that not a single piece of evidence or testimony in the public realm supported the revised scenario.

Nonetheless, Culpeper Commonwealth's attorney Close was keeping Washington clearly in his focus. "It may be that the case was already solved," he told the *Washington Post* two days after the pardon. "There's a huge difference between innocent and pardoned."[5]

There also was a major difference between pardoned and free.

Contacted at Keen Mountain the day after Gilmore's announcement, Earl Washington had little but praise for the man who pardoned him. "I feel great," he told a *Richmond Times-Dispatch* reporter. "I look forward to living in Virginia Beach. . . . I'd like to see my family and my niece. Then, I gotta get me a job." As for Gilmore, "the only thing I'd like to say to Mr. Gilmore is I thank him for doing the tests. He did a good job. The test proves I was innocent."[6]

His attorneys were less grateful. Speaking to the *Washington Post*, Bob Hall called Gilmore's decision "gutless" and argued that Washington's prison sentence in the Weeks case should have been reduced to time served.[7] Eric Freedman was equally incensed. "It's an act of political cowardice and bureaucratic buck passing that compounds the original injustice," the New Yorker said. "No one doubts that Mr. Washington would have been released six or seven years ago on the non-capital charge, which is the governor's excuse for continuing to hold him."[8]

Meanwhile, the family of Rebecca Williams greeted the news of Washington's pardon with confusion. "Now we've got this hell to go through all over again," lamented Helen Richards, Rebecca Williams's mother.[9]

On October 3, the day after Washington was pardoned, corrections department officials promised to recalculate the prisoner's parole eligibility as if he had earned good-time points during his years on death row and at full, rather than half credit, while under a life sentence. That was only fair, everyone agreed. A recalculation might mean that Washington was already eligible for mandatory parole, which occurs in Virginia when a prisoner has served all but six months of a sentence, minus good time.

Regardless of what the department set as Washington's mandatory release date, however, there was strong evidence that he would have been freed years earlier except for the capital conviction. In the 1980s and early 1990s few first-time offenders with a clean prison record—like Washington—were reaching their mandatory parole dates in prison, much less completing their full sentences. With good-time points, some offenders were actually serving as little as one-sixth of their sentences.

Washington likely would have come up for his first parole hearing in 1988 or 1989 and probably would have been given parole a few years later, according to Richard Kern, the Virginia government's leading authority on sentencing and parole practices. When those statutes underwent an extensive tightening in 1994, Kern directed the commission that oversaw the work.

The commission's final report highlighted how unusual it was for Washington to have served seventeen years and four months for the dual crimes of malicious wounding and breaking and entering. According to the report, first-degree murderers released in 1993, a typical prereform year, served an average of 10.3 years out of an average sentence of 35.2 years. Individuals convicted of murder in the second degree served an average of 5.7 years out of average sentences of 16.7 years. As for Washington's two crimes, the average sentence for malicious wounding was 8.3 years and the average time served 2.8 years, and the average sentence for breaking and entering was 6.8 years, with 2.2 served.[10] In other words, the average time served for Washington's crimes was five years. He was in prison longer than the average first-degree murderer.

Might the nature of the attack on Mrs. Weeks justify a longer period in prison? According to Kern, no. Harmful as the crime was, the absence of permanent physical injury simply did not put the assault into the worst category of malicious woundings. "It would be very unusual under the old parole and good-time laws to find anyone in our prison system or any other that would be in prison seventeen years for that act with no prior record," Kern said.[11]

Even under the revised sentencing guidelines that were adopted when parole was essentially abolished in Virginia in 1994, individuals convicted of crimes similar to Washington's served about a decade, Kern said. But Jim Gilmore, the conservative politician, did not want to be seen as cutting short the sentence of a man convicted of assaulting an elderly woman, even if that sentence was imposed in an era when judges kept penalties high because only a fraction of a sentence was served. At the same time, a parole board operating in a new era of shorter sentences, with a higher percentage of time served, was determined to treat Washington's case no differently than any other.

Questioned the day after Gilmore's pardon, Kern calculated that—even without discretionary parole—Washington probably would have reached his mandatory parole date in the Weeks case the previous year. By that assessment, the prisoner should already be free.[12] But the determination involved some judgment calls. No one could say for sure how many good-time credits Washington would have earned. When the corrections department released its calculation two days after the pardon, its judgment was tougher. According to the department, Washington had a mandatory parole date of February 12, 2001, four months away. The parole board could grant discretionary parole earlier, if it chose.[13]

The delay was a red flag to Washington's advocates, who distrusted the state's intentions. They feared that some minor infraction, possibly a trumped up one, would be found to keep Washington behind bars indefinitely. Throughout October and November, as the parole board prepared to evaluate Washington's bid for discretionary parole, his attorneys approached each step with near paranoia. When the board wanted an examiner to interview the prisoner, a routine step in such cases, the team delayed out of fear that the review was a ploy to stall Washington's release. Eventually, the team consented, but not without apprehension.

Shortly before Washington was pardoned, Walter Felton had telephoned parole board Chairman James Jenkins to advise him that a decision in the Hazel Weeks case was likely to be coming the parole board's way soon.[14] A Richmond-area attorney, Jenkins had been appointed by Gilmore to head the Virginia parole board the previous year. Jenkins recognized that many of those who came before the board were the products of miserable childhoods, and he felt some sympathy. At times, he also suspected miscarriages of justice in the files he read. But his chief concern was accountability and the expectation that offenders must pay for their crimes. He was personally acquainted with the effects of violence through an uncle who was murdered during a robbery, and he was particularly unforgiving of crimes affecting children and the elderly.

Aware that the Washington decision would be high-profile, Jenkins studied the case file. He needed to be able to address press inquiries about the matter, and he wanted to know the details of the Weeks case.

Among the documents Jenkins saw was the presentence report in which Deputy D. A. Zeets described the night of Washington's arrest. Over the next several weeks, Jenkins, quoting from that report, would tell various reporters that Mrs. Weeks had been found naked and bleeding. The scarcely veiled insinuation was that there had been an attempted rape. But Jenkins never saw the transcript of the preliminary hearing, held immediately after the break-in and ten months prior to the presentence report. At that hearing, in direct contradiction to his later statement, Zeets said that Mrs. Weeks was already being tended to when he arrived at the house. He said nothing about her having been naked. Nor did anyone else. Jenkins did not read Mrs. Weeks's testimony that she never removed her gown.

Advised later of the discrepancy, Jenkins said it did not alter his view that Washington did not deserve early parole. He was concerned both that Washington hit Mrs. Weeks forcefully enough to break a chair and that he later shot his brother in the foot. Both Earl and Robert Washington termed the shooting an accident, and the charges were dropped, but to Jenkins's mind, Washington stole a gun to shoot his brother and shot him deliberately.

The team was incensed the following year when the Virginia parole board released two killers who had served only a few more years than Washington. One man served twenty-two years after hiring a hit man to kill two people; the other served twenty-six for murdering a Navy enlisted man. "If you hit someone with a chair, you can get almost eighteen years," fumed Hall. "If you kill two people, it nets you only four more."

A typical prisoner coming before the parole board as it was constituted in 2000 could not expect leniency, however, particularly if the offense was a violent one. Since the early 1990s, when Washington first would have been considered for parole, save for the capital conviction, there had been a complete turnabout in parole grant rates. Approved grants dropped from 47 percent of the requests considered in 1990 to 40 percent in 1993 to 8 percent in 2000.[15] When it came to violent crimes, the grant rate was lower, less than 2 percent. Of course, that decline was accompanied by shorter sentences in many cases.

The parole board did not think it was part of its mission to make amends to Washington for the years he had erroneously spent on death row. In the board's view, that responsibility—if there was any—belonged to the governor and the legislature. They decided to assess the Weeks conviction in isolation from any other events in Washington's life. And by that standard, the board decreed three days before Christmas 2000, that Washington ought to be held until his mandatory release date on February 12. The decision, Jenkins acknowledged, would have been more difficult if the release date had not been just six weeks away.

Once again, Washington's attorneys could do nothing more than fume about injustice. Given his status as a first-time offender with a clean prison record, Washington might well be in a category of one as a Virginia prisoner who had served so long for a malicious wounding in which there was no permanent physical injury.[16] Surely, at some level, he deserved dispensation for coming within nine days of execution and erroneously spending nine and a half years on death row. But no one official was willing to put all the pieces together and address them as a whole. Eric Freedman expressed his frustration: "The real culprit here is Gov. Gilmore who tried to take the politically convenient way out by relegating Mr. Washington to the bureaucratic labyrinth rather than standing up to the plate and granting him his long overdue release."[17]

By now, there was an almost rote quality to the defense team's outrage. Compared with more than nine hundred weeks behind bars, what were six more? The state's position was established. It would free Earl Washington, but with no apology, compensation, self-reproach, or a nod toward his humanity. Through his assault of Hazel Weeks, Washington had determined his own fate. Those were the unspoken terms of his release. Given the fact that nothing had compelled Gilmore to order the DNA tests or to honor their results, in the state's view the prisoner should be grateful.

He was. On a calendar attached to his cell wall at the Greensville Correctional Center in Jarratt, Virginia, where he had been moved to await the release, Washington charted the days to freedom. "I mark off every night before I go to bed," he said. "Next morning, I go back and recount."[18] With nineteen days remaining, Washington said he was just beginning to contemplate life outside prison. "I just ain't ready to think about it. I'll think about it the last five days," Washington said. His goal for the remaining time was to steer clear of trouble. "I can sleep for them nineteen days," he said, before pausing to recalculate. "Sleep for eighteen days. The nineteenth day, I'll be gone."

Seated in a small visiting room furnished only with a table and two chairs, Washington laid out a vision of the future as spare as his surroundings. "I can't go back to Fauquier County. That's what Barry says. I got to listen to what Barry says. Only thing Barry tells me, we're going to Virginia Beach. First day, I've got a news conference. If I don't want to do it, I don't have to. As long as he's there, I'll do it. . . . I got a job waiting on me, but I can't tell you what it is. . . . I'll call one of my sisters, let 'em know where I'm at once I get settled in."

One thing Washington claimed to have learned for sure. He could not drink alcohol, at all. "That's most people's biggest fear," he said, citing the prospect that he might again get into trouble under the influence of alcohol. "I learned a lesson from drinking. You get locked up, and you will get set up." His complaint about his years in prison had nothing to do with Hazel Weeks, however. Once again expressing remorse, Washington said he deserved to be punished for hurting Mrs. Weeks. "There's an old saying, 'If I commit a crime, I got to do the time.'"

As Washington's release approached, Virginia officials made clear that he was not to become a national poster-child for the death penalty abolitionist movement, at least not on their time. When permission was requested for Washington to attend a press conference in Washington, D.C., with Virginia Representative Bobby Scott and other supporters of the Innocence Protection Act on the day of the release, the corrections department nixed the idea. Washington might have a pardon in the rape-murder of Rebecca Williams, but in the matter of Hazel Weeks he was just another prisoner going out on supervised parole. The state would set the terms of his comings and goings as long as he was under its control, and for now the only place he was going to was Virginia Beach. Supervised parole would last three years.

In other ways, Washington was not to be treated as a typical prisoner, however. The usual routine was for a paroled offender to walk out of prison into the arms of waiting relatives or to be escorted to the nearest bus station. No such emotional reunion would take place outside the Greensville Correctional Center on the morning of February 12. Corrections officials knew that a contingent of reporters and television cameras would be waiting, along with the defense team and various anti-death penalty activists, to record the moment of Washington's prison exit. The media circus, as far as prison officials were concerned, would have to find another backdrop.

At about 6:45 A.M. on that Monday morning, with a light sleet falling and only a hint of gray lightening the night sky, a corrections department vehicle bearing Earl Washington sped out of a back prison gate and headed for Virginia Beach. Eric Freedman and a handful of reporters stationed at the front gate were unaware of the departure. By the time it became clear an hour or so later that Washington was gone, Freedman could do little more than lament the subterfuge and head for an early afternoon press conference scheduled in Virginia Beach. "All I've ever wanted in this case is to see him come out of the prison gates," complained Freedman, who would have to wait a few more hours for his first face-to-face meeting with the man whose freedom he had pursued for fifteen years.[19]

Other members of the team were assembling for the event as well. Robert Hall, who awakened at 4 A.M. for a radio talk show interview, was heading down from Northern Virginia with his wife, Sally. Barry Scheck and Peter Neufeld had flown in from New York. Gerald Zerkin, like Freedman, went first to Jarratt and then rerouted to Virginia Beach. Barry Weinstein had been up from Georgia, overseeing arrangements, for a couple of days. Marie Deans, now employed as a mitigation specialist exploring the backgrounds of prisoners accused of capital crimes, left her home in Charlottesville early in the morning with Henry Heller, founder of Virginians for Alternatives to the Death Penalty. Representative Bobby Scott, blocked in his plans to bring Washington to the Capitol, was on his way to Virginia Beach as well.

Shortly after 9 A.M., Washington and his escorts walked into Kay Mirick's office at Support Services Inc. There were hugs and shouts of glee as Deans and Weinstein for the first time in their long association saw Earl Washington outside prison walls and with his hands un-chained. What Mirick remembered most from that freezing cold morn-ing, when others were wearing parkas and sweaters, was Washing-ton's attire. He was dressed in a short-sleeved cotton shirt and work pants. He had a $25 check from the Department of Corrections in his pocket, but he had no hat, no coat, no gloves. "He looked startled, like a deer caught in the headlights, like he was walking through a cloud," she said.

A few hours later, the group pulled up in front of the building where reporters and cameras were waiting to record Washington's re-action to his first hours of freedom. Sitting in the car's front seat, now dressed in polo shirt and a second-hand parka, Washington saw the sea of faces and he turned to Deans and Weinstein in panic. Already, Henry Heller was holding the door for him to get out of the car, but Earl seemed frozen. Taking in the scene, Marie put her head close to his and spoke softly. "You know how I am about press conferences," she said. "They make me really nervous. You can't make me go in there by my-self." Drawing in a deep breath, Earl took hold of her hand, and to-gether they faced the crowd.

For Earl Washington, the days that followed were a waking dream of delights and freedoms unimagined in almost two decades behind bars. In some ways, the comforts of this new life, with its furnished apartment, regular meals, and clothes donated by well-wishers ex-ceeded any he had known. He ventured onto the beach. He discovered Chinese and Mexican food. He awoke at 4 A.M. and went outside to smoke a cigarette in the rain. He welcomed two sisters, two nieces, a brother, and assorted other relatives who rented a van and drove to Vir-ginia Beach for a reunion. He began attending a church in Norfolk with a woman whose name he could not remember, but who picked him up every Sunday without fail. "I'm the only black person in the whole church," he confided, marveling at the warmth of his welcome. "People there are real nice," he said. "That's something I've got to deal with, people being nice." He made friends at Support Services Inc., including Mark Carpenter, a staff member who became his work partner. To-gether, they painted and did plumbing and electrical work on the vari-ous houses and apartments owned by the facility. He formed a bond with Carpenter's young son, and he earned his colleague's praise. "He's one of the most pleasant people I've ever worked with, and effi-cient," said Carpenter. "Earl would be welcome to come live in my

house any time if he needed to, and I know he'd do the same for me."
He allowed himself to contemplate the future that had seemed so hazy
a few weeks earlier from a cell at the Greensville Correctional Center.
"I'd like to marry, settle down, have a family before I get too old," he
said. Slowly, some of the wariness and watchfulness ebbed, both for
Washington and for those who had worked so long to bring him to that
point.

All the Support Services Inc. apartments had a name, and Earl
Washington's was called "Hope." It was what had kept him going for
eighteen years. Now, it was the emotion enveloping him and many others as he embarked on the perilous walk of freedom.

15

The Aftermath

THE STORY OF Earl Washington Jr. is more than an account of what happened to one man. It is a lesson in the frailty of human institutions, how they are prone to value expediency over truth, order over complication, official interpretations over private claims. The criminal justice system may, as former Virginia Governor Jim Gilmore once said, do "exceedingly well." But it is still subject to flawed memory, rumor, inexact science, mistaken judgment, and at times outright deceit. The safeguards against false imprisonment and execution are many—among them, a presumption of innocence, the guarantee of legal representation, and access to an elaborate hierarchy of appeals. Sometimes, in the face of that array, the guilty may go free. But one cannot trace the extraordinary series of coincidences and events necessary to free Earl Washington without reaching a parallel truth. Even with multiple protections and even in the face of the supreme penalty of death, the system sometimes fails in another way. The price of America's retention of capital punishment almost certainly is the wrongful execution, here and there, of an innocent man. Such victims most likely live, like Washington, at life's margins. They may have sullied their bond to the larger community, as had Washington through his assault of Hazel Weeks. They probably will have few protective resources, economic, mental, or racial. They are society's expendable men, the secret, shameful underbelly of a popular punishment.

Anyone who doubts the existence of such wrongful convictions should remember what it took to save Earl Washington from such a fate. He was freed not because of a system designed to excise error, but in spite of one committed to affirming its own judgments. The conclusion of British psychologist Gisli Gudjonsson after reviewing one of the most exhaustive studies of wrongful convictions in the United States is consistent with Washington's struggle: "Almost without exception, the defendants were dependent upon the good will of others in proving their innocence. . . . [T]he criminal justice system itself is deficient in discovering, admitting to, and doing something about, errors which they make."[1]

In cases where no such goodwill exists in the form of a committed attorney, an aggressive journalist, or a dedicated friend or relative, the prisoner is doomed. Ironically, the likelihood of unearthing error may be greatest when a death sentence attracts the resources and passion of the abolitionist movement and the pro bono bar. If Washington had been sentenced, from the start, to a life in prison, none of his principal defenders would even have known of his case, and the odds against his release would have skyrocketed.

A striking array of forces converged to free Washington. In the summer of 1985, as his execution approached, a fellow death row inmate filed on his own initiative a civil lawsuit that brought Eric Freedman and a prestigious New York law firm into the case. Freedman arrived just three weeks before Washington's scheduled execution. Had help not emerged, Washington could have died without his habeas appeals being filed. Perhaps at the very last minute Marie Deans would have found someone to represent Washington, but it is unlikely that such a recruit would have offered the quality of representation and commitment that Freedman brought to the case over fifteen years, support that was essential to Washington's eventual release.

Later that fall, if Robert Hall had not discovered the discrepancy between Washington's blood type and the seminal stains on the blue blanket, evidence that was missed at trial and during the direct appeals, Washington almost certainly would have died. Ultimately, the appeals courts rejected the blood evidence as proof of innocence. It was the later DNA tests—not the serological tests—that led to Washington's pardon. But the questions raised by Hall's discovery caused the 4th Circuit appeals court to send the case back to federal district court for a hearing, and the twenty-two-month delay that followed kept Washington alive. During those months, the PCR-DNA process that led to Wilder's commutation was developed as a forensic tool. Without the questions raised by Hall, the 4th Circuit would have rejected Washington's appeal in December 1991. A clemency petition likely would have reached Wilder six or so months later, just before a scheduled execution. That would have been many months before the nation's first PCR-DNA release.

Washington also might have died except for a fluke by which attorney general Mary Sue Terry resigned to run for governor and Gail Marshall and Steve Rosenthal briefly assumed positions of authority within the office. Marshall's skepticism about Washington's guilt and Rosenthal's willingness to approve DNA testing led to such a test in October 1993, immediately after the 4th Circuit issued its final ruling. If Rosenthal had not ordered the test, something he probably did not have the authority to do, only Wilder could have done so. Given Wilder's irritation with Washington's attorneys for cutting short the appeals, the governor might well have refused. Then, Washington's sentence would not have been commuted to life in prison on Wilder's last day in office. Perhaps Wilder's successor would have approved a test; but perhaps not. If not, Washington surely would have died.

While Washington's attorneys would have pressed for STR-DNA testing eventually, they might not have gotten it without the national exposure and momentum created by Ofra Bikel's *Frontline* piece. Washington was at the mercy of whatever governor considered his request. Because of the Twenty-One-Day Rule, he had no recourse in court. It took a barrage of media exposure before the tests were ordered, and even after the DNA of a convicted rapist was found at the crime scene, Gilmore never proclaimed Washington innocent. He simply said that a jury considering all the facts would have reached a different conclusion. Five months after Washington's release, Gilmore's secretary of public safety made clear the limitations of that statement. "Earl Washington is still questionable as to whether he did or did not" commit the crime, said Gary K. Aronhalt. "I have to take issue with the claim that he's innocent."[2]

It was an enormous stroke of luck that a vaginal smear remained in 2000 for testing. And given Washington's tedious and uncertain advance toward freedom, one wonders what the prisoner's mental state would have been by the time of his release had it not been for the steadfast friendship of Barry Weinstein. Many men released from death row have unhappy or failed reentries to society.

Those who argue that the system worked in Washington's case overlook a host of failings: the failure to detect a false confession, the failure to supply Washington with an adequate defense at trial; the failure of every appellate court—save the 4th Circuit appeals court in one limited ruling—to recognize the flaws in the case. It is not reassuring that so many of the state's arguments that prevailed in court, such as the claim that the blue blanket seminal stains belonged to Clifford Williams, were simply wrong. Without advances in scientific testing, no one would ever have known.

As is typical in capital cases, the skill, the knowledge of death penalty law, and the resources brought to bear in Washington's defense were greatest at the point at which those assets were least likely to help. During his trial and direct appeals—the stages on which everything that followed hinged—Washington was represented by an attorney who had never tried a capital case and whose recollection is that he received $1,000 to $2,000, perhaps less, for his services. Spending on expert witnesses and private investigators was zero. In the eight years between August 1985 and September 1993, when the 4th Circuit Court of Appeals issued the last ruling in the Washington case, hundreds of thousands of dollars in pro bono legal fees and tens of thousands of dollars in investigative fees and other ancillary costs were spent by his attorneys on the prisoner's behalf. He was represented by lawyers with detailed knowledge of capital statutes and related court rulings. The help came largely too late. By the habeas stage, the whole exercise, if not a charade, was perilously close to one because the institutional bias tilted so strongly in favor of protecting the integrity of the trial verdict. Defenders of that system point to the importance of honoring the decisions of local judges and the citizens who form juries. Without substantial skepticism, however, a flawed verdict may remain unexposed.

A dozen individuals freed from death row between 1993 and 2002 due to tests of crime-scene DNA show that it is possible to paint a picture in court that appears to be a faithful, realistic rendering of the truth, but is not.[3] Such cases led U.S. Supreme Court Justice Sandra Day O'-Connor to declare in a speech to the Minnesota Women's Lawyer's Group in July 2001: "If statistics are any indication, the system may well be allowing some innocent defendants to be executed."

In the Washington case, as in others, many of those invested in the original conviction maintain their belief in its accuracy, even when doing so requires wildly improbable adjustments. In the aftermath of Earl Washington's release in February 2001, various law enforcement and public officials in Culpeper continued to defend the original guilty verdict. Confused and distraught, the family of Rebecca Williams vacillated on the matter. The motivation for them to embrace the original interpretation was strong. Letting go of a belief in Washington's guilt entailed opening a Pandora's box of questions about Rebecca and Clifford

Williams. The family's safest haven was in the belief that the killer of their mother, wife, and daughter was the stranger originally convicted of the crime.

"I can't talk to nobody. I can't find out nothing," said Clifford Williams six months after Washington's release.[4] His efforts to get information about the renewed investigation were unproductive, he said. Newly remarried, living in a small community not far from Culpeper, Williams was just back from California and a successful visit with the three daughters who were lost to him for many years after their mother's death. His drug dependency and evidence that the girls were being poorly cared for resulted in Helen Richards gaining custody of her granddaughters in the mid-1980s. In 1988, hoping to sever all ties with their father, she quietly moved them to California without telling Clifford of her plans or leaving a forwarding address. He rediscovered them only after his new wife launched a determined search. The three girls and their grandmother, whom they call "mom," all lived in the same trailer park in El Cajon. The two youngest have children. Misty Michelle Phillips, who was eleven months old at her mother's death, described her California childhood as "really good. . . . My mom kept us really busy."[5] Their reunion with their father was "fantastic," she said. His relationship with his daughters "is just starting to grow real good," added Clifford.

The family did not welcome the intrusion of the reopened investigation. Toward Earl Washington, who bore the family's scorn and hatred for years, they were ambivalent. "If he's innocent, let the man go and don't ever bother him again," said Phillips. But in the same conversation, her animosity boiled up. "I think it's absolutely asinine," she said of Washington's release. "They convicted him of my mother's death. They convicted him. He played stupid to get himself out of it."

Clifford Williams and Helen Richards had similar reactions, focusing alternately on Washington's supposed knowledge of the case and the unexplained presence of two DNAs, neither belonging to him. They held on to the possibility of his guilt in part because years of rumor and small-town talk had transformed Washington's supposed knowledge into something far greater than it was. For instance, Williams believed firmly that Washington told investigators the specific radio station to which Rebecca was listening on the morning of her death. He did not. Meanwhile, Richards believed that Washington told police he watched her daughter for weeks before the crime. That is inaccurate. Nothing in the case papers or court transcripts supports such an allegation. But knowing that Richards believed it helps explain why she continued to say, "The things Earl Washington said, he would almost have to be present."[6]

On one thing Richards and Williams agreed. "If they're going to turn this man loose, they ought to get off their seats and find the one who did it," Williams said.

Throughout the Culpeper community, those who continued to believe in Washington's guilt generally did so for three reasons: reluctance to admit error, particularly when it might aid the antideath penalty movement; misconceptions about how much Washington knew; and lack of understanding of how a person would confess falsely to a crime of such magnitude. Puzzling as the confession may seem, the notion of an innocent man claiming crimes he did not commit is far from unique. Individuals with mental retardation are especially prone to want to please those in a superior position, such as a police interrogator. But it is not only individuals with mental challenges who falsely confess. Psychologist Hugo Munsterberg, credited with being the first in his field to identify the phenomenon, described it in 1908 as an emotional shock which distorts memory during interrogation.[7]

The most common cause of false confessions is overzealous police. But there are more subtle, psychological explanations that may have little or nothing to do with police pressure: among them, a bid for notoriety, a desire to protect someone else, guilt over a previous misdeed, mental illness, or a personality highly influenced by suggestion.[8]

In 1986 British psychologist Gudjonsson and colleague N. K. Clark produced a theoretical model for determining when an individual is susceptible to suggestion during a police investigation. They cited three conditions—uncertainty, interpersonal trust, and expectation of success.[9] Washington's retardation aside, all three qualities may have been present as he faced police. Having spent the early evening drinking prior to the break-in at the home of Hazel Weeks, Washington appears to have had only a marginal memory or understanding of what occurred at the Weeks house. *Uncertainty* was a factor as he faced the police. Second, Schrum's level manner with Washington may have created a degree of *interpersonal trust*, whereas a more harsh style might have bred greater resistance, according to the model. And finally, Washington's sense that he was pleasing his interrogators ("OK Earl, that's better . . .") could have created an *expectation of success* in escaping a stressful situation.

"When placed under pressure, many individuals are more likely to serve their immediate self-interest than their long-term ones, even though the former may be to their eventual detriment," Gudjonsson writes.[10]

Interrogative suggestibility and compliance, conditions in which a suspect either accepts a suggestion as true during questioning or agrees to it despite knowledge that it is false, correlate with low intellectual functioning, low self-esteem, anxiety, and lack of assertiveness,[11] all of which could be found in twenty-three-year-old Earl Washington when he faced the Fauquier County deputies after his arrest. To discount even the possibility of a false confession is to ignore a whole history of such behavior in annals of criminal justice.

The discovery of two separate DNAs forced the defenders of the original verdict into ever more convoluted explanations of how Washington could still be involved. No one official argued that Washington and *both* of the men whose DNAs appeared at the crime scene were to blame, or that if there were two culprits, they were the two unidentified men. Those scenarios were properly rejected as far-fetched. But in fact, it was just as far-fetched to place Washington and an accomplice at the scene. A host of evidence pointed to a single perpetrator, and not a single piece of that evidence pointed to Earl Washington Jr. as the man.

What is to be made of the two DNAs? If only one is linked to the crime, then the most likely candidate would seem to be that of the convicted rapist. Peter Neufeld was outraged that, a year and a half after the tests were completed, no charges had been brought against the man. But others on the defense team saw the case as far from airtight. The blue blanket on which the convicted rapist's semen was found was described by Clifford Williams as a "party blanket" that had once been in a van belonging to Hilda Richards. After the van was wrecked, Williams said, the blanket wound up in someone else's trunk and eventually at the Williams home. He did not know when or how it arrived. Given the uncertain whereabouts of the blue blanket over time, it would be risky—on the basis of that evidence alone—for prosecutors to try to place the man at the Williams apartment on the day of the murder. Also, if the rapist is the culprit, then what explains the semen found on Rebecca Williams's body? To suggest without proof that she was having an affair tars a woman unable to defend herself.

The second possibility is that the semen found inside Rebecca Williams's body belonged to her murderer. By that theory, the stains on the blue blanket were deposited by the convicted rapist at some other time and in some other place. Rebecca Williams was not having an affair on the early morning of her death, and Earl Washington was never present. Nothing in that interpretation is inconsistent with the verified facts.

In the two decades since the arrest of Earl Washington Jr., Virginia and many other states have improved their administration of the death penalty somewhat. Standards for the legal representation of defendants in capital cases have been written. The practice of audiotaping or video-taping confessions has gained ground. Some states have adopted provisions for postconviction DNA testing through the courts, rather than gubernatorial clemency. But the changes are neither exhaustive nor universal.

Mere adoption of standards for interrogations or for the selection of defense attorneys in capital cases has not meant that those standards are followed. The presumption in favor of the trial outcome remains inviolate in many state and federal appeals courts. Moreover, the passage of the Anti-Terrorism and Effective Death Penalty Act of 1996, approved in the wake of the Oklahoma City bombing, streamlined the appeals process by setting tighter filing deadlines and limiting various proceedings. Both reduced the likelihood that a wrongful conviction would be detected.

The report in April 2002 of the Illinois Commission on Capital Punishment, established by Governor Ryan in the wake of a series of death row releases in that state, confirmed that the shortcomings in Washington's conviction and appeals are not unique to Virginia. The commission's sober assessment of failings in the administration of capital punishment in that state reflected many of the omissions and lapses evident in the Washington case. "All members of the Commission have emerged from our deliberations with a renewed sense of the extraordinary complexities presented by the question of capital punishment," wrote the group of prominent jurists, prosecutors, and elected and appointed officials at the conclusion of the most serious investigation into the administration of the death penalty yet undertaken by an American state.[12]

What reforms are needed?

Requiring qualified, experienced defense counsel at trial, combined with adequate access to expert resources, is the single most critical reform needed in reducing wrongful convictions in capital cases. Given the weight attached to trial verdicts throughout the appeals process, it is folly to concentrate effort, talent, and resources at the habeas stage. In the Washington case, a defense attorney untrained and inexperienced in capital defense—and nearly uncompensated for his work—botched the job. Hundreds of thousands of dollars worth of pro bono legal work in the subsequent two decades barely salvaged the situation.

The Washington case argues for "concentrating resources and energy at the trial level," said Judge Harvie Wilkinson, member of the 4th Circuit appeals panel. The case is "a cautionary reminder that humans are fallible. . . . You can do the most conscientious job that it's humanly possible to do, and at the end of the day you still have no guarantee that you've been right."[13] Proper representation demands adequate training and compensation, as well as a serious effort to convince major law firms and very able attorneys to extend their pro bono work to trials. "It's not an area for amateurs. It's the kind of thing that only people with a lot of experience should be going into," Wilkinson said.

Mere guidelines do not guarantee attorney competence, however. In Virginia, a study found no independent verification of the credentials of lawyers placed on a list of capital-eligible attorneys.[14] Moreover, Virginia judges are urged to pick from the approved list when appointing indigent counsel, but they are not required to do so. And much as jurists such as Wilkinson might hope for top-notch attorneys to agree to represent defendants in capital trials, the grueling and often dispiriting nature of the work discourages many. Remember also, standards for the appointment of defense attorneys for indigent persons would not have guaranteed better representation for Washington. His attorney was retained, not appointed.

A second needed improvement is the videotaping of interrogations and confessions. Without it, it's impossible to judge whether the police, even unwittingly, supplied Washington with information or led him to statements that appeared damning when viewed in isolation. Attorney Bob Hall points out that Washington was interrogated for about eight to ten hours overall, but his confession could be read in about twenty minutes. "What happened in the remaining, unrecorded hours?"

Barriers to the introduction of new evidence of innocence also ought to be relaxed. When a life is at stake, the inability to consider credible evidence of actual innocence in court, no matter when it is unearthed, makes a mockery of justice. The advent of DNA testing forcefully demonstrates the potential for error in criminal cases. States need to create procedures by which a convicted individual can petition a court, not only for DNA testing that might establish innocence, but for consideration of other types of newly discovered, potentially exculpatory evidence.

Many of those who have watched the process from a front-row seat endorse separating such decisions from gubernatorial clemency. "I sat there so many times and said, why am I doing this and not a court?" said Walter McFarlane, who evaluated dozens of clemency petitions as Wilder's counsel. In the aftermath of Earl Washington's pardon, Virginia adopted a procedure by which prisoners can petition a court for postconviction consideration of DNA evidence. "I personally was very glad to see that," noted Ferrara. As director of the Virginia division of forensic science, "I have watched every governor have to make these terribly difficult decisions on clemency. All of them, every one, agonized over these decisions."

Without Wilder, Earl Washington probably would be dead, and without Gilmore, Washington might be imprisoned for life. He owes them much. But because governors operate in the political realm, their statements and actions are never devoid of politics. That worked to Washington's detriment, both when his attorneys were not given the full results of the first DNA test and in Gilmore's chilly public comments. Courts do not expect 100 percent certitude. But with every iota of doubt about the innocence or the future actions of a person being granted clemency, a politician is risking his own hide. That is not the ideal climate for dispassionately weighing new postconviction evidence.

Growing awareness of the potential for wrongful convictions also ought to make courts highly skeptical of any capital conviction based on a single eyewitness, jailhouse informant, or confession. The work of the Innocence Project underscores the danger of accepting any of those forms of testimony as the sole basis for an execution.[15] If, as in the Washington case, the confession comes from a person with borderline intelligence, "there ought to be almost a presumption that the confession is not valid," said Gail Marshall, who after leaving the Virginia attorney general's office became active in bar association work on the legal needs and rights of the mentally disabled.

The possibility of error increases as long as those charged with representing the state in criminal justice matters remain closed to the possibility of the state's imperfection. While hubris about such matters is not unique to the Old Dominion, officials serving Virginia seem especially impervious to doubt. The attitude was recalled by Judge Dickson Phillips in the aftermath of Washington's pardon. "I remember one of the state's lawyers, how outraged he was that anyone could ever think that anything so terrible as the conviction of an innocent man could ever happen in the state of Virginia," said Phillips, a member of the 4th Circuit panel in the Washington case.[16]

Finally, the starting point for much that went wrong for Earl Washington was the limited understanding within the law enforcement and criminal justice systems of mental retardation. At the Fauquier County sheriff's office on the morning of May 21, 1983, Washington typified an individual with mild retardation confronting law enforcement authorities. Consider the stress most people experience when stopped for a traffic violation, says Ruth Luckasson. Next, "consider the amplified stress of an actual arrest," she writes. "Then, think about the number of resources a person without disabilities can bring to bear to the situation: verbal ability, negotiating skills, access to people who can help, money for a lawyer and expert witnesses, and so forth. Now, superimpose the situation of most people with cognitive limitations: limited verbal ability, reduced personal skills, few social connections, no money for a lawyer, reduced ability to deal with stress, and so forth. The contrast is striking, and the imbalance sets the stage for injustice."[17]

Many law enforcement officials—not only those in Fauquier County, Virginia—are ill-prepared to understand the complexity of such a situation. Because an individual with retardation may appear compliant, agreeable, and capable of answering questions, in contrast perhaps to a person with a mental illness, the officer may not appreciate the impaired cognitive functioning underlying the person's responses. Authors John J. McGee and Frank Menolascino note, "Since most communities have no systematic approach for dealing with individuals with these needs, the suspects enter the criminal justice system without external support and advocacy."[18]

A better alternative, in addition to education, is an advocacy system to support individuals with retardation from the time of arrest. Luckasson points as a model to the Arc of Colorado Springs, which maintains a multidisciplinary support team ready to respond quickly when police officers, lawyers, or judges identify a prisoner with a mental disability.[19] A few other state and local Arcs have similar programs, but they only work if there is cooperation from law enforcement and criminal justice authorities. By contrast, in Great Britain individuals believed to have a mental illness or retardation must be assisted by a supportive adult, perhaps a relative or a lawyer, during police interrogations.

Despite progress since 1983, work also remains in developing broader acceptance of competency and evaluation standards appropriate to the mentally retarded. Many of the doctrines involving competence to stand trial, to plead guilty, to confess, to waive rights, and so on, were developed in response to individuals with mental illness, not mental retardation. When an evaluation occurs, the person making the assessment must understand the ways in which even mild mental retardation can impact a confession or a guilty plea.[20] The Culpeper court ordered an overall evaluation of Washington's competency to stand trial, but no expert ever focused on an equally critical and separate point, the reliability of his confession.

On June 20, 2002, the U.S. Supreme Court struck a mighty blow in favor of the mentally disabled by banning the execution of offenders who are retarded. But this high profile decision is only a beginning. The key will be in the extent to which defense attorneys are able to get skilled assessments of clients and persuade juries of intellectual deficits and gaps in adaptive behavior.

Even if every precaution is taken to insure a proper outcome, can wrongful executions be entirely avoided? That question is at the center of the ongoing national debate on the future of the death penalty. Given human fallibility, the answer is probably no, particularly when those charged with capital crimes are so often from outside society's mainstream. The only way to ensure that innocent people are not executed is to join other developed nations in halting the practice.

What does the future portend for Earl Washington?

Of the various strokes of good fortune that mixed with bad in his life, none was luckier than the chance meeting of Kay Mirick and Ruth Luckasson. After years behind bars, the ability to rebuild a life is often lost. It would have been dangerous for Washington to return to the bosom of the community and family in which his earlier trouble had occurred. He would have arrived home as a forty-year-old man without work experience or training in any but the most elementary jobs. His siblings, struggling to keep their own lives afloat, could offer little beyond moral support and, at worst, a rehash of the life he had left behind.

Instead, when Earl Washington arrived in Virginia Beach on February 12, 2001, awaiting him were a home, a job, and a community of people ready to meet him halfway in creating relationships and a productive life. He rose to the challenge, performing well as a handyman and work partner of Mark Carpenter, learning to negotiate many of the tasks and skills necessary for independent living. Fortunately, Support Services Inc. existed to fill the void.

Immediately after Washington's release, Mirick fielded telephone calls from a few Virginia Beach residents who were worried and angry. The thrust of their comments was, "How dare I bring this ex-con in? No one knew what he was capable of," she said. Her reply was conciliatory. "I don't think you know him. Keep watching." In the next eighteen months, Washington thrived. He became an employee, rather than a customer of Support Services Inc., and his monthly earnings, combined with a small government disability check, covered most of his monthly bills. He learned a variety of skills, including his favorites—painting and steam-cleaning carpets. His network of friendships broadened. He mastered some of the amenities of modern life from automatic coffee pots to cell telephones.

He was not completely independent, however. Shortcomings remained. He could not manage a checkbook, so Support Services Inc. functioned as a bank, doling out allowances and overseeing bill payment. He failed the written test for a driver's license, although he was still trying. "Can Earl open a bank account by himself? Probably not," said Weinstein. "Can Earl rent an apartment by himself? Probably not." But could he live a useful life in a setting designed to capitalize on his strengths and compensate for his weaknesses? Yes.

The prevailing definition of mental retardation, approved by the American Association on Mental Retardation in 1992, has several corollaries. Two are particularly pertinent to Earl Washington.[21] First, limitations often coexist with strengths. For instance, throughout his life, observers noted a kindly temperament. "He is now in a place where that matters. One of his real strengths now matters," Luckasson said.

The second is that, with good support over a sustained period, the ability of the person to function in society will generally improve. That is also hopeful. "People with mental retardation can learn things over time, and he has had a long time to decide how he wants to live his life," Luckasson said.

Sustained support is critical, however. Washington's success in the period following his release demonstrated the difference nurture can make. If those pillars—a job, a home, a community, transportation—were lost, then Washington's future would be more precarious.

Earl Washington's prospects for a full life grew on May 4, 2002. As light filtered through majestic stained glass windows at the First Presbyterian Church of Norfolk and a guitarist strummed, he exchanged wedding vows with Pamela Marie Edwards, a sweet-faced, thirty-nine-year-old woman who shares his mild retardation. The couple were introduced over the telephone about a year earlier by a mutual friend. Their romance blossomed rapidly, and when a newspaper article reported their plans to marry, an assortment of strangers came forward to help. Almost everything at the wedding and reception—clothing, flowers, a tiered wedding cake, a white limousine, photographs, food, and music—was donated by well-wishers. The audience was a rare blend of black and white, retarded and not, wealthy and poor.

"You've come a long way, Earl. This moment now is a testament to the way God has brought your path straight," said the Reverend Tim Roberts. A chorus of voices echoed, "Amen."

The end of the Earl Washington story lies not in that fairy-tale moment but in chapters still unfolding, both in individual lives and in American jurisprudence.

"It's a matter of immense relief to us that an innocent man was not executed, but it's also a very sad case in another way because no one should ever be imprisoned for the length of time he was for a crime they didn't commit," said Judge Wilkinson. "It's also a very tragic case for the (Williams) family because the perpetrator has never been found and all that time was wasted. We escaped the very worst outcome, but at the same time there's been no good outcome because years of Mr. Washington's life were wrongly taken away and the poor family has yet to achieve any closure. I just feel sorry for a lot of different reasons."

It is a curious thing how lives can intersect and be altered forever in an instant. Earl Washington Jr., an impoverished day laborer; Hazel Weeks, an elderly widow; and Rebecca Williams, a teenage mother of three, had almost nothing in common except their roots in Virginia's

Piedmont. And yet, one week in May 1983, they became connected in a way no one could have predicted and none of them would have chosen. Over the following decades, memories of the explosive events faded for many. But their story lived on in legal annals. U.S. Supreme Court Justice John Paul Stevens, in fact, cited the case to bolster his majority opinion in *Atkins v. Virginia* that executions of the mentally retarded involve unacceptable risk. For a handful of people, who experienced the events more intimately, no reminders of the case were needed.

In Warrenton on a hot day in July 2001, Jimmy Weeks sat in his superintendent's office at the department of public works and gave his final word on his mother's assault. Weeks is a small man with an unflinching gaze and unvarnished speech. "The only thing I'd like to say is that she did not deserve what happened, because she had befriended him," he said.

Not long before, Weeks's son had suggested to him that it might be about time to put the painful episode to rest. "You know, probably Mamaw would have forgiven him by now and everybody should just let it lie," the son said.

And what did Jimmy Weeks think of that?

Briefly, a grin appeared. "You never agree totally with your son. That's against all the rules."

He turned serious again. "It's been twenty years almost and I'm getting tired of hearing about it. I can't change anything, nothing. If you ask me if I feel any remorse for the punishment that he got for my mother, I do not. This other crime, I don't know anything about the other one, other than what I read in the paper."

At the Hillcrest Memorial Gardens outside Culpeper, Eleanor Pullen checked the paper in her hand and strode purposefully through the grass, two paces to the west, four to the north. With the toe of her sandal, she explored the growth, searching for the orb marking the spot where Rebecca Williams was buried.

It was a shame, Pullen said, that no formal marker had been erected, but these things happen. Kneeling, she explored the ground with her fingers, then pushed back the grass blades to reveal the disk. In the afternoon sunlight, the shadow of a maple tree reached almost to the spot. "There," she said.

Pullen had never met the Williams family, but she had not forgotten Rebecca's death or Earl Washington's arrest. In fact, she marked her employment at the gardens by his January 1984 trial, three months after she began work. The event was so mesmerizing that Pullen wrote a song, shipped it off to a music company, and spent $300 recording it. Her sympathies were entirely with Rebecca Williams.

Now, eighteen years later, the tape and the words were still stored in a brown envelope in the office. She fitted the tape into a player and turned up the volume on the guitar music.

> *This is a true story, I'm sorry to say.*
> *It all happened on a warm summer's day.*
> *Her husband was at work at the time.*
> *Such a tragic thing had never entered his mind.*
>
> *The oldest child was at school that day,*
> *While her two smaller children were at home, busy at play.*
> *Never had they expected to witness such a sight*
> *Their dear mother murdered by a big man's might.*

At the time, Pullen thought a future in hell was none too harsh for Washington. Then came the DNA tests. Now she did not know what to think. "I might be wrong. I don't know," she said, shrugging. Mostly, she hoped people would not forget Rebecca Williams. "You heard about it for a while, and then it just sort of died," she said.

A few weeks after their wedding, Earl and Pam Washington sat in a fast-food restaurant in Virginia Beach and ruminated about their meeting, their future, the unlikely course of their lives. By earlier standards, Washington was almost garrulous, keeping up a running banter with his wife over day-to-day trivialities. Sometimes he lapsed into dialogue, repeating various sides of a conversation.

One story went like this. A few days earlier he and Mark Carpenter, the best man at his wedding, had walked into a hardware store.

"I see you got your bodyguard," Washington quoted the man behind the counter.

"He's not my bodyguard. He's my brother," replied Carpenter, who is a slender, white man.

Washington found the exchange satisfying. "None of this bodyguard stuff," he said.

The talk turned to children. Earl would like to have four, two boys and two girls.

Pam, whose twenty-one-year-old daughter lives with and has been adopted by her mother, would like two.

"Two," she said.

"Four," Earl replied.

"Have it your way then."

He would name one of the girls Pam Marie, after his wife and mother. The boys would be Earl Washington Jr. II and Earl Washington Jr. III.

Everyone laughed. How would he tell them apart?

"I will know which is which, you best believe that. I'm going to say, 'Second, come here. Third, you come here.' If I ever pass away then a son's got my name, keep it alive."

So far, adjusting to life after prison had been easier than expected, Washington said. Things cost more. The pace was a bit faster. But he was proud of his accomplishments. "I've stayed out of trouble. Got a good job. I'm about good people every day. I've got a good woman in my life who tries hard to keep me out of trouble."

Pam ducked her head at the praise.

Asks what she liked best about her husband, she glanced at him, then said softly, "His looks, kind of humor, his intelligence."

Earl's answer about Pam was shorter. "Everything," he said.

Sitting in that normal place on an average day, with his wife across the table, it was easy to recognize in Earl Washington the worth that was there, visible to anyone inclined to see.

Notes

NOTES TO CHAPTER I

1. Affidavit of Marie M. Deans, August 23, 1985, contained in *Washington v. Sielaff*, petition for a writ of habeas corpus, filed August 27, 1985, Circuit Court of Culpeper, 91-L-85.

2. Marie M. Deans interview with author in Charlottesville, Va., May 7, 2001.

3. For summaries of the Earl Washington case, see Tim McGlone, Matthew Dolan, and Bill Sizemore, "A Near Fatal Injustice," *Virginian-Pilot* (January 22, 2001): A1. Also see Brooke A. Masters, "Missteps on Road to Justice," *Washington Post* (December 1, 2000): A1. And see Frank Green, "Washington Released," *Richmond Times-Dispatch* (February 13, 2001): B1.

4. Marie Deans interview, May 7, 2001.

5. Peter Bacque, "Prison History: Written in Dirt," *Richmond Times-Dispatch* (September 12, 1992).

6. Paul W. Keve, *The History of Corrections in Virginia* (Charlottesville: University of Virginia Press, 1986), 25–26.

7. Ibid., 190. Also see Joint Legislative Audit and Review Commission, "Review of Virginia's System of Capital Punishment," a report to the Governor and the General Assembly (January 15, 2002): 5–6.

8. "More Charges Filed in Uprising," *Richmond Times-Dispatch* (September 20, 1985). For detailed story of the Briley brothers and their execution, see Daryl Cumber Dance, *Long Gone: The Mecklenburg Six and the Theme of Escape in Black Folklore* (Knoxville: University of Tennessee Press, 1987).

9. For Morris O'Dell Mason, see Emily Reed, *The Penry Penalty: Capital Punishment and Offenders with Mental Retardation* (Lanham: University Press of America, 1993), 81–82.

10. Earl Washington interview with author in Virginia Beach, Va., March 29, 2001.

11. Austin Sarat, *When the State Kills: Capital Punishment and the American Condition* (Princeton: Princeton University Press, 2001), 160–162.

NOTES TO CHAPTER 2

1. Helen Richards telephone interview with author, August 2001.
2. Clifford Williams telephone interview with author, August 1, 2001.
3. "Culpeper Woman Killed," *Star-Exponent* (June 5, 1982): A1.
4. Helen Richards telephone interview, August 2001.
5. For accounts of Rebecca Williams's morning, see "Culpeper Woman Killed," A1. Also see "Murder Remains Total Mystery," *Star-Exponent* (June 16, 1982), and trial testimony of Doris Campbell and Helen Richards.
6. Dr. James C. Beyer testimony in Earl Washington trial transcript, 770–776.
7. Paul Brundage testimony in Earl Washington trial transcript, 477–482.
8. Officer J. L. Jackson testimony in Earl Washington trial transcript, 482–496.
9. Kenneth H. Buraker testimony in Earl Washington trial transcript, 496–498.
10. Clifford Williams testimony in Earl Washington trial transcript, 499–502.
11. "Culpeper Woman Killed."
12. C. Reese Wilmore testimony in Earl Washington trial transcript, 592–636.
13. "Murder Probe Goes On," *Star-Exponent* (June 9, 1982).

NOTES TO CHAPTER 3

1. Philip J. Schwarz, *Twice Condemned: Slaves and the Criminal Laws of Virginia, 1705–1865* (Baton Rouge: Louisiana State University Press, 1988), 197.
2. Eugene M. Scheel, *Culpeper: A Virginia County's History through 1920* (Orange: Green Publishers, 1982), 158.
3. Karen Ibrahim, Karen White, and Courtney Gaskins, *Fauquier County, Virginia Register of Free Negroes 1817–1865*, 1993.
4. Family records are found in Dee Ann Buck, *Birth Registry, Fauquier County, Virginia, 1853–1896*, 1996, and Dee Ann Buck, *Death Registry, Fauquier County, Virginia, 1853–1896*, 1996. Also see Fauquier County, Va., Register of Marriages, stored at the Library of Virginia, Richmond, Va.
5. Mary Mudd Jones interview with author in Bealeton, Va., December 5, 2001.

6. Schwarz, *Twice Condemned*, 38.

7. Ibrahim, *Fauquier County*, i.

8. Schwarz, *Twice Condemned*, 92.

9. Scheel, *Culpeper*, 159.

10. Ibid., 162–163.

11. William W. Barr, "The Freedmen of Elk Run," *Fauquier Magazine* (March 1989): 4.

12. Nancy C. Baird, ed., *Journals of Amanda Virginia Edmonds: Lass of the Mosby Confederacy, 1859–1867* (Stephens City, Va.: Commercial Press, 1984).

13. P. A. L. Smith, *Fauquier County, Virginia Memories* (Hartford, Ky.: McDowell Publishers, 1979), 11. For other histories of Fauquier and Culpeper counties, see D-Anne Evans, *Train Whistles and Hunting Horns: The History of the Plains, Virginia* (Middleburg: Piedmont Press, 1994). Also see Fauquier County Bicentennial Committee, *Fauquier County, Virginia, 1759–1959* (Warrenton: Virginia Publishing Co., 1959); and T. O. Madden, *We Were Always Free: The Maddens of Culpeper County, Virginia* (New York: Vintage Books, 1993).

14. "Twenty Local People among the Richest in America," *Fauquier Democrat* (December 1, 1983): A1.

15. "Warrenton Seen as Model Town," *Fauquier Democrat* (April 14, 1983): A1.

16. School records obtained from Director of Pupil Personnel, Fauquier County Schools, in conjunction with trial of Earl Washington Jr. Release form October 4, 1983.

17. Molly Cupp, social history of Earl Washington Jr., prepared for defense team, 1993.

18. Frances Glaettli telephone interview with author, October 17, 2001.

19. Don Huffman interview with author in Bealeton, Va., September 14, 2001.

20. Medical records obtained in conjunction with trial of Earl Washington Jr. Release form signed October 4, 1983.

21. Molly Cupp, social history.

22. Earl Washington Jr. interview with author in Virginia Beach, Va., October 17, 2001.

23. Alfreda Pendleton interview with author in Remington, Va., September 5, 2001.

24. Earl Washington interview with author at Greensville Correctional Center, Jarratt, Va., January 24, 2001.

25. Shirley Cuesenberry interview with author in Bealeton, Va., September 5, 2001.

26. "Identity of Murder Suspect Shocks Long-Time Neighbors," *Culpeper News* (May 26, 1983).

27. For additional understanding of mental retardation, see Robert L.

Schalock, *Adaptive Behavior and Its Measurement* (Washington, D.C.: American Association of Mental Retardation, 1999). Also see Alexander Tymchuk, K. Charlie Lakin, and Ruth Luckasson, *The Forgotten Generation: The Status and Challenges of Adults with Mild Mental Retardation* (Baltimore: Paul H. Brookes, 2001); and Ronald L. Taylor, *Assessment of Individuals with Mental Retardation* (San Diego: Singular Publishing Group, 1997).

28. Ruth Luckasson letter to Barry A. Weinstein, December 17, 1993, contains evaluation submitted as part of 1993 clemency petition.

NOTES TO CHAPTER 4

1. Transcript of Mrs. Hazel Weeks's testimony at preliminary hearing on charges brought against Earl Washington Jr., Warrenton, Va., June 23, 1983.

2. James H. Weeks III interview with author in Warrenton, Va., July 27, 2001.

3. Transcript of Deputy Denny Zeets's testimony at preliminary hearing in Warrenton, Va., June 23, 1983.

4. Cathy Dyson, "Deputies Arrest Alleged Rapist," *Fauquier Democrat* (May 26, 1983).

5. Transcript of Deputy A. L. Robinson's testimony at preliminary hearing in Warrenton, Va., June 23, 1983.

6. Earl Washington Jr. interview with author at Greensville Correctional Center, Jarratt, Va., January 24, 2001.

7. Joel Williamson, *A Rage for Order: Black/White Relations in the American South since Emancipation* (New York: Oxford University Press, 1986). In his discussion of the rise of Radicalism in the post–Civil War period, Williamson observes:

> In the Radical mind, the single most significant and awful manifestation of black retrogression was an increasing frequency of sexual assaults on white women and girl children by black men. Above all else, it was this threat that thrust deeply into the psychic core of the South, searing the white soul, marking the character of the Southern mind radically and leaving it crippled and hobbled in matters of race long after the mark itself was lost from sight. (p. 84)

8. Richard A. Rutyna, "The Capital Laws of Virginia: An Historical Sketch," paper presented to the Virginia State Crime Commission Advisory Committee on Capital Punishment (September 17, 1973): 33.

9. Ibid., 35.

10. James Jenkins telephone interview with author, October 2000.

NOTES TO CHAPTER 5

1. Terry Schrum interview with author on September 6, 2001 in Fauquier County, Va.

2. Terry Schrum police notes of interview with Earl Washington Jr., May 22, 1983.

3. C. Reese Wilmore testimony in Earl Washington trial transcript, 592–636.

4. Jonathan Lynn interview with author in Warrenton, Va., June 27, 2001.

5. Richard Bonnie, "The Competency of Defendants with Mental Retardation to Assist in Their Own Defense," in Ronald W. Conley, Ruth Luckasson, and George Bouthilet, eds., *The Criminal Justice System and Mental Retardation* (Baltimore: Paul H. Brookes, 1992), 108–110. Bonnie, director of the Institute of Law, Psychiatry and Public Policy at the University of Virginia, argues that "Substantial reliability concerns are raised whenever a defendant with mental retardation pleads guilty." At worst, responses may be dictated more by limited conceptual skills and submission to authority than truth. "In cases involving defendants with subnormal intelligence, special precautions are required to offset the many factors that propel the system toward efficient outcomes rather than reliable ones" (p. 108).

6. S. Allen Cubbage interview with author in Warrenton, Va., September 14, 2001. The wall in Cubbage's office contained certificates acknowledging his completion of basic and advanced courses in "Interviewing and Interrogation." Asked what he was taught about interviewing individuals with mental deficiencies, he replied: "I don't know that that's ever been addressed, now that I think back."

NOTES TO CHAPTER 6

1. Linda Marie Bache testimony in trial transcript, *Commonwealth of Virginia v. Earl Jr. Washington*, 315–318.

2. Jury selection in *Commonwealth v. Washington* is covered in pages 172–446 of the trial transcript.

3. Kathleen Hoffman, "Washington's Jury Set for Case Today," *Star-Exponent* (January 19, 1984): A1.

4. Author interview with Village Apartments property manager in Culpeper, Va., September 19, 2001.

5. John Scott interview with author in Fredericksburg, Va., August 23, 2001.

6. Transcript of motions hearing, *Commonwealth of Virginia v. Earl Jr. Washington*, August 2, 1983.

7. Transcript of motions hearing, *Commonwealth of Virginia v. Earl Jr. Washington,* November 2, 1983, 102. The conclusions of James C. Dimitris and Arthur Centor are contained in an October 21, 1983 letter to Judge David F. Berry. The letter is part of the trial record, stored in the Circuit Court clerk's office, Culpeper, Va.

8. Ibid., 108.

9. Transcript of motions hearing, *Commonwealth v. Washington,* November 29, 1983, 159. See also Motion for Change of Venue, dated September 22, 1983. Motion includes three articles from the Culpeper *Star-Exponent,* describing Washington's arrest in Fauquier and his subsequent charging in the death of Rebecca Williams. The earliest ("Suspect Charged in Area Murder, Rape," May 24, 1983) was coauthored by Gary Close, a journalist who by the time of Washington's pardon in 2000 had become Culpeper County Commonwealth's attorney. His subsequent role in the case is described in chapters 13 and 14.

10. Kathleen Hoffman, "Bennett Beats Gentry to Prosecutor's Office," *Star-Exponent* (November 9, 1983): A1.

11. Bennett opening statement in trial transcript, 471.

12. Brundage testimony in trial transcript, 477–481.

13. Jackson testimony in trial transcript, 482–495.

14. Buraker testimony in trial transcript, 496–498.

15. C. Williams testimony in trial transcript, 499–502.

16. Beyer testimony in trial transcript, 508–516.

17. Campbell testimony in trial transcript, 517–520.

18. Deal testimony in trial transcript, 560–564.

19. Richards testimony in trial transcript, 520–523.

20. Schrum testimony in trial transcript, 568–589.

21. Hart testimony in trial transcript, 589–592. Later, 637–639.

22. Wilmore testimony in trial transcript, 592–636.

23. Pendleton testimony in trial transcript, 662–666.

24. Washington testimony in trial transcript, 639–662.

25. Bennett closing statement in trial transcript, 710–718, and rebuttal, 720–724.

26. Scott closing statement in trial transcript, 718–720.

27. Pendleton testimony in trial transcript, 793–799, and 861–867.

28. Centor testimony in trial transcript, 781–793.

29. Richards testimony in trial transcript, 852–860.

NOTES TO CHAPTER 7

1. For a complete account of the Mecklenburg escape, see Joe Jackson and William F. Byrd, *Dead Run: The Untold Story of Dennis Stockton and America's Only Mass Escape from Death Row* (New York: Times Books, 1999).

2. Joe Giarratano letter to author, dated March 31, 2001.

3. Investigator S. Allen Cubbage notes of Earl Washington confession, dated May 23, 1983. Also see Warrenton Police preliminary investigative report on felonious assault of Eugena Hecker, November 12, 1982. Both documents are contained in Earl Washington's 1993 petition for executive clemency.

4. Warrenton Police Department supplementary investigative report involving Lynn Rawlings's rape. Written by S. Allen Cubbage, May 2, 1983.

5. Affidavit of Jonathan S. Lynn, December 27, 1993.

6. Jonathan Lynn interview with author in Warrenton, Va., June 27, 2001.

7. Paul W. Keve, *The History of Corrections in Virginia* (Charlottesville: University of Virginia Press, 1991), 191.

8. Richard A. Rutyna, "Virginia: An Historical Sketch," paper presented to the Virginia State Crime Commission advisory committee on capital punishment (September 17, 1973): 1.

9. Ibid., 7–28.

10. Ibid.

11. Daniel J. Flanigan, *The Criminal Law of Slavery and Freedom 1800–1868* (New York: Garland Publishing, 1987), xxx.

12. Rutyna, "Virginia," 31.

13. Ibid.

14. Ibid., 33.

15. Ibid.

16. Joint Legislative Audit and Review Commission (JLARC), "Review of Virginia's System of Capital Punishment," a report to the Governor and General Assembly (January 15, 2002): 5–6.

17. John Bessler, *Death in the Dark: Midnight Executions in America* (Boston: Northeastern University Press, 1997), 60–61.

18. Philip J. Schwarz, *Twice Condemned: Slaves and the Criminal Laws of Virginia, 1705–1865* (Baton Rouge: Louisiana State University Press, 1988), 319–320.

19. Eric Rise, *The Martinsville Seven: Rape, Race and Capital Punishment* (Charlottesville: University of Virginia, 1995), 3.

20. Richard B. Sherman, *The Case of Odell Waller and Virginia Justice, 1940–42* (Knoxville: University of Tennessee Press, 1992), 6.

21. Ibid., 12.

22. Ibid., 31.

23. Ibid., 22.

24. Ibid., 4.

25. Ibid.

26. Ibid., 90.

27. Ibid., 160.

28. Rise, *The Martinsville Seven*, 7ff.

29. Ibid., 23.

30. Ibid., 5.

31. Ibid., 102.

32. Ibid., 118.

33. Ibid., 138.

34. JLARC, "Review of Virginia's System of Capital Punishment," 27–28. The study showed that racial disparities disappeared altogether in the rate at which prosecutors sought the death penalty in capital-eligible murder cases between 1995 and 1999.

35. Frank Green, "Execution Moratorium Urged," *Richmond Times-Dispatch* (April 15, 1999): B1.

36. Eric Freedman, *Habeas Corpus: Rethinking the Great Writ of Liberty* (New York: New York University Press, 2002).

37. Laura LaFay, "Unequal, Unfair and Irreversible: The Death Penalty in Virginia," a report of the American Civil Liberties Union of Virginia (April 2000): 23–27. LaFay outlines a series of procedural limitations on judicial review in Virginia.

38. James S. Liebman, Jeffrey Fagan, and Valerie West, "A Broken System: Error Rates in Capital Cases, 1973–1995," Columbia School of Law (June 12, 2000): 47.

39. Liebman, "A Broken System," 68–70.

40. Ibid., 70.

41. JLARC, "Review of Virginia's System of Capital Punishment," IV.

42. Ibid, 53–83.

43. The Death Penalty Information Center (www.deathpenaltyinfo.org) maintains up-to-date statistics on executions nationally. See also LaFay, "Unequal, Unfair."

44. Giarratano letter, March 31, 2001.

45. *Washington v. Commonwealth*, 323 S.E.2nd 577: Virginia 1980.

46. Giarratano letter, March 31, 2001.

NOTES TO CHAPTER 8

1. Marty Geer e-mail correspondence with author May–June 2001. Chronology confirmed through legal time records maintained by Marty Geer.

2. Eric Freedman interview with author in New York City, April 15, 2001.

3. Ibid. Also, Jay Topkis telephone interview from New York City with author, May 29, 2001, and John "Jack" Boger telephone interview from Raleigh, N.C., with author, April 27, 2001.

4. Letter from Robert N. Baldwin, executive secretary of the Supreme Court of Virginia to Mary P. Devine, staff attorney division of legislative services, General Assembly of Virginia, September 16, 1985.

5. For information on Joe Giarratano, see June Arney, "Bloody Boot Prints Led Him to Doubt His Own Confession," *Virginian-Pilot* (June 26, 1994): A15; Coleman McCarthy, "Life Sentence, No Time Off for Innocence," *Baltimore Sun* (July 23, 2000); James J. Kilpatrick, "Why Kill Joe Giarratano Now?" *Virginian-Pilot* (January 30, 1991): A9.

6. Scott Elliot Rogers, "Limiting the Relief Available to Indigent Death Row Inmates Denied Meaningful Access to the Courts: *Murray v. Giarratano*, 109 S.Ct. 2765 (1989)," *Florida State University Law Review* (Winter 1990): 41.

7. Joe Giarratano's actions involving Earl Washington are described in correspondence from Giarratano to the author, December 8, 2000, March 31, 2001, and April 15, 2001. See also correspondence between Joe Giarratano and William Sizemore, December 18, 2000.

8. For a full account, see Anthony Lewis, *Gideon's Trumpet* (New York: Random House, 1964).

9. Marty Geer correspondence, May–June 2001.

10. *Giarratano v. Sielaff*, Civil Action no. 85-0655-R, filed in U.S. District Court for the Eastern District of Virginia, received by clerk's office on July 3, 1985, formally filed on August 6, 1985.

11. Letter from Joseph Giarratano to the Hon. Robert R. Merighe [*sic*], re. *Giarratano v. Sielaff*, Civil Action no. 85-0655-R, August 19, 1985.

12. "Facts about the Death Penalty," Death Penalty Information Center (September 24, 1999).

13. *Washington v. Sielaff*, petition for a writ of (state) habeas corpus, filed August 27, 1985, in Virginia: Circuit Court of Culpeper, 95-L-85.

14. *Washington v. Sielaff*, order by Judge Lloyd Sullenberger, entered August 27, 1985 in Virginia: Circuit Court of Culpeper, 91-L-85.

15. Citations in *Giarratano v. Murray*: *Giarratano v. Murray*, 668F Supp. 511 (E.D. Va. December 18, 1986) (no. CIV.A. 85-0655-R). Judgment affirmed by: *Giarratano v. Murray*, 847 F 2d 1118, 57 USLW 2011 (4th Cir. (Va.) June 03, 1988) (no. 87-7518, 87-7519). Rehearing denied (January 22, 1990). Certiorari granted by: *Murray v. Giarratano*, 488 U.S. 923, 109 S.Ct. 303, 102L.Ed2d 322 (U.S. Va. October 31, 1988) (no. 88-411). And judgment reversed by: *Murray v. Giarratano*, 492 U.S. 1, 109 S. Ct. 2765, 106 L.Ed 2d 1, 57 USLW 4889 (U.S. Va. June 23, 1989) (no. 88-411).

16. Excerpts from *Giarratano v. Murray* trial, July 10–11, 1986 in the U.S. District Court for the Eastern District of Virginia. Testimony of James Kulp, 268.

NOTES TO CHAPTER 9

1. Marie Deans interviews with author in Charlottesville, Va., May 7, 2001 and by telephone, October 31, 2000, November 3, 2000, and January 31, 2002. See also Greg Schneider, "Suffering with Death-Row Prisoners Awaiting the Chair," *Virginian-Pilot* (September 17, 1992): A1.

2. Robert Hall telephone interview with author, June 8, 2001.

3. Sally Hall interview with author in Richmond, Va., January 18, 2002.

4. Robert Hall e-mails to author, May 1, 2001 and January 21, 2002.

5. Laura LaFay, "Unequal, Unfair and Irreversible: The Death Penalty in Virginia," a report of the American Civil Liberties Union of Virginia (April 2000): 30.

6. Robert Hall e-mails to author, May 1, 2001 and January 21, 2002.

7. Certificates of analysis in Rebecca Williams case, Bureau of Forensic Science, Commonwealth of Virginia, dated 6–11–82, 6–23–82, 6–28–82, 8–19–82, 8–27–82, 11–10–82, 2–28–83, 5–26–83, 8–12–83, 8–26–83, and 9–8–83.

8. Joint Legislative Audit and Review Commission, "Review of Virginia's System of Capital Punishment," a report to the Governor and the General Assembly (January 15, 2002): 72–73.

9. Transcript of preliminary hearing in Culpeper, Va., June 30, 1983, 35–36.

10. Memorandum to the Court, filed in *Washington v. Sielaff*, written by Robert T. Hall, November 21, 1985.

11. Order of Virginia Supreme Court, filed in Culpeper Circuit Court, December 3, 1984.

12. *Washington v. Sielaff*, Motion to Dismiss, filed in Culpeper Circuit Court, September 27, 1985, 3.

13. Ibid., 4.

14. Ibid., 1–16.

15. *Washington v. Sielaff*, Answer to Respondent's Motion to Dismiss and Memorandum of Law in Support of Petition for a Writ of Habeas Corpus, November 28, 1985, 1–63.

16. A rare exception was the case of Wilbert Lee Evans who was sentenced to die for the fatal shooting of a deputy sheriff during an attempted escape from the Alexandria jail in 1981. During sentencing, the local Commonwealth's attorney urged the jury to impose the death penalty, based on Evans's "future dangerousness" to society. The prosecutor introduced evidence of a series of previous crimes in North Carolina as proof that Evans could not be trusted to live. The jury voted for death.

The only problem was that some of the information was incorrect, a fact the prosecutor later acknowledged having known when he made his jury presentation. When the case reached the Virginia Supreme Court on direct appeal and the U.S. Supreme Court in a bid for certiorari, no one mentioned the mistakes.

While Evans's direct appeal was pending, the Virginia Supreme Court ruled in *Patterson v. Commonwealth*, 222 Va. 653, 283 S.E. 2d 212 (1981), that error in sentencing in a capital case must result in the automatic reduction of a death sentence to life imprisonment. Virginia's capital statute at the time held that a death sentence must be imposed by the same jury that determined guilt. Since it would be impossible to reconvene juries months or years later, sentencing error in capital cases meant that the Commonwealth had no choice but to substitute the lesser penalty, the justices held.

When the prosecutor's misrepresentation in the Evans case became public, the attorney general's office took the rare step of acknowledging error, but not until emergency legislation had been pushed through the General Assembly allowing resentencing by a different jury if a death sentence was set aside due to error.

As noted by Justice Thurgood Marshall in a dissent when the case reached the U.S. Supreme Court, the state did not notify Evans that it was confessing error until March 28, 1983, the same day the governor signed into law a bill allowing a new jury to be convened for a resentencing in a capital case. Whether or not the timing was deliberate, Marshall said, the failure to disclose prosecutorial misconduct earlier "constituted egregious conduct that seriously harmed Evans," who later was executed.

Such was the degree to which the Virginia attorney general's office had willingly acknowledged error in previous cases.

17. Ibid., 13.

18. *Washington v. Sielaff*, Second Motion to Dismiss, December 31, 1985, 12.

19. Ibid., 14.

20. Ibid., 16.

21. Ibid., 15–18.

22. *Washington v. Sielaff*, Transcript of Hearing on Respondent's Motion to Dismiss, before Judge Lloyd Sullenberger, Culpeper Circuit Court, September 17, 1986, 24.

23. Ibid., 28–35.

24. Letter from Judge Lloyd C. Sullenberger to Robert T. Hall and Linwood T. Wells Jr., November 12, 1986.

25. Thomas R. Morris, *The Virginia Supreme Court: An Institutional and Political Analysis* (Charlottesville: University of Virginia Press, 1975). "Perhaps the most politically significant role of the state Supreme Court is to confer legitimacy on the public policy decisions of other government agencies," writes Morris. "The court has not ventured far from public opinion—if public opinion is defined in terms of a majority vote of the legislature—in its decisions."

26. A graphic illustration of that commitment was Carrico's authorship in 1966 of a decision upholding Virginia's miscegenation law prohibiting racially mixed marriages. In his opinion in *Loving v. Virginia*, 206 Va. 924 (1966), Justice

Carrico made clear his disdain for judicial activism. Explaining why he did not intend to override an earlier decision by the Virginia Supreme Court in support of the miscegenation law, he wrote: "A decision by this court reversing the Naim case . . . would be judicial legislation in the rawest sense of that term. Such arguments are properly addressable to the legislature, which enacted the law in the first place, and not to this court, whose prescribed role in the separated powers of government is to adjudicate, and not to legislate." The U.S. Supreme Court reversed, striking down the Virginia law as a violation of the Fourteenth Amendment and ending miscegenation laws nationwide.

27. Order of the Virginia Supreme Court, February 28, 1988, in *Washington v. Sielaff*, Circuit Court no. 91-L-85/2456 H.C.

NOTES TO CHAPTER 10

1. Neil A. Lewis, "A Court Becomes a Model of Conservative Pursuits," *New York Times* (May 24, 1999): A1.

2. James S. Liebman, Jeffrey Fagan, and Valerie West, "A Broken System: Error Rates in Capital Cases, 1973–1995," Columbia University School of Law (June 12, 2000).

3. Mark Johnson, "A Courtly Upholding of Law's Rightness," *Richmond Times-Dispatch* (January 10, 1999).

4. Margaret Edds, "A Newspaper's Evolving Tradition," *Virginian-Pilot* (October 18, 1998).

5. Eric Freedman interview with author in New York, N.Y., April 15, 2001.

6. Frank Green, "Lawyers Say Confession Details May Have Been Offered by Police," *Richmond Times-Dispatch* (June 5, 1990).

7. Johnson, "A Courtly Upholding."

8. Frank Green, "Low-Profile 4th Circuit Makes Presence Felt—Quietly," *Richmond Times-Dispatch* (March 12, 1989).

9. *Washington v. Murray*, 952 F.2d 1472 (4th Cir. 1991).

10. Ibid., 1477–78.

11. Ibid., 1478.

12. Ibid., 1479.

13. Marie Deans interview with author in Charlottesville, Va., May 7, 2001.

14. Gerald Zerkin interview with author in Richmond, Va., June 1, 2001.

15. *Washington v. Murray*, C.A. no. 88-0956-AM, transcript of trial proceedings before Judge Claude M. Hilton, 4–9.

16. Ibid., 11.

17. Ibid., 12–13.

18. Ibid., 24.

19. Ibid., 84.

20. Ibid., 97.

21. Ibid., 63.

22. Ibid., 98.

23. Ibid., 110–111.

24. Ibid., 112–113.

25. *Washington v. Murray,* memorandum opinion by Judge Claude M. Hilton, July 29, 1992, 5.

26. Ibid., 3.

27. Ibid., 5.

28. Frank Green, "Lawyer Competency Is at Issue in Appeal; Judges Throw Out Some Tough Questions," *Richmond Times-Dispatch* (June 10, 1993).

29. Eric Freedman telephone interview with author, January 8, 2002.

30. *Washington v. Murray,* 4 F.3d 1285 (4th Cir. 1993), 1286.

31. Ibid., 1291.

32. Ibid., 1293.

33. Ibid.

34. Ibid., 1294.

35. Brooke Masters, "Missteps on Road to Injustice," *Washington Post* (December 1, 2000): A1.

NOTES TO CHAPTER 11

1. Barry Weinstein telephone interview with author, January 28, 2002.

2. Barry Weinstein telephone interviews with author, June 7, 2001 and January 28 and 29, 2002.

3. Barry Scheck e-mail to author, February 2, 2002.

4. www.deathpenaltyinfo.org/innoc.html, February 9, 2002.

5. Brooke A. Masters, "DNA Testing in Old Cases Is Disputed," *Washington Post* (September 10, 2000): A1.

6. Barry Scheck, Peter Neufeld, and Jim Dwyer, *Actual Innocence* (New York: Doubleday, 2000), 73.

7. Gail Marshall interview with author in Orange, Va., December 7, 2001.

8. Stephen Rosenthal interview with author in Richmond, Va., January 3, 2002.

9. Letter from Stephen D. Rosenthal to Robert T. Hall, dated June 2, 1993.

10. Letter from Stephen D. Rosenthal to Robert T. Hall, dated September 28, 1993.

11. Letters from Gerald T. Zerkin to Stephen Rosenthal, dated October 5, 1993 and October 13, 1993.

12. Gerald Zerkin interviews with author in Richmond, Va., June 1, 2001 and January 13, 2002.

13. Letter from Gerald T. Zerkin to Walter A. McFarlane, dated October 26, 1993.

14. Gerald Zerkin interview, June 1, 2001.

15. Robert Hall e-mail to author, January 14, 2002.

16. Stephen Rosenthal interview, January 3, 2002.

17. Certificate of Analysis, Virginia Division of Forensic Science, from Jeffery D. Ban to John H. McLees Jr., October 25, 1993.

18. Frank Green, "Guilt in Doubt in Rape, Slaying," *Richmond Times-Dispatch* (October 26, 1993).

19. Ibid.

20. Ibid.

21. Bill Miller, "Virginia Death Row Inmate Awaits More Tests," *Washington Post* (October 27, 1993): D3.

22. Green, "Guilt in Doubt."

23. Frank Green, "DNA Case Appeals May Be Dropped in Pardon Bid," *Richmond Times-Dispatch* (October 27, 1993).

24. Advisory to the Media, Office of the Governor, October 26, 1993.

25. Ibid.

26. L. Douglas Wilder telephone message to author, January 2002.

27. Letter from Robert T. Hall to Gov. L. Douglas Wilder, December 2, 1993.

28. Letter from Dr. David H. Bing to Robert T. Hall, December 8, 1993.

29. Draft of letter from Alan Abeson, executive director Arc, to Gov. L. Douglas Wilder.

30. William Raspberry, "Full Pardon for Earl Washington Jr.," *Washington Post* (January 5, 1994): A19.

31. James Weeks III interview with author in Warrenton, Va., July 27, 2002.

32. Lynn Waltz, "New DNA Analysis Key to Possible Pardon," *Virginian-Pilot* (January 14, 1994): D4.

33. Marie Dean telephone interview with author, January 31, 2002.

34. Letter from Hall to Wilder, December 2, 1993.

35. "Governor Wilder Orders State Employees to Disregard Directive Seeking Their Resignations," media advisory, December 15, 1993.

36. For an account of the Roger Keith Coleman case, see John C. Tucker, *May God Have Mercy: A True Story of Crime and Punishment* (New York: W. W. Norton, 1997).

37. Tyler Whitley, "Pardon Thought to Get Wilder Off Political Hot Seat," *Richmond News Leader* (February 20, 1991).

38. Jim Mason, "Data Appear to Hurt, Not Help, Inmate's Appeal," *Richmond News Leader* (April 9, 1992).

39. Advisory to the Media, Office of the Governor, December 29, 1993.

40. Frank Green, "Aid Offered in Washington's Case," *Richmond Times-Dispatch* (January 7, 1994).

41. Jonathan Lynn affidavit, dated December 27, 1993.
42. Barry Scheck e-mail to author, February 2, 2002.
43. Letter from Dr. Henry A. Erlich to Barry Weinstein, January 13, 1994.
44. Frank Green, "Fate Hangs by a Thread of DNA," *Richmond Times-Dispatch* (January 13, 1994).

NOTES TO CHAPTER 12

1. Barry Weinstein telephone interviews with author, January 28 and 29, 2002.
2. Conditional pardon order by Gov. L. Douglas Wilder in the case of Earl Washington Jr., January 14, 1994.
3. Eric Freedman telephone interview with author, January 8, 2002.
4. Marie Deans interviews with author in Charlottesville, Va., May 7, 2001, and by telephone on January 31, 2002.
5. Robert Hall interview with author in Richmond, Va., January 18, 2002.
6. Walter McFarlane interview with author in Richmond, Va., March 13, 2002.
7. Earl Washington telephone interview with author, March 3, 2002.
8. Greg Schneider, "Suffering with Death-Row Prisoners Awaiting the Chair," *Virginian-Pilot* (September 17, 1992): A1.
9. Joe Jackson, "Virginia Inmates on Death Row Lose Chief Ally," *Virginian-Pilot* (September 4, 1993): D1.
10. Barry Weinstein telephone interview with author, June 7, 2001.
11. Conditional pardon order, January 14, 1994.
12. Frank Green, "Death Penalty Foes Endure Rough Season," *Richmond Times-Dispatch* (March 27, 1994).

NOTES TO CHAPTER 13

1. Ofra Bikel telephone interview with author, March 25, 2002.
2. Jonathan Alter, "The Death Penalty on Trial," *Newsweek* (June 12, 2000): 24–34. Also, "DNA Fingerprinting Methods," www.encyclopedia.com/articles /03711Methods.html, April 1, 2001.
3. Walter Felton interview with author in Williamsburg, Va., March 25, 2002.
4. Transcript of *Frontline* program #1808, "The Case for Innocence," aired January 11, 2000. Written, produced, and directed by Ofra Bikel.
5. Certificate of Analysis, Virginia Division of Forensic Science, from Jeffrey D. Ban to Walter A. McFarlane, January 14, 1994.

6. Walter McFarlane interview with author in Richmond, Va., March 13, 2002.

7. Robert Hall telephone interview with author, March 27, 2002.

8. "Earl Washington: Set Him Free," an editorial in the *Virginian-Pilot* (January 20, 2000): B10.

9. Letter from Gerald T. Zerkin to Walter S. Felton Jr., January 27, 2000.

10. Margaret Edds, "Freeing Washington Would Destroy Myth of Justice," *Virginian-Pilot* (April 16, 2000).

11. Letter from Gerald T. Zerkin to Walter S. Felton Jr., May 1, 2000.

12. "Why Not?" an editorial in the *Richmond Times-Dispatch* (May 6, 2000).

13. For a description of the Jefferson DNA results, see Warren Fiske, "Jefferson Fathered Slave: DNA Results All But Settle 200-Year-Old Controversy about 3rd U.S. President," *Virginian-Pilot* (November 1, 1998): A1.

14. Charles Zewe, "Bush Recommends Reprieve for Death Row Inmate," CNN.com (June 1, 2000).

15. Frank Green, "Gilmore Orders New DNA Testing," *Richmond Times-Dispatch* (June 2, 2000).

16. Kay Mirick interview with author in Virginia Beach, Va., October 2001.

17. Letter from Kay Mirick to Barry A. Weinstein, June 30, 2000.

18. Certificate of Analysis from Jeffrey D. Ban to Walter Felton Jr., September 8, 2000.

19. Gary Close interview with author in Williamsburg, Va., July 9, 2001.

20. Frank Green, "Lawyers Request Pardon," *Richmond Times-Dispatch* (September 7, 2000).

21. Michael Hardy, "Gilmore Holding DNA Evidence Results Could Clear Inmate with Life Term," *Richmond Times-Dispatch* (September 26, 2000).

NOTES TO CHAPTER 14

1. "Statement of Governor Jim Gilmore Regarding the Pardon of Earl Washington," released by the governor's press office, October 2, 2000. For accounts of the Gilmore pardon, see Brooke Masters, "DNA Clears Condemned Va. Inmate," *Washington Post* (October 3, 2000): A1. Also see "Based on DNA evidence, Gilmore Pardons Inmate for Rape, Murder," *Virginian-Pilot* (October 3, 2000): A1. And see Frank Green, "DNA Clears Washington," *Richmond Times-Dispatch* (October 3, 2000): B1.

2. Barry Weinstein telephone interview with author, March 22, 2002.

3. Marie Deans telephone interview with author, April 15, 2002.

4. Eric Freedman telephone interview with author, April 1, 2002.

5. Brooke Masters, "Va. Inmate to Get Back 'Good Time,'" *Washington Post* (October 4, 2000): B1.

6. Frank Green, "Pardoned Inmate Is Grateful, but Washington Wonders When He'll be Released," *Richmond Times-Dispatch* (October 4, 2000).

7. Masters, "DNA Clears Condemned."

8. Green, "DNA Clears Washington."

9. Masters, "DNA Clears Condemned."

10. Governor's Commission on Parole Abolition and Sentencing Reform, final report, August 1994.

11. Rick Kern telephone interview with author, April 29, 2002.

12. Green, "Pardoned Inmate Is Grateful."

13. Tim McGlone, "Pardoned Prisoner to Stay Put a Bit Longer," *Virginian-Pilot* (October 5, 2000): A1.

14. James Jenkins telephone interview with author, April 29, 2002.

15. Grant rates for fiscal 1988 through 2002 received from Linda Blackwell, secretary to the chairman of the Virginia parole board, April 29, 2002.

16. A request by the author for the number of first-time offenders, convicted on a primary offense of malicious wounding in 1983 or earlier, who were still in a Virginia prison in November 2000, was rejected by the Department of Corrections under the Freedom of Information Act. See "Prison Officials Hide behind a Wall of Secrecy," editorial in the *Virginian-Pilot,* November 19, 2000.

17. Frank Green, "Early Release Denied," *Richmond Times-Dispatch* (December 23, 2000): B1.

18. Earl Washington Jr. interview with author at Greensville Correctional Center, Jarratt, Va., January 24, 2001.

19. Tim McGlone, "Former Death-Row Inmate Released into Spotlight," *Virginian-Pilot* (February 13, 2001): A1.

NOTES TO CHAPTER 15

1. Gisli Gudjonsson, *The Psychology of Interrogations, Confessions and Testimony* (Chichester: John Wiley & Sons, 1992), 211. The study to which Gudjonnson refers was conducted by H. A. Bedau and M. L. Radelet and was reported in an article, "Miscarriages of Justice in Potentially Capital Cases," *Stanford Law Review,* 40 (November 1987): 21–179. That study is expanded in Michael Radelet, Hugo Bedau, and Constance Putnam, *In Spite of Innocence: Erroneous Convictions in Capital Cases* (Boston: Northeastern University Press, 1992).

2. Frank Green, "Lawyer Stresses Power of DNA Tests," *Richmond Times-Dispatch* (July 17, 2001).

3. "Innocence: Freed from Death Row," www.deathpenaltyinfo.org, May 17, 2002.

4. Clifford Williams telephone interview with author, August 1, 2001.

5. Misty Michelle Phillips telephone interview with author, August 2001.

6. Helen Richards telephone interview with author, August 2001.

7. Munsterberg's pioneering work is described in Hugo Munsterberg, *On the Witness Stand: Essays of Psychology and Crime* (Garden City: Doubleday, 1908).

8. Gudjonsson, *The Psychology of Interrogations*, 272.

9. Gisli Gudjonsson, Isabel Clare, Susan Rutter, and John Pearse, *Persons at Risk during Interviews in Police Custody: The Identification of Vulnerabilities* (London: Sage, 1985), 67–94.

10. Ibid., 163.

11. Gudjonsson, *The Psychology of Interrogations*, 163.

12. "Report of the Governor's Commission on Capital Punishment," presented to Illinois Gov. George H. Ryan, April 2002.

13. J. Harvie Wilkinson III interview with author in Charlottesville, Va., January 7, 2002.

14. Laura LaFay, "Unequal, Unfair and Irreversible: The Death Penalty in Virginia," a report of the American Civil Liberties Union, 12.

15. Barry Scheck, Peter Neufeld, and Jim Dwyer, *Actual Innocence* (New York: Doubleday, 2000).

16. Brooke Masters, "Missteps on Road to Injustice," *Washington Post* (December 1, 2000): A1.

17. Ruth Luckasson, "The Criminal Justice System and People with Mild Cognitive Limitations," in Alexander Tymchuk, K. Charlie Lakin, and Ruth Luckasson, eds., *The Forgotten Generation: The Status and Challenges of Adults with Mild Cognitive Limitation* (Baltimore: Paul H. Brookes Co., 2001), 349.

18. John J. McGee and Frank J. Menolascino, "The Evaluation of Defendants with Mental Retardation in the Criminal Justice System," in Ronald W. Conley, Ruth Luckasson, and George N. Bouthilet, eds., *The Criminal Justice System and Mental Retardation* (Baltimore: Paul H. Brookes Co., 1992), 62.

19. Luckasson, "The Criminal Justice System," 353.

20. Ibid., 350.

21. Robert L. Schalock, *Adaptive Behavior and Its Measurement* (Washington, D.C.: American Association on Mental Retardation, 1999), 185.

Recommended Reading

Acker, James, Robert Bohm, and Charles Lanier. *America's Experiment with Capital Punishment*. Durham: Carolina Academic Press, 1998.

Baird, Nancy C. *Journals of Amanda Virginia Edmonds: Lass of the Mosby Confederacy, 1859–1867*. Stephens City: Commercial Press, 1984.

Baldus, David, George Woodworth, and Charles Pulaski. *Equal Justice and the Death Penalty*. Boston: Northeastern University Press, 1990.

Bedau, Hugo Adam. *The Death Penalty in America: Current Controversies*. New York: Oxford University Press, 1997.

———. *The Death Penalty in America*, 3rd ed. New York: Oxford University Press, 1982.

Bedau, Hugo Adam, and Michael L. Radelet. "Miscarriages of Justice in Potentially Capital Cases." *Stanford Law Review* 40 (November 1987): 21–179.

———. "The Myth of Infallibility: A Reply to Markman and Cassell." *Stanford Law Review* 41 (November 1988): 161–170.

Borchard, Edwin. *Convicting the Innocent*. New Haven: Yale University Press, 1932.

Bressler, John. *Death in the Dark: Midnight Executions in America*. Boston: Northeastern University Press, 1997.

Brown, Edmund G. (Pat) with Dick Adler. *Public Justice, Private Mercy: A Governor's Education on Death Row*. New York: Weidenfeld & Nicolson, 1989.

Carter, Dan T. *Scottsboro: A Tragedy of the American South*. Baton Rouge: Louisiana State University Press, 1979.

Cassell, Paul G. "The Guilty and the 'Innocent': An Examination of Alleged Cases of Wrongful Conviction from False Confessions." *Harvard Journal of Law and Public Policy* (spring 1999): 523.

Cole, David. *No Equal Justice: Race and Class in the American Criminal Justice System*. New York: New Press, 1999.

Conley, Ronald W., Ruth Luckasson, and George Bouthilet, eds. *The Criminal Justice System and Mental Retardation*. Baltimore: Paul H. Brookes, 1992.

Dance, Daryl Cumber. *Long Gone: The Mecklenburg Six and the Theme of Escape in Black Folklore*. Knoxville: University of Tennessee Press, 1987.

Flanigan, Daniel J. *The Criminal Law of Slavery and Freedom, 1800–1868*. New York: Garland Publishing, 1987.

Freedman, Eric. *Habeas Corpus: Rethinking the Great Writ of Liberty*. New York: New York University Press, 2002.

Gudjonsson, Gisli. *The Psychology of Interrogations, Confessions and Testimony*. Chichester: John Wiley & Sons, 1992.

Gudjonsson, Gisli, Isabel Clare, Susan Rutter, and John Pearse. *Persons at Risk during Interview in Police Custody: The Identification of Vulnerabilities*. London: Sage, 1985.

Guild, Jane Purcell. *Black Laws of Virginia*. Lovettsville: Willow Bend Books, 1996.

Haines, Herbert H. *Against Capital Punishment: The Anti-Death Penalty Movement in America, 1972–1994*. New York: Oxford University Press, 1996.

Jackson, Joe, and William F. Byrd. *Dead Run: The Untold Story of Dennis Stockton and America's Only Mass Escape from Death Row*. New York: Times Books, 1999.

Joint Legislative Audit and Review Commission. "Review of Virginia's System of Capital Punishment," a Report to the Governor and the General Assembly, January 15, 2002.

Kamisar, Yale. *Police Interrogation and Confessions: Essays in Law and Policy*. Ann Arbor: University of Michigan Press, 1980.

Keve, Paul W. *The History of Corrections in Virginia*. Charlottesville: University of Virginia Press, 1986.

LaFay, Laura. "Unequal, Unfair and Irreversible: The Death Penalty in Virginia," a Report of the American Civil Liberties Union of Virginia, April 2000.

Latzer, Barry. *Death Penalty Cases: Leading U.S. Supreme Court Cases on Capital Punishment*. Boston: Butterworth-Heinemann, 1998.

Leo, Richard A., and Richard J. Ofshe. "The Consequences of False Confessions: Deprivations of Liberty and Miscarriages of Justice in the Age of Psychological Interrogation." *Journal of Criminal Law and Criminology* 88 (winter 1998): 429.

Lewis, Anthony. *Gideon's Trumpet*. New York: Random House, 1964.

Liebman, James S., Jeffrey Fagan, and Valerie West. "A Broken System: Error Rates in Capital Cases, 1973–1995." Columbia School of Law, June 12, 2000.

Lifton, Robert Jay, and Greg Mitchell. *Who Owns Death?* New York: William Morrow, 2000.

Madden, T. O. *We Were Always Free: The Maddens of Culpeper County, Virginia*. New York: Vintage Books, 1993.

Markman, Stephen J., and Paul G. Cassell. "Protecting the Innocent: A Response to the Bedau-Radelet Study." *Stanford Law Review* 41 (November 1988): 121–160.

McCloskey, James. "Convicting the Innocent." *Criminal Justice Ethics* 8 (winter/spring): 1–9.

Mello, Michael. *The Wrong Man: A True Story of Innocence on Death Row*. Minneapolis: University of Minnesota Press, 2001.

———. *Dead Wrong: A Death Row Lawyer Speaks Out against Capital Punishment*. Madison: University of Wisconsin Press, 1997.

Miller, Gene. *Invitation to a Lynching*. Garden City, N.Y.: Doubleday, 1975.

Miller, Kent, and Michael Radelet. *Executing the Mentally Ill: The Criminal Justice System and the Case of Alvin Ford*. Newbury Park: Sage, 1993.

Morris, Thomas R. *The Virginia Supreme Court: An Institutional and Political Analysis*. Charlottesville: University of Virginia Press, 1975.

Munsterberg, Hugo. *On the Witness Stand: Essays of Psychology and Crime*. Garden City: Doubleday, 1908.

Prejean, Helen. *Dead Man Walking*. New York: Random House, 1993.

Protess, David, and Rob Warden. *A Promise of Justice*. New York: Hyperion, 1998.

Radelet, Michael, Hugo Bedau, and Constance Putnam. *In Spite of Innocence: Erroneous Convictions in Capital Cases*. Boston: Northeastern University Press, 1992.

Reed, Emily. *The Penry Penalty: Capital Punishment and Offenders with Mental Retardation*. Lanham: University Press of America, 1993.

Rise, Eric. *The Martinsville Seven: Rape, Race and Capital Punishment*. Charlottesville: University of Virginia, 1995.

Sarat, Austin. *When the State Kills: Capital Punishment and the American Condition*. Princeton: Princeton University Press, 2001.

Schalock, Robert L. *Adaptive Behavior and Its Measurement*. Washington, D.C.: American Association of Mental Retardation, 1999.

Scheck, Barry, Peter Neufeld, and Jim Dwyer. *Actual Innocence*. New York: Doubleday, 2000.

Scheel, Eugene M. *Culpeper: A Virginia County's History through 1920*. Orange: Green Publishers, 1982.

Schwarz, Philip J. *Twice Condemned: Slaves and the Criminal Laws of Virginia, 1705–1865*. Baton Rouge: Louisiana State Univesity Press, 1988.

Sherman, Richard B. *The Case of Odell Waller and Virginia Justice, 1940–42*. Knoxville: University of Tennessee Press, 1992.

Smith, J. David. *Minds Made Feeble: The Myth and Legacy of the Kallikaks*. Rockville: Aspen Systems, 1985.

Smith, P. A. L. *Fauquier County, Virginia Memories*. Hartford: McDowell, 1979.

Solotaroff, Ivan. *The Last Face You'll Ever See*. New York: HarperCollins, 2001.

Taylor, Ronald L. *Assessment of Individuals with Mental Retardation*. San Diego: Singular Publishing Group, 1997.

Tucker, John C. *May God Have Mercy: A True Story of Crime and Punishment*. New York: W. W. Norton, 1997.

Tymchuk, Alexander, K. Charlie Lakin, and Ruth Luckasson. *The Forgotten Generation: The Status and Challenges of Adults with Mild Mental Retardation.* Baltimore: Paul H. Brookes, 2001.

Von Drehle, David. *Among the Lowest of the Dead: The Culture of Death Row.* New York: Times Books, 1995.

White, Welsh S. *Life in the Balance: Procedural Safeguards in Capital Cases.* Ann Arbor: University of Michigan Press, 1984.

Williamson, Joel. *A Rage for Order: Black/White Relations in the American South since Emancipation.* New York: Oxford University Press, 1986.

Index

About the Author

MARGARET EDDS is an editorial writer and former political reporter for the *Virginian-Pilot* in Norfolk. She is a graduate of Tennessee Wesleyan College and the author of two previous books, *Claiming the Dream* and *Free at Last*. She and her husband, Bob Lipper, have three children and live in Richmond, Virginia.